INSPIRE / PLAN / DISCOVER / EXPERIENCE

AMSTERDAM

AMSTERDAM

CONTENTS

DISCOVER 6

EXPERIENCE 66

NEED TO KNOW 220

Left: Bikes locked up on a bridge in autumn
Previous page: Montelbaanstoren seen from the Singel
Front cover: Canal houses illuminated at dusk

DISCOVER

Amsterdam's skyline at sunset

WELCOME TO AMSTERDAM

With its reflective waterways, tilting canal houses and humpback bridges, Amsterdam is undeniably picturesque. But this city contains multitudes: museums and street art, cruises and cycle rides, Dutch cuisine and world street food. Whatever your dream trip to Amsterdam includes, this DK Eyewitness Guide is the perfect travel companion.

1 A boat moored on a canal at sunset.

2 A canal reflecting the Red Light District's illuminations.

3 A couple relaxing outside a colourful café.

4 Characterful houses lining one of the canals.

Amsterdam is a city where both the past and the present are keenly felt. Majestic 17th-century mansions are perfectly preserved, while 20th-century warehouses have been transformed into quirky entertainment complexes. The vast Rijksmuseum, with its Old Masters, sits beside the Stedelijk Museum, which displays puzzling contemporary art installations. Infamously hedonistic, the city's nightlife encompasses so much more than the Red Light District. As well as relentless night-clubs, there are first-class concert venues, including the innovative Muziekgebouw aan 't IJ.

Beyond Amsterdam, postcard-pretty villages and heritage-rich cities are never far away. Windswept beaches, flat, windmill-dotted fields and striped bulbfields punctuate the Dutch landscape. The cities have plenty to offer too. There's ultramodern Rotterdam and historic Haarlem, stately Den Haag and laid-back Leiden. World-class museums await, including the Mauritshuis and Utrecht's museum of Miffy – the little white rabbit.

With so many different things to discover and experience, Amsterdam can seem overwhelming. We've broken the city down into easily navigable chapters, with detailed itineraries, expert local knowledge and colourful, comprehensive maps to help you plan the perfect visit. Whether you're staying for a weekend, a week, or longer, this DK Eyewitness Guide will ensure that you see the very best Amsterdam has to offer. Enjoy the book, and enjoy Amsterdam.

REASONS TO LOVE AMSTERDAM

It's undoubtedly pretty. It's renowned for its nightlife. It moves on bicycles and boats. Ask any Amsterdammer and you'll hear a different reason why they love their city. Here, we pick some of our favourites.

1 RIJKSMUSEUM

Few art collections can rival the concentrated brilliance of Amsterdam's most famous museum. Don't miss Rembrandt's masterful *The Night Watch* *(p124)*.

CRUISING THE CITY'S CANALS 2

Admire the unique façades of canal houses and listen to the water lapping against your boat while you explore the rings of attractive waterways *(p48)*.

3 FUNKY STREET ART

Graffiti has been given a veneer of respectability in recent years, but there are always exciting and raw works to be found when you know where to look, including these works by BRONIK and Ives.One *(p34)*.

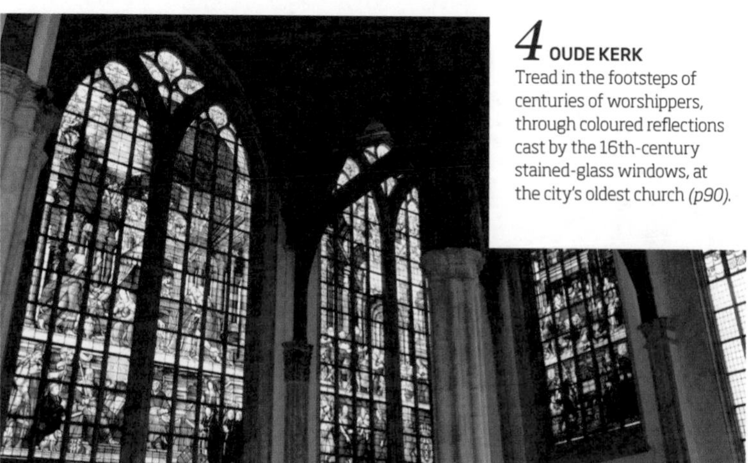

4 OUDE KERK

Tread in the footsteps of centuries of worshippers, through coloured reflections cast by the 16th-century stained-glass windows, at the city's oldest church *(p90)*.

MUSEUM HET REMBRANDTHUIS 5

Visit this moving museum to discover the real man behind the paintings. You can almost feel Rembrandt's hand on your shoulder as you walk around the artist's former home *(p94)*.

SAMPLING JENEVER 6

Savour the taste of the rich, malty grandfather of gin in a warmly lit *proeflokaal*. In the 17th century, customers could sample *jenever* in these tasting rooms before buying it.

JOODS HISTORISCH MUSEUM 7

This emotive complex of synagogues reflects the wealth and depth of the city's Jewish heritage *(p92)*.

ALL-NIGHT NIGHTLIFE 8

Don't miss out on the beating heart of this nocturnal city. Discover raunchy burlesque clubs, upscale piano bars, a pulsating LGBT+ scene and pumping rock clubs *(p40)*.

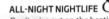

9 STREET FOOD AT ALBERT CUYPMARKT

Savour everything from traditional soused *haring* (herring), served with raw onions and gherkins, to dishes from Asia, Africa, South America, the Middle East and the Mediterranean at this market *(p145)*.

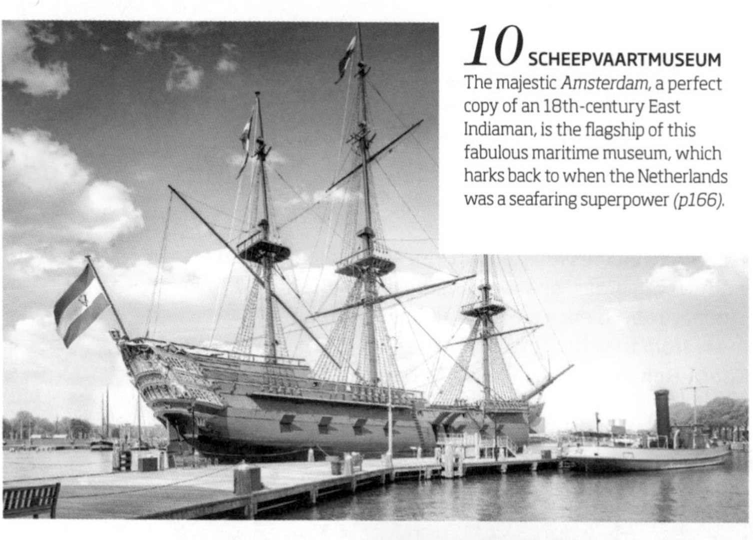

10 SCHEEPVAARTMUSEUM

The majestic *Amsterdam*, a perfect copy of an 18th-century East Indiaman, is the flagship of this fabulous maritime museum, which harks back to when the Netherlands was a seafaring superpower *(p166)*.

CYCLING AROUND NOORD 11

A trip to the Dutch capital wouldn't be complete without enjoying the national pastime: cycling. Venture out on two wheels to the graffiti-adorned streets of Noord, pausing at offbeat cafés *(p44)*.

VAN GOGH MUSEUM 12

Marvel at the golden layers of *Sunflowers*, the dizzying perspective of *The Bedroom*, and the contrasting colours of *Irises* at this temple to the Dutch artist *(p128)*.

EXPLORE AMSTERDAM

This guide divides Amsterdam into eight colour-coded sightseeing areas, as shown on the map below. Find out more about each area on the following pages. Away from the city, Beyond Amsterdam *(p184)* covers Noord-Holland, Zuid-Holland, Utrecht and Gelderland.

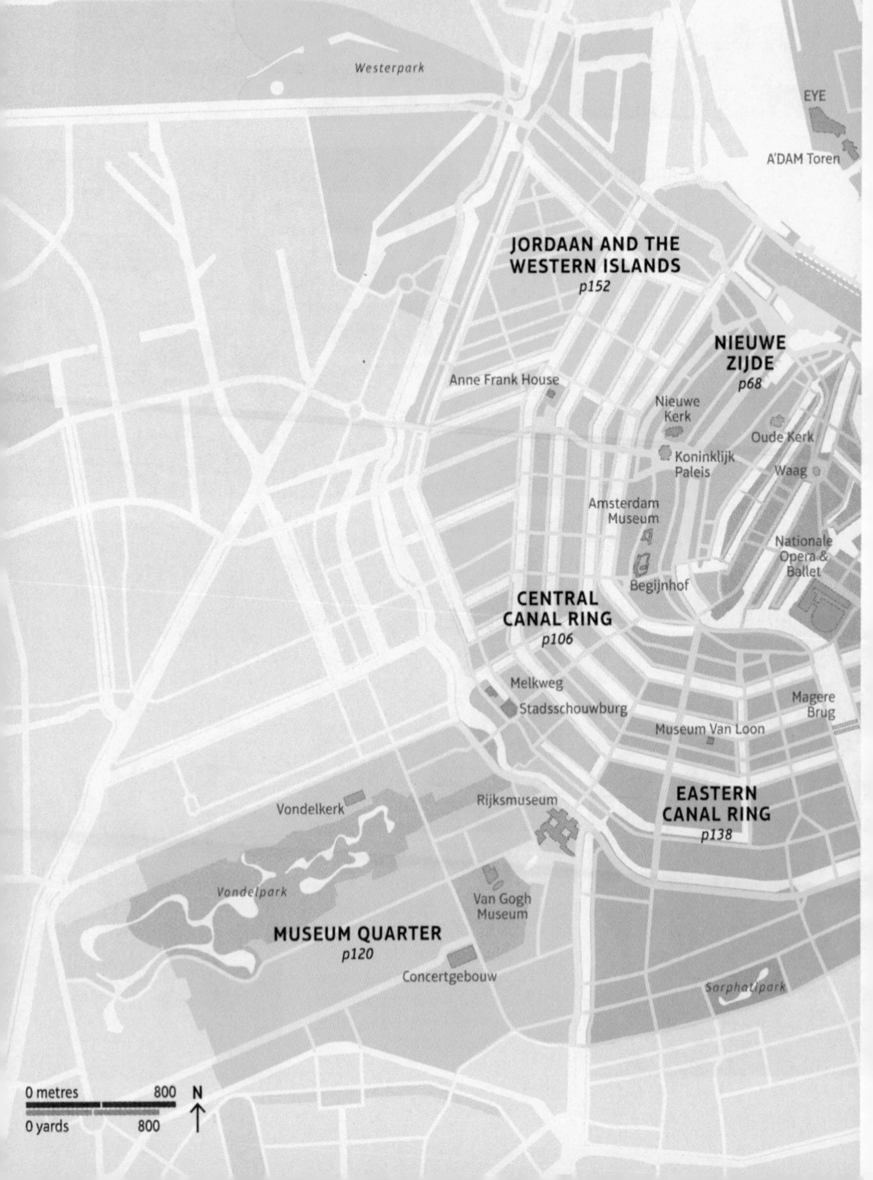

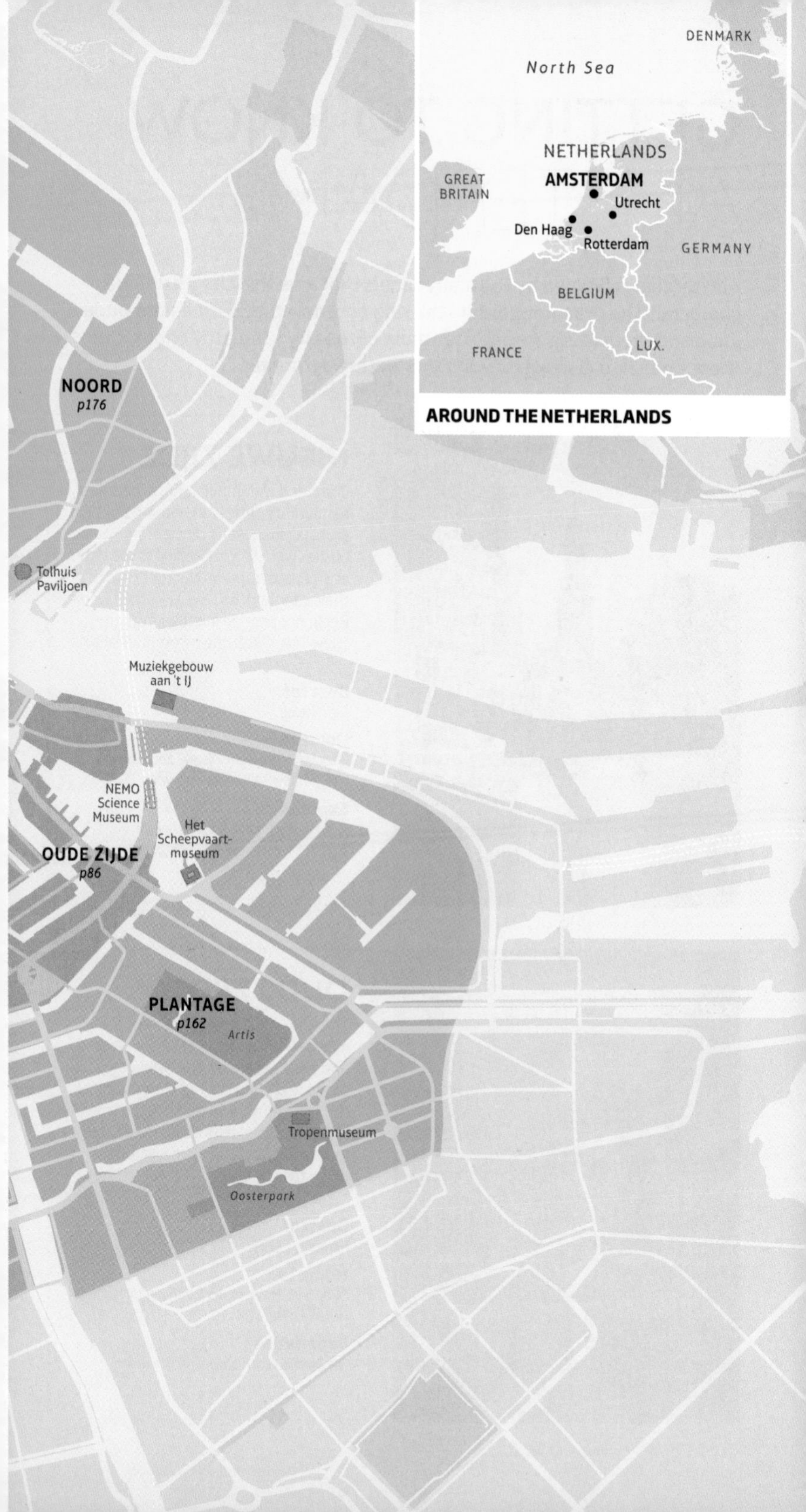
DENMARK
North Sea
NETHERLANDS
GREAT BRITAIN
AMSTERDAM
Utrecht
Den Haag
Rotterdam
GERMANY
BELGIUM
FRANCE
LUX.
AROUND THE NETHERLANDS
NOORD
p176
Tolhuis Paviljoen
Muziekgebouw aan 't IJ
NEMO Science Museum
Het Scheepvaart-museum
OUDE ZIJDE
p86
PLANTAGE
p162
Artis
Tropenmuseum
Oosterpark

GETTING TO KNOW AMSTERDAM

Amsterdam is divided by the many canals that give this city its unique character. The Grachtengordel - the ring of canals that defines the Oude Zijde and Nieuwe Zijde - encloses most of the city's top attractions, but there's much to discover beyond this watery perimeter.

PAGE 68

NIEUWE ZIJDE

Crammed with hotels, shops, bars and restaurants, this is Amsterdam's busiest tourist district. At its centre, Dam Square bustles with visitors heading to the sights as street performers clamour to grab their attention. Enclaves like the serene Begijnhof provide a refuge from the "New Side's" relentless commercialism.

Best for
Sightseeing

Home to
Amsterdam Museum, Nieuwe Kerk, Begijnhof, Museum Ons' Lieve Heer op Solder

Experience
Jenever *at a traditional* proeflokaal

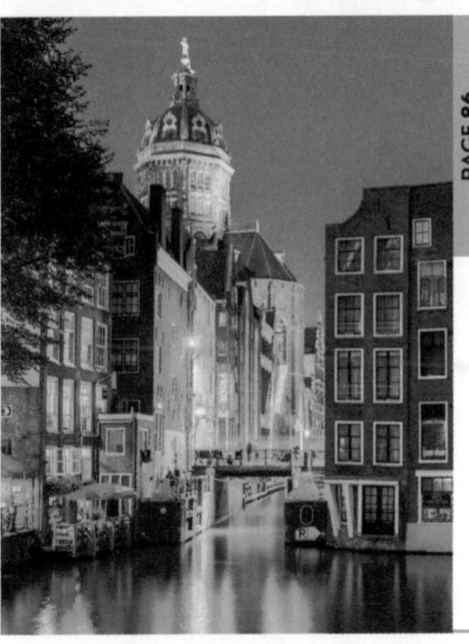

PAGE 86

OUDE ZIJDE

The "Old Side" is an oddball: an intensely urban quarter where piety and porn sit side by side. While the glow of the Red Light District almost bathes the 14th-century Oude Kerk, the smell of incense does battle with the all-too familiar scent of marijuana wafting down the streets.

Best for
Heritage

Home to
Oude Kerk, Museum Het Rembrandthuis, Joods Historisch Museum

Experience
The Zeedijk – the main drag of Chinatown

PAGE 106

CENTRAL CANAL RING

Curving between the IJ and the Amstel like concentric ripples in a pond, the Singel, Herengracht, Keizersgracht and Prinsengracht canals define Amsterdam's central canal ring. Compared with the cramped Nieuwe Zijde, there's a more spacious feel to this part of the city. Leidseplein – the area's hub – is packed with open-air cafés, but the square really comes into its own after dark, when music bars and dance clubs attract throngs of visitors and a sprinkling of locals. In summer, the party scene spills out onto the waterside streets, giving the area a fizzing atmosphere.

Best for
Canal trips and scenic strolls

Home to
Anne Frank House

Experience
A ride along the area's picturesque canals aboard a pedal-driven "canal bike"

PAGE 120

MUSEUM QUARTER

For lovers of high culture, the Museumplein is what Amsterdam is all about. Three world-class museums and one of the world's great concert halls stand around a calm green space. Visitors flock here to the square to pose by the Iamsterdam sign, admire Old Masters in the Rijksmuseum and modernists in the Stedelijk Museum, but the Van Gogh Museum is the quarter's true star. Away from the Museumplein, you'll find elegant streets defined by wealth and taste.

Best for
World-class art and classical music

Home to
Rijksmuseum, Van Gogh Museum, Stedelijk Museum

Experience
The wealth of art on display in Musemplein, before having a picnic in Vondelpark

→

PAGE 138

EASTERN CANAL RING

The Singel and the Amstel canals define this district, while Vijzelstraat and Vijzelgracht cut a straight line through its heart. At the north end of Vijzelstraat is a sight much loved by visitors – the Bloemenmarkt, with its floating flower vendors. South of Singelgracht – in the De Pijp area – the landscape changes. Striking modern architecture replaces the graceful Golden Age canal-house façades. This is Amsterdam's most multicultural neighbourhood and Albert Cuypmarkt sits at its core, where the air is clouded with enticing scents and vendors call to passersby.

Best for
Offbeat museums and multicultural street food

Home to
Museum Willet-Holthuysen

Experience
The delicious variety of street food on offer along Albert Cuypmarkt for a taste of the multicultural heritage of the Netherlands

PAGE 152

JORDAAN AND THE WESTERN ISLANDS

Gentrification has taken over much of the once-raffish Jordaan. Old-style taverns are now almost outnumbered by chic boutiques and galleries. As a result, bohemian-minded artists, artisans, performers and other creative types now favour the streets around Westerpark. Despite the chiming of Westerkerk's bells, the atmosphere here is more hedonistic than holy, with dozens of bars, cafés, galleries and eateries satisfying every desire of a hip clientele.

Best for
Quirky shops and galleries

Home to
Historic hofjes *and* bruin cafés *("brown cafés")*

Experience
An art exhibition, funky dance perfomance or food festival at the vibrant Westergasfabriek cultural complex

PAGE 162

PLANTAGE

East of the Amstel, this immaculately planned peninsula of tree-lined avenues and gracious 19th-century buildings contrasts with the cramped streets of Oude Zijde, which is only a block or two away. At its centre are the green spaces of Artis – the city's zoo – and Hortus Botanicus Amsterdam, which kids will love exploring. On the gentrified Entrepotdok waterfront, centuries-old warehouses have been turned into upscale apartments. Where the waters of the Nieuwevaart and the Oosterdok meet, a flotilla of historic ships lies at anchor.

Best for
A family day out

Home to
Het Scheepvaartmuseum, Tropenmuseum

Experience
A concert at the innovative Muziekgebouw aan 't IJ concert hall

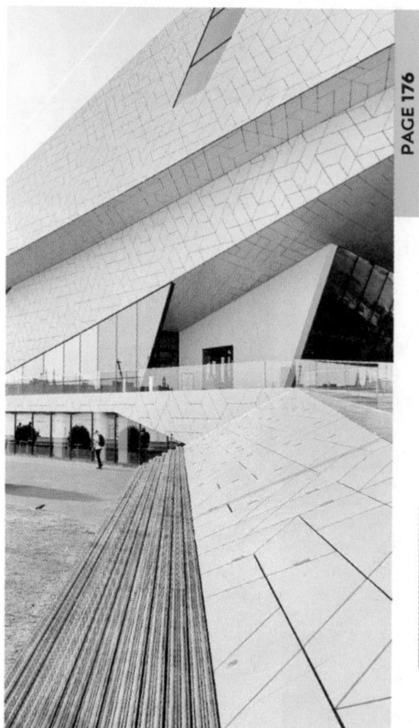

PAGE 176

NOORD

This edgy neighbourhood is a five-minute ferry ride across the IJ from the city centre. Noord is a rejuvenated dockland with a youthful, post-industrial vibe. Former factories and warehouses have been transformed into performance venues, ateliers and galleries, eateries and boutique hotels. Street art enlivens once-derelict buildings, flea markets take over formerly sleepy streets and locals lounge on deckchairs on a man-made beach. The 100-m- (328-ft-) high A'DAM Toren, with its trendy clubs and revolving restaurant, is the district's emblematic landmark of transformation.

Best for
Edgy culture and nightlife

Home to
A'DAM Toren

Experience
New horizons on the highest swing in Europe at A'DAM Toren

1 A *rondvaartboot* cruising down a canal.

2 A performer in Leidseplein.

3 The Art Deco interior of Café Americain.

4 Tulips for sale at the Bloemenmarkt.

Amsterdam may be a compact city, but it's packed with must-see sights and unique experiences. These itineraries will inspire you to make the most of your visit.

5 HOURS

Morning

Whether arriving in the city centre from the airport or by train, Centraal Station is the perfect gateway to the heart of this vibrant city. Historically, Amsterdam has been shaped by the water, so choose to explore the city for the first time by boat, rather than on foot. The Open Haven, in front of the station, is the best place to hop on a canalboat *(p48)*. There are lots of options to choose from, including multi-stop boats that connect all the major museums for those who want to cover a lot of sights in a short space of time. For a more relaxed introduction to the city, glass-topped *rondvaartboten* (tour boats) offer trips that last anywhere from one hour to 90 minutes, with multilingual commentary that highlights the opulent Golden Age architecture of the Herengracht, Prinsegracht and Keizersgracht canals, the splendour of the Golden Bend *(p116)* and canal-side landmarks. You'll cruise past the striking spires of the Westerkerk *(p115)*, and Munttoren *(p80)*, as well as the pretty floating Bloemenmarkt *(p146)*.

Afternoon

After leisurely taking in the city, hop off your boat at Leidseplein – a square filled with street performers eager for applause – where you'll find plenty of pleasant places for a lunch break. Sit back at one of the open-air cafés and watch the free entertainment *(p35)*. The nearby Café Americain *(p115)*, with its fountain and striped awnings, is a good choice. If the weather is problematic, the interior, with its vibrant stained glass, will not disappoint. After savouring your meal, you'll be ready to continue discovering the city's highlights. Many canal cruise companies offer combination tickets that give you fast-track access to the vast Rijksmuseum *(p124)*. Rembrandt's *The Night Watch* has pride of place in the museum's Gallery of Honour, but book a guided Highlights of the Rijksmuseum tour to take in other masterpieces, such as Rembrandt's *The Jewish Bride*, Frans Hals's *The Wedding Portrait* and *The Merry Drinker*, and Jan Vermeer's serenely luminous *The Kitchen Maid* and *Woman Reading a Letter*. The perfect end to your first day in the city.

←

1 Discovering the past at the Joods Historisch Museum.

2 The Nationaal Monument dominating Dam Square.

3 Café de Sluyswacht's outdoor seating.

4 Cantonese cuisine at Oriental City.

2 DAYS

Day 1

Morning The Dam is the natural starting point for your voyage of discovery around Amsterdam. Pay your respects to Dutch victims of World War II at the Nationaal Monument *(p80)*, then stroll down Rokin to the Amsterdam Museum *(p74)*. For a quick glimpse of the diverse collection, head straight for the Amsterdam Gallery, which is free to enter. After admiring the Old Masters here, say hello to *'T Lieverdje*, a cheeky bronze personification of Amsterdam, on the Spui. Next, take a peek into the tranquil Begijnhof *(p78)*, where Het Houten Huis is one of Amsterdam's oldest houses.

Afternoon Pause for lunch on the Spui at Café Luxembourg *(www.cafeluxembourg.amsterdam)*, a classic brasserie. Order prawn croquettes and *bitterballen* (fried meatballs). Make your way along the canal-lined streets to the Museum Quarter in time for the 3:30pm guided tour of the Van Gogh Museum *(p128)*. Discover more about one of the world's most famous artists while exploring one of the largest collections of his works.

Evening For tasty street dining, amble a couple of blocks along Stadhouderskade, turning right into Ferdinand Bolstraat. Here, and in the Albert Cuypstraat *(p145)*, you'll be spoiled for choice.

Day 2

Morning A visit to the Joods Historisch Museum *(p92)* is a humbling reminder of how much the city owes to the Sephardic and Ashkenazi Jews who found a tolerant refuge here as early as the 15th century. In sharp contrast, the Waterlooplein Market *(p102)* around the corner is a worldly clutter of flea-market stalls. Browsers can find everything here: vintage clothing, ethnic jewellery, antiques, curios and even pornography.

Afternoon The waterside Café de Sluyswacht is the perfect place for a snack before strolling to the Museum Het Rembrandhuis *(p94)*. Take your time gaining an insight into the home life of Amsterdam's greatest painter, before embarking on a leisurely walk along Sint Antoniesbreestraat to the Nieuwmarkt *(p97)*. Pause at In de Waag *(p102)* for a coffee before walking along Zeedijk – the main thoroughfare of Chinatown.

Evening This area is dotted with Chinese, Indonesian and Thai eateries. Oriental City *(www.oriental-city.com)* is favoured by locals and specializes in Cantonese and Szechuan food. Feast on the fabulous dim sum, with deliciously warming fillings. After dinner, wind up at In de Wildeman *(p83)*, one of the city's finest *proeflokalen*, for an after-dinner glass of *jenever*.

1 A family cycling in Amsterdam.

2 Kids exploring NEMO Science Museum's roof terrace.

3 Enjoying Pllek's beach.

4 "Tale of the Whale" at Het Scheepvaartmuseum.

1 DAY
by bike

Morning

A trip to Amsterdam wouldn't be complete without a day spent in the bike saddle. Traversing the centre may seem daunting, especially if you are travelling as a family, so instead head to the laid-back Noord. First, pick up your ride from one of the many rental agencies near Centraal Station. Parents with tots and toddlers can rent bikes with child seats or trailers. There are also options for older kids, including off-road BMX wheels for adventurous teens *(p44)*. Next, board one of the blue-and-white ferries that shuttle between Centraal Station and Noord *(p42)*. No ticket is needed, and bikes go free. Take in the contrasting scenes of the canal-lined centre and the industrial north as you cross the IJ river. After a 20-minute cruise, disembark and ride for ten minutes to NDSM *(p181)*, a former shipyard that is now a cultural hotbed. Lock up your bike here. The painted shipping containers house plenty of quirky shops and galleries, but the main attraction for kids is Pllek, which has an artificial beach. For one weekend each month, IJ-Hallen (next to NDSM) hosts Europe's largest flea market. It's a fantastic place for anyone who likes a pre-loved bargain *(p182)*.

Afternoon

Stroll down to Café Noorderlicht for a family lunch *(p183)*. Sit inside the light interior if it's cold and drizzling or relax in its grassy beer garden on a balmy summer day. After lunch, collect your bike, board a ferry back to Centraal Station, then cross the Oosterdok via the bike-friendly Mr J J van der Veldebrug bridge. Ahead is what looks like a fabulous starship at anchor, but is in fact the NEMO Science Museum *(p99)*. Packed with hands-on, cutting-edge tech, this innovative museum will delight all the family. Best of all, the museum has a huge rooftop café. Rest tired legs here, while admiring the panoramic views of Oude Zijde and Plantage, before cycling on. The next stop is Het Scheepvaartmuseum *(p166)*. The flagship attraction here is the *Amsterdam*, an immaculate reconstruction of a three-masted 18th-century merchant vessel. Actors dressed in period costume bring to life the world of sailors aboard a Dutch East Indiaman in Amsterdam's colonial heyday. Children will love the interactive "Tale of the Whale" exhibition. After an energetic day, return your bike to the rental agency, which will be less than ten minutes away.

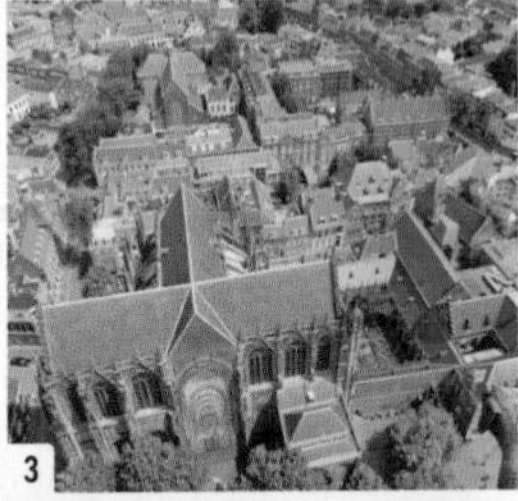

←

1 The lavish lounge of Hotel des Indes.

2 Flowers blooming in front of the Binnenhof in Den Haag.

3 The view from the Domtoren in Utrecht.

4 A lady admiring a painting at the Mauritshuis.

2 DAYS

beyond Amsterdam

Day 1

Morning Buy a prepaid OV Chipkaart travelcard, sold at stations, newsagents and supermarkets. It's a half-hour hop from Centraal Station to Utrecht, which is one of the oldest cities in the Netherlands *(p216)*. Make a beeline for the Domtoren *(p216)*, a Gothic masterpiece that dominates the city. There's a magnificent view from the top of the 112-m- (367-ft-) high tower – but getting there involves climbing 456 steps. Feet firmly back on solid ground, walk down Lange Nieuwestraat to the red-brick Museum Catharijneconvent *(p216)*. Once inside the 16th-century monastery, built for the Knights of St John, check out the gold and silver church ornaments, jewelled crucifixes and reliquaries in the collection.

Afternoon For lunch, wander along the Oudegracht canal to Meneer Smakers *(p216)*, which serves artisan burgers – including veggie versions. On the way back to the station by way of Steenweg, pause at the Museum Speelklok *(p216)*. Within this church is a magical collection of musical mechanisms.

Evening It's a 38-minute ride to dignified Den Haag *(p202)*. Check in at the grand Hotel des Indes *(p205)*, freshen up, then sip a champagne cocktail before indulging in a five-course tasting dinner in the hotel's elegant Restaurant des Indes *(p206)*.

Day 2

Morning Start the day with a lavish breakfast at the hotel, then set off to discover the stately charm of Den Haag. Start at the Mauritshuis, a six-minute walk away *(p204)*. Gems of the small, but superb, collection include Vermeer's *Girl with a Pearl Earring* and Rembrandt's *The Anatomy Lesson of Dr Nicolaes Tulp*. After treading the wooden-floored galleries, join a guided tour of the stately Binnenhof located just next door *(p202)*. After finding out more about how the country is governed, walk around the reflective Hofvijver to Garoeda *(p206)*. Sample Indonesian cooking at this culinary classic, which opened in 1949.

Afternoon It's time to leave this classy city. Leiden is under 15 minutes from Den Haag, so there's plenty of hours left in the day to explore this university town *(p198)*. From the station, take in the picturesque canals and student hang-outs as you head towards the town centre. First, visit the Rijksmuseum van Oudheden *(p201)*, with its rich collection of antiquities, then the 15th-century Pieterskerk *(p200)*, which is just around the corner.

Evening After a busy day of sightseeing, relax with a drink at the Grand Café Van Buuren *(p200)* on Stationsweg, before embarking on the 40-minute journey back to Amsterdam.

Pieter Mondriaan

Boldly coloured squares and rectangles are the hallmarks of "Piet" Mondriaan's work. Mondriaan (1870-1944) was one of the driving forces behind De Stijl - the Dutch movement that explored the clarity and purity of straight lines. His *Composition in Red, Black, Blue, Yellow and Grey* (1920) is one of the gems of the Stedelijk Museum's collection *(p130)*.

Mondriaan's *Composition in Red, Black, Blue, Yellow and Grey*

AMSTERDAM FOR ART LOVERS

With its picturesque canal scenes and liberal atmosphere, it's easy to see why this city has been a haven for artists for centuries. In Amsterdam's museums, you'll find both flashy 17th-century portraits and cutting-edge 20th-century works, while street artists are making the city their canvas.

Vincent van Gogh

Vincent van Gogh (1853-90) began painting in the Netherlands, but his most famous works were inspired by Arles. The sun-soaked colours of Provence can be seen in *Sunflowers* (1888) and *Vincent's Bedroom in Arles* (1888). Continually blighted by depression, he tragically ended his life before his brilliance was recognized. The Van Gogh Museum is an unmissable stop for any art fan *(p128)*.

OFFBEAT ART GALLERIES

Electric Ladyland
Tweede Leliedwarsstraat 5 electric-lady-land.com
This fluorescent art gallery is a treat for those who love all things psychedelic.

Street Art Museum
The world's largest street art-museum is housed in a former warehouse next to NDSM *(p181)*.

Kochxbos
Eerste Anjeliersdwarsstraat 36
kochxbos.nl
Visit Kochxbos for collectable graphic art and 21st-century surrealism.

↑ A visitor admiring Vermeer's *Girl with a Pearl Earring* in the Mauritshuis

Jan Vermeer

Delft-born Johannes (Jan) Vermeer (1632-75) is one of the superstars of the Golden Age *(p127)*. With works such as *The Love Letter* (1666), Vermeer helped to create a new form of genre painting where objects in everyday scenes became symbols. In *The Love Letter*, which hangs in the Rijksmuseum *(p124)*, the lute represents carnal love. Vermeer's best-known work, *Girl With a Pearl Earring* (1665), is housed in the Mauritshuis in Den Haag *(p204)*.

Did You Know?

The I amsterdam City Card grants you free entry to many museums *(p229)*.

↑ The Van Gogh Museum housing *Vincent's Bedroom in Arles (inset)*

Rembrandt van Rijn

Born in Leiden, Rembrandt Harmenszoon van Rijn (1606-69) moved to Amsterdam in 1631, where he found many wealthy patrons. *The Night Watch* (1642) is his most venerated work and you can admire it, and many of his other paintings, in the Rijksmuseum *(p124)*, but for an insight into the artist's life, head to the Museum Het Rembrandthuis *(p94)*.

→ *The Night Watch* dominating the Rijksmuseum's Gallery of Honour

De Machine, an interactive logistics exhibit, at NEMO Science Museum

AMSTERDAM FOR FAMILIES

Many cities claim to be family-friendly, but Amsterdam really does offer a huge mix of attractions and activities that won't fail to keep the kids entertained. It's not just museums either; there are parks and urban beaches, as well as plenty of opportunities for cycling and fun on the water.

Open-Air Fun

Amsterdam is a green city and spaces like the Vondelpark *(p133)*, Westerpark *(p160)* and Oosterpark *(p172)* have free activity areas that are perfect when children need to burn off excess energy. In Noord, kids will love Pllek – an urban beach where films are screened in the summer *(p181)*. Beyond the city, at the open-air Zuiderzee Museum *(p190)*, old-style barges transport families back to the early 20th century, where re-enactors in traditional costume demonstrate local crafts.

People relaxing on a sunny day at Pllek in Noord

Rainy-Day Activities

Child-friendly museums are the perfect places to head if the weather turns sour. At The Little Orphanage *(p75)*, young visitors can experience the life of a 17th-century orphan, including milking a cow. Interactive exhibits at NEMO Science Museum *(p99)* are both educational and entertaining. Kids can protect Earth from meteorites, blow bubbles big enough to stand in and don their lab coats to perform experiments. Tropenmuseum Junior *(p169)* transports visitors to Morocco, where they explore a medina and try their hand at mosaics. Miffy, the small white rabbit, comes to life at Nijntje Museum in Utrecht *(p217)*. Here little ones can listen to storytellers and play.

←

A father and son making model gears at the NEMO Science Museum

EAT

The Pancake Boat

Cruise with pancakes.

P11 Ms. van Riemsdijkweg

pannenkoekenboot.nl

Kinderkookkafé

Kids are the chefs here.

A8 Vondelpark 6B

kinderkookkafe.nl

NEMO Rooftop Café

An open-air terrace.

J4 Oosterdok 2

nemoscience museum.nl

INSIDER TIP

Nature Calls

Apart from inside museums, the best places to find toilets are train stations, cafés and department stores. Be prepared to pay 50 cents or to buy a drink.

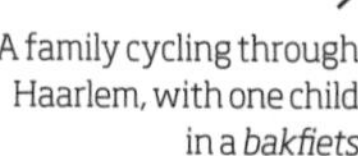

→

A family cycling through Haarlem, with one child in a *bakfiets*

Active Fun

With little traffic, cycling is a great way to explore the city *(p44)*. Younger children can ride in front of parents in a child-friendly *bakfiets* bike trailer. Numerous companies rent tandems and other bikes for all ages, and families can escape to parks like Vondelpark and Amsterdamse Bos to find countless traffic-free cycle paths. Cycling isn't restricted to the streets - pedal-powered "canal bikes", seating four or more, are a super way to explore Amsterdam's canals *(p48)*.

AMSTERDAM FOR FOODIES

Raw herring and *bitterballen*, street food from four continents and some of the finest restaurants in Europe – Amsterdam really is a mecca for foodies looking to tickle their taste buds. Here we look at some of the city's must-eats.

Dutch Classics

Smelling of the sea, with a soft texture inside the crispy exterior, *haring* (salted raw herring) has been a popular Dutch snack since the Middle Ages. It's best savoured in June when the first fish of the season land on street stalls, such as Stubbe's Haring. *Bitterballen* is another local pick-me-up. These deep-fried meat croquettes are filled with comforting gravy and dipped in a bowl of mustard. For lunch or dinner, order *erwtensoep*, also called *snert* – a thick soup of split peas and sausage – or *stamppot*, a hearty dish of mashed potatoes, crispy bacon and winter greens. Looking for something sweet? *Pannenkoeken* (pancakes) are the answer.

↑ Crispy, golden *bitterballen* with mustard

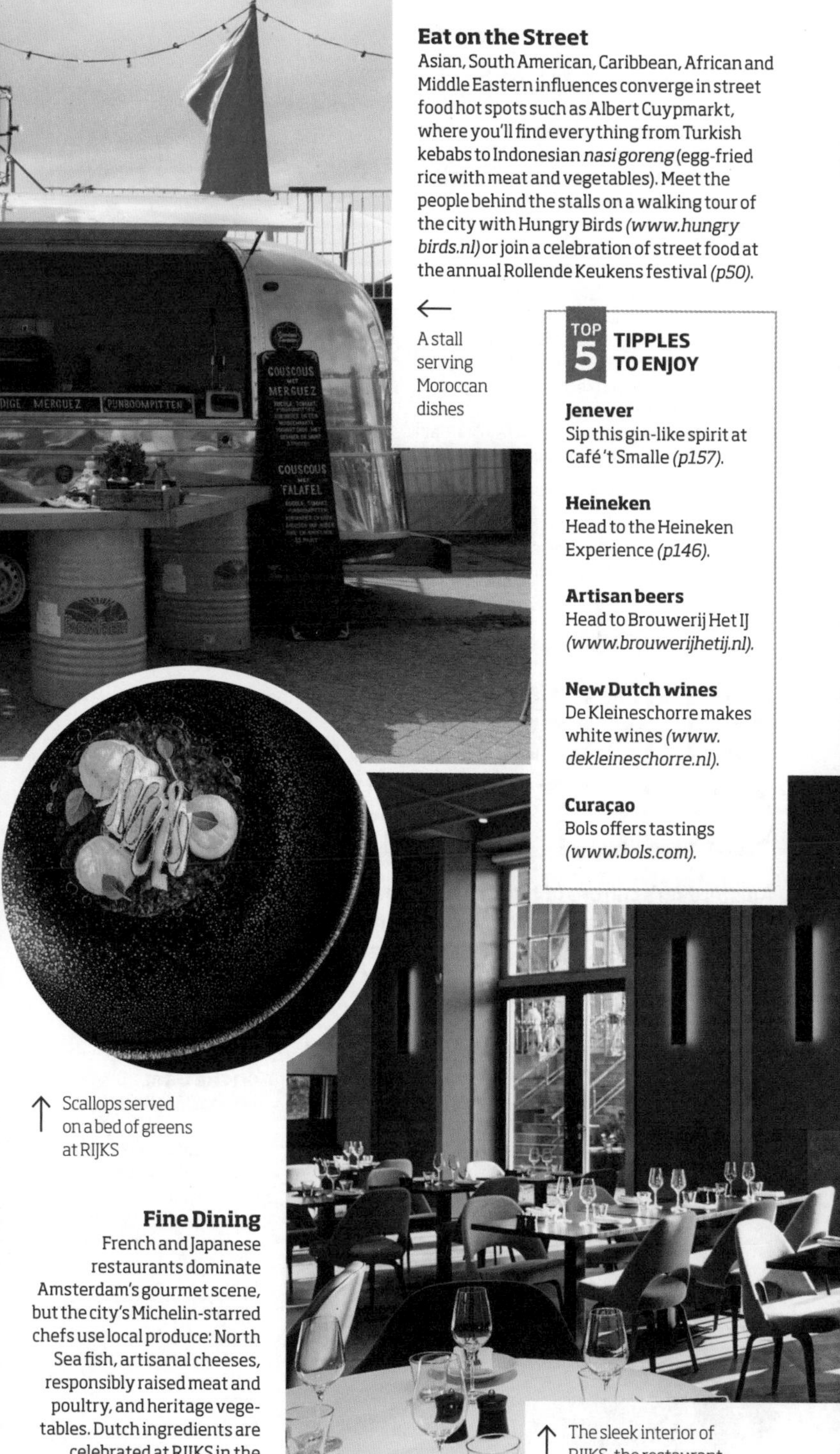

Eat on the Street

Asian, South American, Caribbean, African and Middle Eastern influences converge in street food hot spots such as Albert Cuypmarkt, where you'll find everything from Turkish kebabs to Indonesian *nasi goreng* (egg-fried rice with meat and vegetables). Meet the people behind the stalls on a walking tour of the city with Hungry Birds *(www.hungrybirds.nl)* or join a celebration of street food at the annual Rollende Keukens festival *(p50)*.

← A stall serving Moroccan dishes

TOP 5 TIPPLES TO ENJOY

Jenever
Sip this gin-like spirit at Café 't Smalle *(p157)*.

Heineken
Head to the Heineken Experience *(p146)*.

Artisan beers
Head to Brouwerij Het IJ *(www.brouwerijhetij.nl)*.

New Dutch wines
De Kleineschorre makes white wines *(www.dekleineschorre.nl)*.

Curaçao
Bols offers tastings *(www.bols.com)*.

↑ Scallops served on a bed of greens at RIJKS

Fine Dining

French and Japanese restaurants dominate Amsterdam's gourmet scene, but the city's Michelin-starred chefs use local produce: North Sea fish, artisanal cheeses, responsibly raised meat and poultry, and heritage vegetables. Dutch ingredients are celebrated at RIJKS in the Rijksmuseum *(p124)*.

↑ The sleek interior of RIJKS, the restaurant of the Rijksmuseum

Street Art

What was once an anti-establishment act is now enshrined in two of Amsterdam's most popular museums. The street art museum at NDSM *(p181)* houses large-scale murals from artists from around the world, while Banksy is the star of Moco Museum's collection *(p132)*. Captured on canvas, his iconic *Battle of the Beanfield* dominates the entrance hall. Despite these innovative museums, the best way to see street art is in the wild. Alltournative Amsterdam's enthusiastic local guides take graffiti fans on adventurous tours around the city's kaleidoscopic mural art scene *(www.alltournative-amsterdam.com)*. If just viewing the pieces isn't enough, pick up a spray can in a graffiti workshop run by a local street artist with Fun Amsterdam *(www.funamsterdam.com)*.

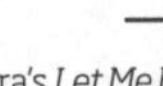

Eduardo Kobra's *Let Me Be Myself* on the outside of the street art museum in NDSM

Did You Know?

The Diary of Anne Frank is the book most read by young people in Kobra's native Brazil.

AMSTERDAM FOR STREET CULTURE

Amsterdam's culture of tolerance has made the city a vibrant centre for cutting-edge street art and theatre. In the 1960s, open-air performances and graffiti were consigned to the countercultural scene, but in the 21st century, street culture has become part of the modern zeitgeist.

Living Statues on the Dam

Take a selfie with a stock-still, periwigged personification of Marie Antoinette, Rembrandt, or a panoply of other historical or fictional figures on the city's bustling central square. The colourful cast of players changes by the hour. Be aware that performers expect to be given a few euros if you take a photograph with them.

Passersby wondering at the discipline of a performer on Dam Square

TOP 3 STREET ART PIECES

Let Me Be Myself (2016)
Eduardo Kobra's Kaleidoscopic mural of Anne Frank adorns the exterior of NDSM's street art museum *(p181)*.

Art Wall Tuinstraat (2012)
The artist Parra has painted a quirky calligraphy on the walls facing a school playground at Tuinstraat 172.

Untitled (2009)
A four-storey, comic-style mural by The London Police is found on the gable end of the canal house at 70 Prinsengracht.

Skateboard Displays at Marnix Bowl

Skateboarders and graffiti artists meet at Marnix Bowl, the city's biggest purpose-built skatepark. Spectators watch in awe as the boarders and BMX-riders pull daredevil stunts on psychedelic ramps.

→

Marnix Bowl, decorated with colourful graffiti by Lastplak Collective

Street Musicians on Leidseplein

Leidseplein is the best place in Amsterdam to watch the city's street performers. Sitting at alfresco café tables, visitors can kick back to the sounds of street bands playing everything from freestyle jazz to hardcore ragga. Buskers appreciate a donation if you enjoy their performance.

→

A street musician entertaining the public with his double bass

P J H Cuypers

Petrus J H Cuypers (1827-1921) placed his stamp on 19th-century Amsterdam with Centraal Station (1889) and the Rijksmuseum *(p124)*. Both red-brick buildings are now sources of pride for Amsterdammers, but when they were built Cuypers's Neo-Renaissance designs offended some who would have favoured a more austere style.

The exterior of P J H Cuypers' grand Centraal Station at night

AMSTERDAM'S ARCHITECTURE

From historic churches to modernist complexes, there's more to Amsterdam's architecture than its iconic canal houses.

The striking green exterior of the NEMO Science Museum ↓

Renzo Piano

Italian architect Renzo Piano (b 1937) transformed the city's waterfront with the NEMO Science Museum *(p99)*. This dazzling, maritime-inspired leviathan looks very much like the giant hull of a ship, with its prow jutting 30 m (98 ft) over the glittering Oosterdok.

INSIDER TIP
Take a tour

Visitors can join an architect-led private tour of new neighbourhoods, such as IJburg, with Architecture Tours *(www.architecturetours.nl)*.

Hendrick de Keyser

This Golden Age architect (1565–1621) was appointed as the city's municipal architect in 1612 and is responsible for the Zuiderkerk *(p98)* and Westerkerk *(p115)*, as well as Delft's Town Hall *(p208)*. His work characterizes the transition from the ornamental style of the Dutch Renaissance to the Classicism of the 17th century.

→

People walking and skating on a frozen canal near Westerkerk

The Amsterdam School

These idealistic architects believed that they could transform lives with their designs. They built distinctive estates like the Dageraad complex (1923) and Het Schip *(p160)*. Piet Kramer (1881–1961) and Michel de Klerk (1884–1923) were leading lights of the movement.

←

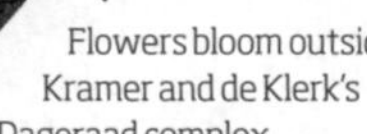

Flowers bloom outside Kramer and de Klerk's Dageraad complex

H P Berlage

Hendrik Petrus Berlage (1856–1934) employed clean, functional lines in his new stock exchange – Beurs van Berlage *(p82)*. The structure marked a forward-looking departure from the Revivalist style that dominated the skyline in the late 19th century.

→

The red-brick exterior of Beurs van Berlage, with its iron and glass roof

▽ Picnic in the Park

The best-known and most accessible of the city's parks, Vondelpark *(p133)* is to Amsterdam what Hyde Park is to London or Central Park to Manhattan. It's near to the Museumplein, so it's a perfect place to relax and have a leisurely picnic after an immersive cultural experience.

△ A Winter Stroll

Hortus Botanicus Amsterdam *(p171)*, with its vast collection of flora, is ideal for a walk in winter. Visitors can escape inclement weather in the botanical garden's glass-domed Palm House, built in 1912, and in huge space-age conservatories that recreate tropical, subtropical and desert climates.

AMSTERDAM OUTDOORS

Although the city is compact and intensely urban, Amsterdammers spend much of their time outdoors. There are tiny green enclaves within its very centre, green expanses not far from the city's heart and breezy North Sea beaches within easy reach.

◁ Cycle through Woodland

The journey to Amsterdamse Bos (by train to Schiphol Airport, and then on bus 180 or 186) takes less than ten minutes from the city centre. Planned in the 1920s, this 1,035-hectare (2,557-acre) expanse of woodland, streams and lakes is a refuge for many wild birds and animals. The best way to explore the park is to either walk or cycle the 145 km (90 miles) of paths that crisscross this natural oasis.

▽ Beautiful Bulbfields

From January to May, the bulbfields around Keukenhof erupt in wondrous strips of colour, attracting visitors from around the world *(p196)*. For the best views of the spectacle, hire a bike and ride from Haarlem to Leiden alongside the flower-laden fields.

▷ Peace and Quiet

A tiny green enclave in the heart of the city, Begijnhof was created in 1346 to be a place of religious reflection *(p78)*. No tour groups are allowed in the grounds of the *hofjes*, making it the perfect place for a break from the bustling streets of Nieuwe Zijde.

◁ Urban Beaches

Beaches may not be the first things that come to mind when you think of Amsterdam, but there are several dotted around the city. The beach on the North shore of Sloterplas lake, 40 minutes away by tram, is best for swimming due to its calm waters. Pllek, however is our pick of the city's beaches *(p181)*. Located in Noord, it attracts foodies to its restaurant, cinemagoers to its summer screenings and eager sunseekers when the temperature rises. Pllek hosts live music events every week, ranging from laid-back acoustic sessions in their restaurant to full-blown parties that'll keep you dancing till the early hours.

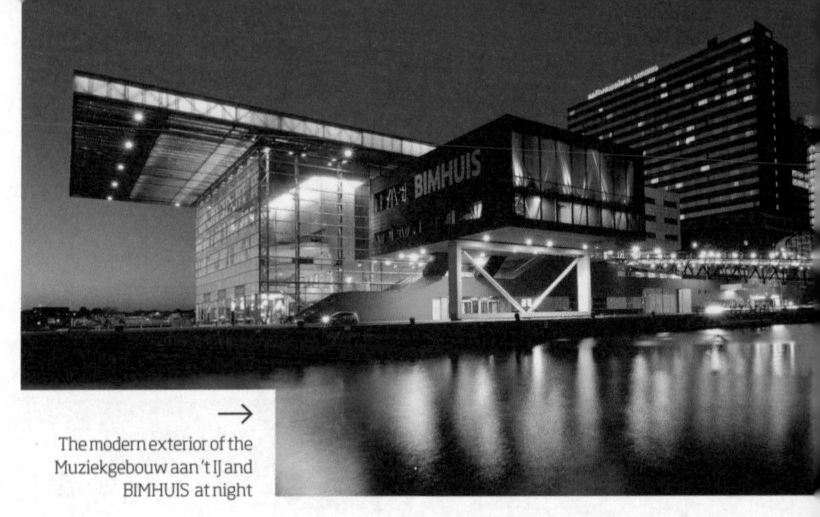

→ The modern exterior of the Muziekgebouw aan 't IJ and BIMHUIS at night

AMSTERDAM AFTER DARK

The Red Light District may be the first thing that comes to mind when you think of Amsterdam at night but clubs have been buzzing here since the 1960s and there's a thriving LGBT+ scene. For a more laid-back atmosphere, jazz can be heard in huge venues, as well as drifting along the side streets.

Club Life

Amsterdam's club scene embraces dance music of every kind, from old-school rock and roll to the latest grime sounds. Paradiso, which opened in the city's hippy heyday has a hedonistic vibe, with the emphasis on cutting-edge sounds and all-nighters *(www.paradiso.nl)*. A more recent addition to the city, Jimmy Woo has a tough door policy, so dress to impress *(www.jimmywoo.com)*. Named after the Greek goddess of the night, Club NYX is one of Amsterdam's top LGBT+ venues *(www.clubnyx.nl)*.

↑ Revellers enjoying a night out at Jimmy Woo

Amsterdam Live

There are plenty of opportunities to hear live music in Amsterdam, from intimate venues to extravagant concert halls. The opulent Concertgebouw has been hosting performances since 1888 and boasts unparalleled acoustics *(p132)*. Meanwhile, modern Muziekgebouw aan 't IJ *(p170)* has spaces for both large and small audiences. The BIMHUIS, which shares the Muziekgebouw aan 't IJ's stunning building, attracts the world's biggest names in jazz. If you prefer to see undiscovered acts, head to Café Casablanca, which claims to be the oldest and most famous jazz club in the Netherlands *(www.cafecasablanca.nl)*. On the edge of the Red Light District, it has a suitably funky atmosphere.

← Dancing to a live music performance at BIMHUIS

DRINK

Nachtcafés stay open until 4 or 5am.

Bloemenbar

Comfy sofas and soft music make Bloemenbar a great place to chill.

E6 Handboogstraat 15 bloemenbar.nl

Nota Bene Café

A favourite of the local student population.

E6 Voetbogstraat 4

Nachtcafé de Biecht

This *bruin café* plays the sounds of the 70s and 80s.

G7 Kerkstraat 346

INSIDER TIP

Free to Enter

The Amsterdam Nightlife Ticket offers free admission to more than 20 clubs for €10 *(www.amsterdamnightlifeticket.com)*.

→ The plain exterior of Melkweg belying its vibrant events

Cultural Complexes

Since the 1970s, Melkweg - a versatile entertainment venue - has staged alternative performances, including world music, experimental theatre and contemporary dance. Famed for its impromptu raves in the 1980s, Westergasfabriek - the former gasworks - is now a well-organized creative hub with a diverse programme of events *(www.westergasfabriek.nl)*. Tolhuistuin also occupies a repurposed building - Shell's former canteen *(www.tolhuistuin.nl)*. It's a laid-back, intimate venue with theatres and exhibition spaces.

Take a Ferry Across the IJ

Rather than splurging on a canalboat cruise through the city centre, ride the free ferry across the IJ instead. Board the blue-and-white ferry bound for NDSM from Centraal Station and enjoy the amazing views of A'DAM Toren and EYE, giving you an insight into the modern face of Amsterdam.

←

A blue-and-white ferry motoring towards Noord's A'DAM Toren and EYE

AMSTERDAM ON A SHOESTRING

Although Amsterdam can be an expensive city, savvy visitors can find plenty of things to see and do free of charge or at a fraction of the price.

Performances in the Park

In summer, the Vondelpark Open Air Theatre hosts free contemporary and modern dance, drama, classical, pop and jazz concerts, as well as stand-up comedy *(p133)*. Many performances are in English.

325

food stalls can be found at Albert Cuypmarkt.

People picnicking near the monument in Sarphatipark ↓

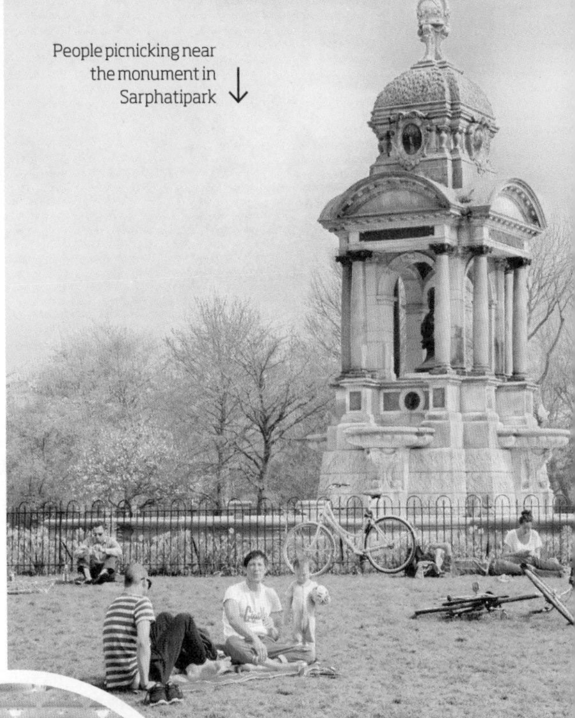

Have a Picnic

A ten-minute walk from Museumplein, Albert Cuypmarkt *(p145)* offers a bewildering choice of ready-made snacks and other picnic ingredients. From freshly baked bread and organic cheeses to fresh fruit, cured herring and pastries, you'll find the perfect picnic elements at these stalls. Take your purchases to the nearby Sarphatipark and while away the afternoon.

Lunchtime Sounds

The Muziekgebouw aan 't IJ *(p170)* serves up a free midday concert once a month, while the Concertgebouw *(p132)* hosts one every Wednesday. Not constrained to lunchtime? The BIMHUIS offers at least one free evening concert, workshop or jam session every week.

← An audience watching an orchestra at the Concertgebouw

↑ A band performing at the Vondelpark Open Air Theatre

Art on the Cheap

No tickets are needed to enjoy works by Rembrandt and other masters in the Amsterdam Gallery at the Amsterdam Museum *(p74)*. As well as a collection of Golden Age paintings of city militiamen and prominent citizens, the world's only free "museum street" also displays 21st-century group portraits.

→ Barbara Broekman's carpet in the Amsterdam Gallery

AMSTERDAM FOR CYCLING

Amsterdam's love affair with the bicycle started in the 1960s, when countercultural groups started promoting bikes as an alternative to the cars that threatened to destroy the city's character. Dedicated cycle lanes and pancake-flat terrain make the city bike-friendly for visitors and locals.

TOP 5 RULES OF THE ROAD

Stay Right
Always use the bicycle lane on the right-hand side of the road.

Stick to the Road
Don't ride on footpaths or pavements.

Be Aware
Be careful of other road users.

Lock It Up
Whenever possible, lock your bike up at an official city cycle rack.

Safety First
Always wear a helmet and high-visibility vest, which are provided by bike rental companies.

Kids on Wheels

Families with tots need a *bakfiets* – the ultra-sensible Dutch two-wheeled toddler transporter that lets parents carry younger children in a child-safe box at the front of the bike. Escape the busy cyclelanes of the crowded centre in the leafy Amsterdamse Bos, with its 145 km (90 miles) of footpaths, cycleways and picnic spots *(p38)*. Alternatively, see the city with We Bike Amsterdam, which runs child-friendly tours on two wheels *(www.webikeamsterdam.com)*.

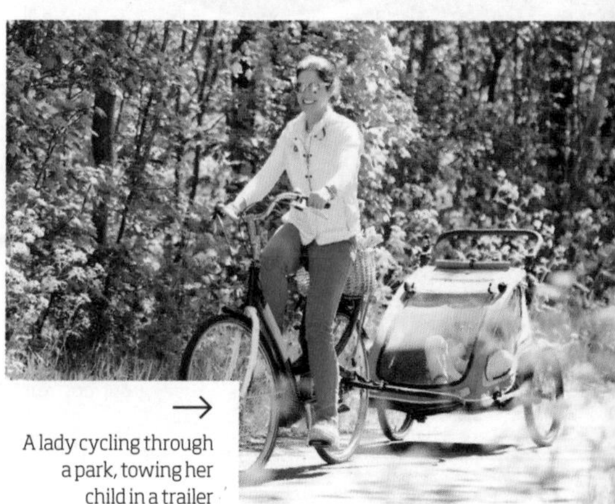

→ A lady cycling through a park, towing her child in a trailer

Bicycles Made for Two

Couples can rent tandem bicycles for romantic rides along Amsterdam's canal rings or the banks of the Amstel. But these routes can get busy with tourists and commuters. For a little peace and quiet, hop on a ferry across the IJ to explore the pretty villages on the outskirts of Noord, such as Ransdorp and Nieuwendam. You can rent a bicycle for two from Black Bikes *(www.black-bikes.com)*.

Couple cycling on a tandem bike down an urban street

WHITE BIKES

Despite the support of Beatle John Lennon and his partner Yoko Ono, the idealistic Witte Fietsenplan ("white bike plan") was short-lived. The anarcho-hippy Provo group wanted to make thousands of white-painted bikes freely available to Amsterdammers, but the city council refused to fund the project and most of the first 50 "white bikes" vanished. Despite this, the scheme boosted support for cycling in Amsterdam and the city now has dozens of bike rental companies - although it still has no city-wide, nonprofit bike-share system.

Going Electric

Cyclists who want to go further without running out of energy can rent ecofriendly bikes with battery-powered electric motors. Many hotels, cafés and restaurants have charging points so cyclists can top up their batteries while taking a break. Rent an electric bike from Black Bikes.

Pausing with an electric bike

Did You Know?

You can download recommended cycling routes at www.iamsterdam.com.

Taking a break from cycling through the wild Zuid-Kennemerland National Park

Off-Road Cycling

Most cycle routes in Amsterdam are on the flat. Bikers who want to pick up the pace can rent BMX bikes to burn round rugged trails on the outskirts of Amsterdamse Bos. For a real breath of fresh air, take the train to Haarlem, rent a bike at the station, then dive into the dunes and woodlands of the Zuid-Kennemerland National Park *(www.rentabikehaarlem.nl)*.

▽ **The Harbour View**
The NEMO Science Museum's rooftop terrace is the ideal vantage point for early morning shots of the Oosterdok, boats at anchor in Het Scheepvaartmuseum and the waterfront *(p99)*.

△ **The Most Photogenic Bridges**
It's a tough call deciding which of Amsterdam's canal bridges is the most picturesque. Fortunately, Blauwbrug *(p145)* and Magere Brug *(p149)* are close together so you can easily take a picture of both. Illuminated after nightfall, Magere Brug is the perfect subject for an after-dark shot.

AMSTERDAM FOR PHOTOGRAPHERS

As one of the world's most photogenic cities, there are iconic shots around every corner in Amsterdam. Here we reveal the wheres and whens to help you snap the perfect picture of this city.

△ **The Classic Canal Image**
Shoot the perfect image of the 17th-century buildings that line Amsterdam's canals from the west side of Herengracht, close to the corner of Leidsestraat. Early evening light is best.

▽ The Colourful Bulbfields

Tulips, daffodils and crocuses bloom for just a few weeks in spring and early summer in Zuid-Holland's bulbfields *(p196)*. This is also when the Keukenhof gardens are at their best. Visit the fields or gardens in March or April for perfect swathes of colour.

▷ The Prettiest Houses

The almshouses surrounding the Begijnhof's inner courtyard are arguably the most charming buildings in Amsterdam *(p78)*. Each of the 47 tall townhouses is distinct, making the photographic opportunities here endless. Plan to visit around midday for the best light. Note that visitors are restricted to the space around the church; the courtyard is only accessible to the inhabitants of these houses.

▽ The Artist's Inspiration

Montelbaanstoren, on the north side of Oudeschans, was one of Rembrandt's favourite subjects *(p98)*. It's not difficult to see why, as this striking tower dominates the wide Oudeschans canal. Snap Montelbaanstoren in the morning, from midway across Keizersbrug, or from the corner of Oudeschans and Oostersekade.

△ The Sunset Panorama

Take the high-speed elevator to A'DAM Toren's Lookout for the ultimate sunset shot over the city skyline *(p180)*. The reflective water of the IJ makes the perfect foreground for a picture of the historic canal rings.

Canal Cruises

Most *rondvaartboten* (cruise boats) offer a multilingual commentary on the history of the city. They also have glass roofs that can be opened in fine weather. To see the city's highlights by day, board a Stromma cruise from one of many locations in the city centre, including Prins Hendrikkade, opposite Centraal Station, and Damrak *(www.stromma.nl)*. Feeling romantic? Indulge in one of the sumptuous fine dining cruises run by Amsterdam Jewel Cruises *(www.amsterdam jewelcruises.com)*.

→

A *rondvaartboot*, with a classy dinner service *(inset)*, passing under a bridge

AMSTERDAM ON THE WATER

Set on the point where the Amstel river flows into the IJ, and characterized by its canal rings, water is everywhere you turn in this city. From do-it-yourself pedalboats to fabulous dinner cruises, there are many ways to enjoy Amsterdam's waterways, nearby lakes and the North Sea.

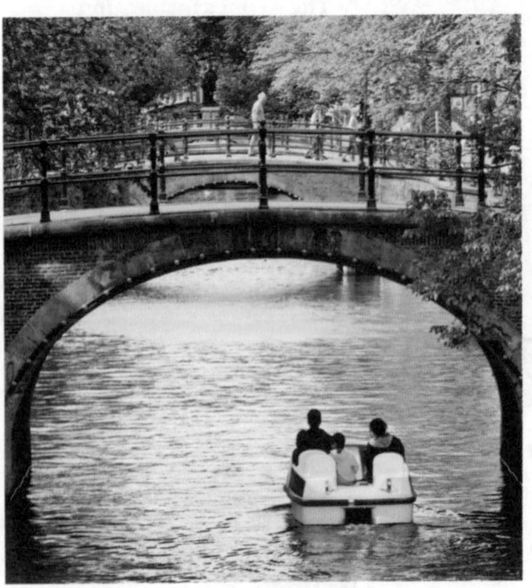

Pedalboats

To navigate Amsterdam's canals at your own pace, rent a two- or four-seater "canal bike". As well as being eco-friendly, pedalboats can help to burn off any excess energy. In summer, this is a great way for everyone, especially families, to discover waterways that the big canal cruisers can't reach. Stromma hires out pedal-boats by the hour and pick-up points are found at the tourist hot spots: Rijksmuseum, Westerkerk, Leidseplein and Keizersgracht.

A family enjoying a four-seater pedalboat on Amsterdam's canal ring

2018

Amsterdam's canals last froze over in this year.

A hop-on, hop-off boat leaving from Centraal Station

Hop-on, Hop-off

Create your own, 24-hour personalized canal tour using Stromma's hop-on, hop-off boats. Chugging around the city's inner waterways, you can disembark at whichever keynote sights you wish to explore.

TOP 3 HISTORIC VESSELS

Amsterdam
Visitors can climb aboard this full-scale replica of a Dutch East Indiaman at Het Scheepvaart-museum *(p166)*.

Zuiderzee
The last original, two-masted, schooner-rigged barge in the Netherlands is available for private charter for 20 to 34 people *(p191)*. Dinner, drinks and snacks are provided.

Tugboats
These veteran vessels, now moored at the Maritiem Museum Rotterdam *(p212)*, were once used in the city's historic harbour.

Traditional sailing boats moored at a dock in the city

Sailing Trips

Take a sunset cruise or spend the day on the calm waters of the Markermeer *(p191)* aboard *Zuiderzee* – a traditional *tjalk* sailing barge *(www.zuiderzee.eu)*. More adventurous sailors can venture into the Ijsselmeer or Waddenzee on *Aaltje Angelina* – a 22-m (72-ft) gaff-rigged *stevenaak (www.aaltjeengelina.nl)*.

A YEAR IN AMSTERDAM

JANUARY

△ **National Tulip Day** *(early Jan)*. Tulip growers create a vivid pop-up garden on Dam Square.

Jumping Amsterdam *(end Jan)*. International showjumping competitions take place at Amsterdam RAI.

FEBRUARY

△ **Chinese New Year** *(mid-Feb)*. Traditional lion dances snake through Nieuwmarkt and fireworks light up the skies.

Herdenking Februaristaking *(25 Feb)*. Commemoration on J D Meijerplein of the brave actions of dockworkers against the Nazis' deportation of Jews during World War II.

MAY

Herdenkingsdag *(4 May)*. Commemorations for victims of World War II are held throughout the Netherlands.

△ **Rollende Keukens Festival** *(mid-May)*. A lively celebration of Dutch street food is held outside Westergasfabriek.

JUNE

Holland Festival *(mid-Jun)*. Concerts, plays, opera and ballet are staged at theatres and concert halls throughout Amsterdam.

△ **Amsterdam Roots Festival** *(late Jun)*. This celebration of world music, dance, film and drama is held in Oosterpark, as well as under cover in Paradiso, Melkweg and BIMHUIS.

SEPTEMBER

△ **Amsterdam Heritage Days** *(1st or 2nd weekend)*. Historic buildings, including Oude Kerk, open their doors to the public free of charge.

Amsterdam Fringe Festival *(early to mid-Sep)*. Experimental theatre and performance, in English, Dutch and no language at all, is staged at various venues throughout the city.

OCTOBER

Amsterdam Dance Event *(mid-Oct)*. More than 100 club venues throughout Amsterdam take part in the world's biggest event for electronic club music fans.

△ **TCS Amsterdam Marathon** *(late Oct)*. Thousands of professional and amateur runners circle the city in this gruelling race, which is over 42 km (26 miles) long.

MARCH

△ **Opening of Keukenhof** *(early Mar).* Tulips, daffodils and hyacinths bloom at this garden near Lisse in Zuid-Holland.

Wonderland Festival *(mid-Mar).* Electro sounds rule at this massive dance rave in Jordaan's Westerpark.

Stille Omgang *(2nd or 3rd Sat).* A silent night-time procession down Rokin celebrates the Miracle of Amsterdam.

Roze Filmdagen *(throughout).* Watch the latest LGBT+ films at Ketelhuis cinema in Westerpark.

APRIL

Tulip Festival *(throughout).* Rare and colourful tulips on display in parks and other locations throughout Amsterdam, including EYE, Hermitage Amsterdam, Hortus Botanicus, Museum Van Loon and Rijksmuseum.

Imagine Film Festival *(mid- to end Apr).* Fantasy, horror and science fiction set the tone at this film fest at EYE.

△ **Koningsdag** *(27 Apr).* Amsterdam becomes one big street, and boat, party on King Willem-Alexander's birthday.

JULY

Comedy Train International Summer Festival *(early Jul).* International stand-up comedians perform at Toomler Theater.

△ **Summer Concerts** *(Jul–Aug).* Classical music is showcased at Concertgebouw.

AUGUST

Hortus Festival *(Thu in Jul & Aug).* Music is performed in the Hortus Botanicus and the botanical gardens in Leiden and Rotterdam.

△ **Pride Amsterdam** *(late Jul–early Aug).* Huge celebrations of LGBT+ solidarity take place throughout the city.

NOVEMBER

△ **Sinterklaas Parade** *(2nd or 3rd Sat).* Santa Claus, or St Nicholas, arrives by boat at St Nicolaasbasiliek to mark the beginning of the festive season.

DECEMBER

Christmas Markets *(throughout).* Stalls selling gifts and seasonal food and drink are set up throughout the city, and an ice-skating rink is erected on Museumplein.

Amsterdam Light Festival *(Dec to mid-Jan).* Artists illuminate city-centre canals with colourful light installations.

△ **New Year's Fireworks Display** *(31 Dec).* Dazzling pyrotechnics light up the sky over the Amstel.

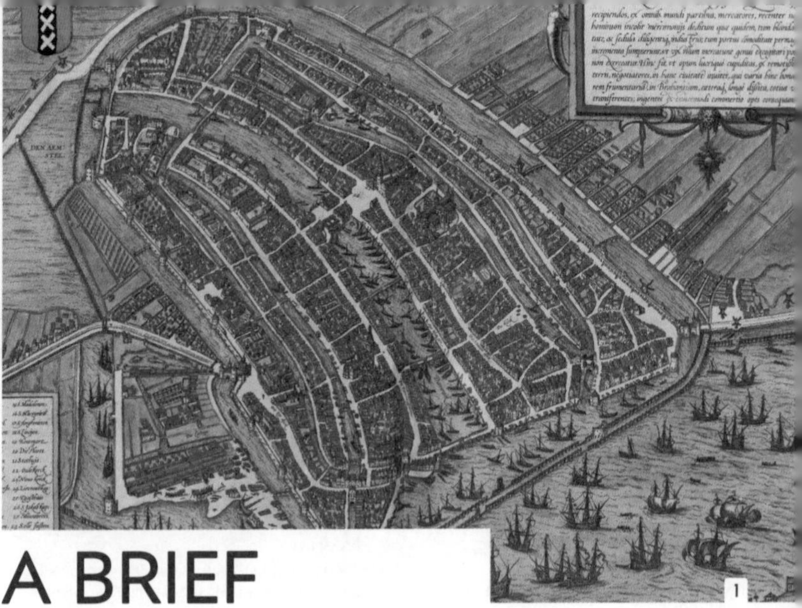

1

A BRIEF HISTORY

Upstart Amsterdam grew quickly from its 13th-century roots in uninhabited marshland. By the 17th century it was in the flushes of its Golden Age as one of Europe's wealthiest cities. Although no longer an imperial hub, Amsterdam today is still a global financial capital and a city where freedom reigns.

Amstelledamme Becomes Amsterdam

Work began in 1264 on the dam of the Amstel river which gave the settlement its name: Amstelledamme. By the 14th century, the town was known as Amsterdam and was prosperous enough to build the imposing Oude Kerk *(p90)*. Amsterdam's second important place of worship – the Nieuwe Kerk *(p72)* – was built in the late 14th century. But the wooden church, along with most of the town, was destroyed by the second of two great fires that swept Amsterdam in 1421 and 1452. Further conflagrations ravaged the town in the early 16th century and in 1521, the city council banned wooden buildings to prevent further disasters.

1 Map showing Amsterdam in 1582.

2 15th-century houses in the Begijnhof.

3 Depiction of the Nieuwe Kerk on fire by Egbert Lievensz van der Poel (1645).

4 Portrait of Prince William of Orange.

Timeline of events

1264

Work begins on the first dam on River Amstel.

1306

Oude Kerk consecrated.

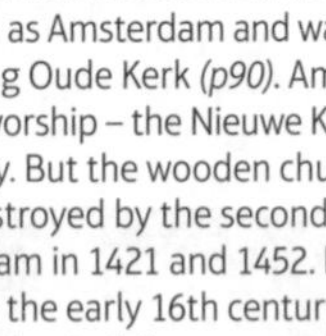

1452

Second fire destroys much of the city, including the wooden Nieuwe Kerk.

1477

Amsterdam becomes part of the Holy Roman Empire under the Habsburgs.

1522

Habsburg Emperor Charles V attempts to crush the Reformation in the Netherlands.

Towards Independence

Amsterdam became part of the Holy Roman Empire via a dynastic marriage in 1477, but the relationship didn't remain peaceful for long. By 1500, the Protestant Reformation swept through Europe and, between 1522 and 1550, some 30,000 Dutch Protestants were killed under Philip II of Spain. In 1568, Prince William of Orange or William the Silent – *stadhouder* (governor) of the provinces of Holland, Zeeland and Utrecht – led the Protestants in the Dutch Revolt (also known as the Eighty Years' War). At first, pragmatic Amsterdam sided with the Spanish, but in 1578 the city switched its allegiance to the rebels in an event known as the Alteration. Amsterdam became the fiercely Protestant capital of an infant Dutch Republic in 1581.

In the following years, the Republic suffered a series of disasters, including the siege of Maastricht. Having grown unpopular, William of Orange was assassinated by one of Philip II's supporters in 1584 *(p208)*. William's sons, Maurice and Frederick Henry, continued his cause. After 80 years of struggle, it was only under Frederick Henry's son William II, Prince of Orange, that independence was granted to the Netherlands in 1648.

Did You Know?

Only 400 of Maastricht's population of 30,000 survived the Spanish siege of 1579.

1543

Charles V unifies the Low Countries - the Netherlands, Belgium and Luxembourg.

1568

War breaks out after the Spanish Duke of Alva executes the Protestant Dukes of Egmont and Hoorn.

1578

Amsterdam shifts allegiance to the Protestant rebels.

1581

Amsterdam becomes the capital of the Dutch Republic.

1584

Prince William of Orange assassinated in Delft.

Boom Times

The 17th century ushered in a prosperous Golden Age for Amsterdam. Dutch admirals ruled the seas, trouncing English and French fleets; Abel Tasman, and other Dutch navigators, explored the globe; and the West India Company and United East India Company (Vereinigde Oostindische Compagnie or VOC) pioneered a worldwide merchant empire.

The new Dutch middle class grew resentful of the ruling House of Orange. In 1795 the Patriots – a radical political faction inspired by the Enlightenment – formed the Batavian Republic, with French support. Napoleon Bonaparte ultimately took control and in 1808 he placed his brother Louis on the Dutch throne.

The Age of Industrialization

After its liberation in 1813, the Netherlands regrouped around the exiled House of Orange and William I was crowned as the first king of the Netherlands in 1815. Recovery was slow, but conquests in the East Indies gave a new industrial economy access to resources including oil, rubber and tin.

↑ A'DAM Toren, the former headquarters of the Shell oil company

Timeline of events

1602

Amsterdam merchants form the United East India Company to trade with Asia.

1626

West India Company acquires Manhattan and founds New Amsterdam.

1648

Peace of Munster ends war with Spain.

1652–54

Commercial rivalry between England and the Netherlands leads to First Anglo-Dutch War.

1666–67

The Netherlands victorious in Second Anglo-Dutch War.

War and Occupation

The Netherlands hoped to remain neutral during World War II, but this wish was dashed when Germany invaded in May 1940. During the occupation, which lasted until May 1945, Jews were deported to concentration camps and gestures of resistance, such as the 1941 dockers' strike, were crushed.

A New Golden Age

Amsterdam forgot colonialism and embraced a European future after the Dutch East Indies – now Indonesia – gained independence in 1949. Fast motorways linked it to its neighbours and the completion of the Amsterdam-Rhine canal encouraged trade. Attracted by a thriving economy, workers from the former Dutch colonies and European Union flocked to the cosmopolitan city, causing a housing crisis.

Urban rejuvenation programmes have eased Amsterdam's overcrowding problem by creating new places to live and work, such as IJburg. For global companies, Amsterdam is appealing because of its multinational workforce and its transport links, which make it a gateway to the rest of the EU.

1 Engraving of the West India Company's building. ↑

2 *Amsterdam* is a replica of a 18th-century ship.

3 The Nationaal Monument in Dam Square.

4 A barge motors on the Amsterdam-Rhine canal.

Did You Know?

The city's population reached a peak of 869,000 in the 1960s, its highest to date.

1678

Franco-Dutch War ends with the Treaty of Nijmegen, leaving the Netherlands undefeated.

1795–1813

The Netherlands under French control.

1815

William I crowned first king of the Netherlands.

1919

Women given right to vote.

1940

Germany invades the Netherlands.

41-TV-RJ

Two women strolling along Egelantiersgracht

A CANAL WALK

With the increase in wealth and civic pride in Amsterdam during the city's 17th-century Golden Age, an ambitious plan was formed to build a splendid ring of canals round the city. Conceived in 1609, and added to in 1664 by Daniel Stalpaert, the scheme grew to encompass wide canals lined with opulent townhouses in a variety of architectural styles. These houses reflect the wealth of the inflating merchant class who prospered from the spoils of the United East India Company and West India Company at that time.

A walk along the canals takes in these merchants' mansions, as well as unbelievably narrow houses and wonderful examples of the Amsterdam School of architecture. The diverse façades, reflected in the glass-like canals, have come to represent the city for people around the world.

The following pages guide you along the Singel, Keizersgracht, Herengracht, Reguliersgracht and Prinsengracht canals. Listen to the sounds of the waterways and feel their bustling energy as you explore the arteries of this water-fuelled city.

1

2

Did You Know?

The Yab Yum brothel once made €40,000 in one night.

A CANAL WALK
DAM SQUARE TO KEIZERSGRACHT

Distance 850 m (0.5 miles) **Nearest tram** Dam **Time** 10 minutes

The walk along Amsterdam's finest canals begins in Dam Square. Leave the square by walking down Paleisstraatpast, passing the Koninklijk Paleis *(p79)*. Cross Nieuwezijds Voorburgwal and Spuistraat, and turn left to stroll along the left bank of Singel.

This canal served as a moat around the city until 1585, when Amsterdam expanded. The Singel is the nexus of the city's second-largest Red Light District. As you walk along, you'll pass both opulent mansions and former brothels, including the infamous Yab Yum.

A L van Gendt designed this massive stone office block at No 239 Singel for trader Julius Carle Bunge. Known as the Bungehuis, it was completed in 1934.

The double-fronted 17th-century canal house at No 265 Singel has been rebuilt several times since it was first constructed.

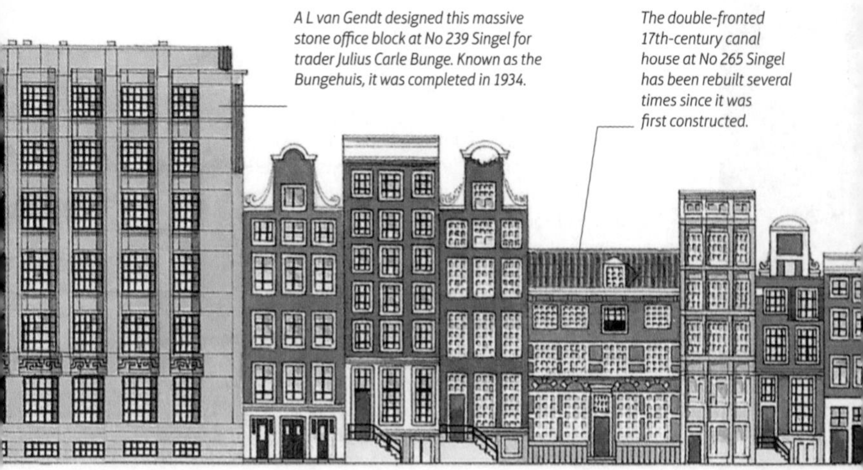

1 The imposing Bungehuis office block is located at No 239 Singel.

2 A vibrant orange boat floats down the Singel, passing the diverse façades that line this canal.

3 The Singel is home to the Bloemenmarkt *(p146)* which floats on the water.

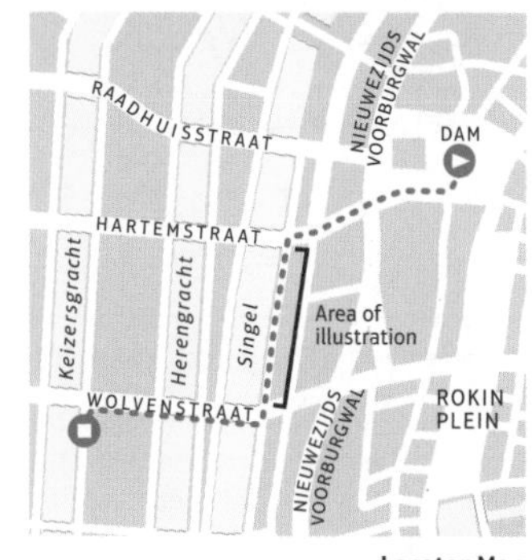

Locator Map

After passing the contrasting 18th-century façades of Nos 317 and 319 Singel, turn right onto Oude Spiegelstraat to cross Herengracht. Walk along Wolvenstraat until you reach Keizersgracht. Turn the page to continue your stroll along the waterways.

The step gable at No 279 Singel dates from the 19th century. Most of the houses along this canal were built between 1600 and 1665.

These houses, Nos 289–293, stand on an alley once called Schoorsteenvegersteeg (chimney sweeps' lane), which was home to many immigrant chimney sweeps in the 19th century.

This infamous former brothel, which was exclusive, occupied the 17th-century canal house at No 295 Singel. The interior has been preserved as a museum.

1

2

A CANAL WALK
KEIZERSGRACHT TO HERENGRACHT

Distance 700 m (765 yards) **Nearest tram** Spui **Time** 10 minutes

Keizersgracht is known as "the emperor's canal" and with good reason. A stroll along this canal takes in highly decorated façades, including No 319, which is covered with scrolls, vases and garlands.

After marvelling at the tiny 345a Keizersgracht, cross Huidenstraat to reach the magnificent section of the canal illustrated below.

Turn left on to Leidsestraat to head along the Leidsegracht, which marks the end of

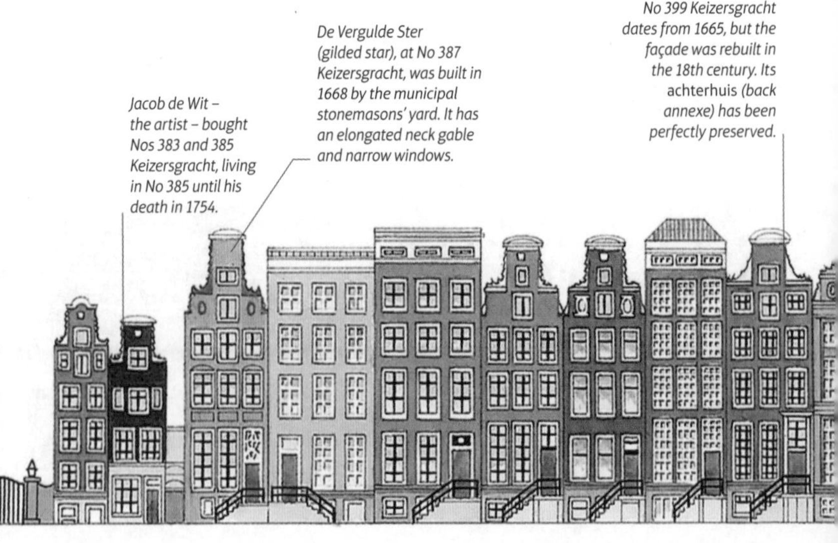

Jacob de Wit – the artist – bought Nos 383 and 385 Keizersgracht, living in No 385 until his death in 1754.

De Vergulde Ster (gilded star), at No 387 Keizersgracht, was built in 1668 by the municipal stonemasons' yard. It has an elongated neck gable and narrow windows.

No 399 Keizersgracht dates from 1665, but the façade was rebuilt in the 18th century. Its achterhuis *(back annexe) has been perfectly preserved.*

3

1 No 401 Keizersgracht has a highly decorated gable, with friezes of cherubs.

2 Boats are moored alongside Nos. 401 and 403 Keizersgracht.

3 A *rondvaartboot* passes under the bridge on Keizersgracht that crosses over the Leidsegracht canal.

WOLVENSTRAAT
Herengracht
NIEUWEZIJDS VOORBURGWAL
Singel
Keizersgracht
Prinsengracht
HUIDENSTRAAT
Area of illustration
Leidsegracht

Locator Map

Daniel Stalpaert's city expansion plan of 1664. It has a mixture of fine 17th- and 18th-century canal houses. Walk to Koningsplein, then take the left bank of the Herengracht. On the next page, the stroll will continue on Herengracht.

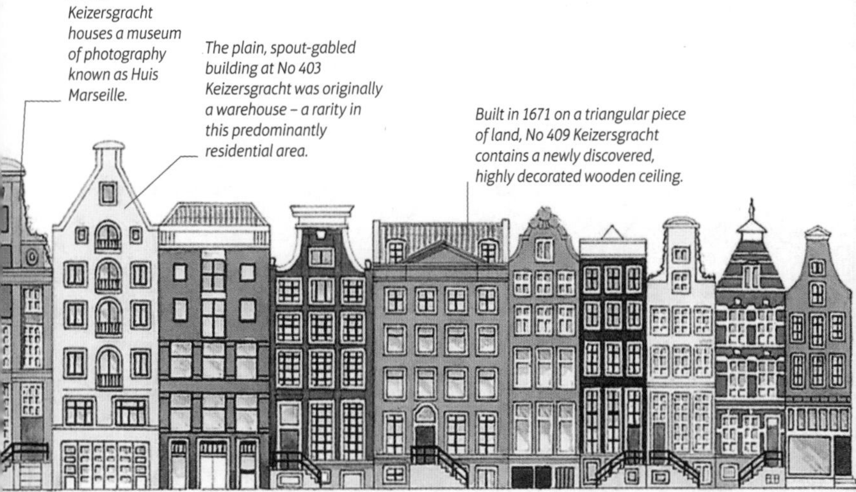
No 401 Keizersgracht houses a museum of photography known as Huis Marseille.
The plain, spout-gabled building at No 403 Keizersgracht was originally a warehouse – a rarity in this predominantly residential area.
Built in 1671 on a triangular piece of land, No 409 Keizersgracht contains a newly discovered, highly decorated wooden ceiling.

1

2

A CANAL WALK
HERENGRACHT TO REGULIERSGRACHT

Distance 550 m (600 yards) **Nearest tram** Koningsplein **Time** 5 minutes

A walk eastwards along Herengracht towards Thorbeckeplein winds past grand, wide-fronted mansions. The most prestigious plots on the canal are known as the Golden Bend *(p116)*, which is illustrated below. Admire this most picturesque section of the canal, while listening to the *rondvaarten* motoring past, creating lapping waves.

The house at No 491 Herengracht was built in 1671. The façade, rebuilt in the 18th century, is decorated with scrolls, vases and coats of arms.

The 17th-century house at No 493 was given a Louis XV-style façade in 1767 by Anthony van Hemert.

The façade of No 495 Herengracht was rebuilt and a balcony added by Jean Coulon in 1739 for burgomaster and art expert Jan Six.

The Kattenkabinet at No 497 Herengracht was created by financier B Meijer in 1984. It is devoted to exhibits featuring the cat in art.

After crossing Vijzelstraat, you'll pass the house where Peter the Great stayed in 1716 and the asymmetrical building at Nos 533–7. Look out for the small houses

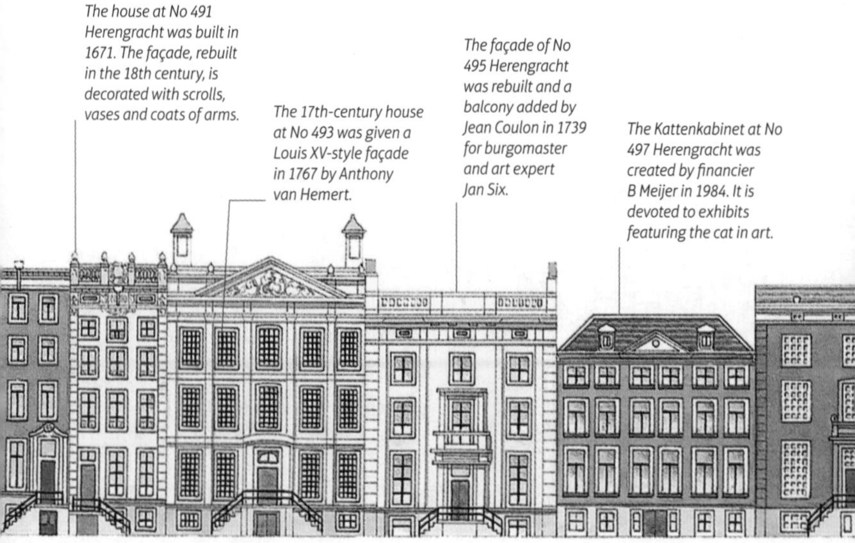

[1] Verdant trees line the canal in front of No 493 Herengracht.

[2] The Kattenkabinet represents itself with a simple black-and-white sign, showing a cat walking away from the viewer.

[3] The grand exteriors of No 497 - the Kattenkabinet - and No 499 Herengracht.

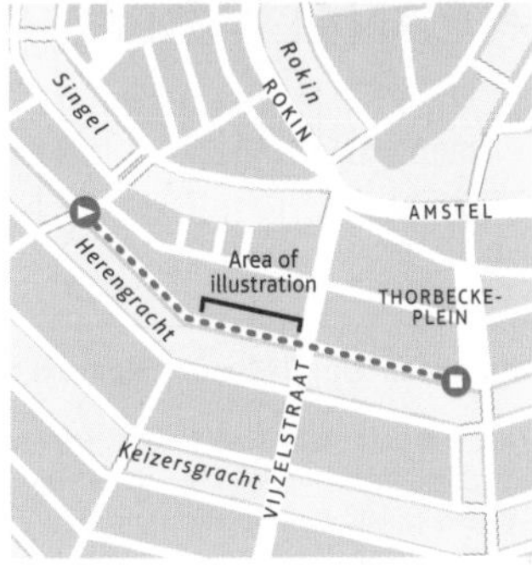

Locator Map

at the corner of Herengracht and Thorbeckeplein which contrast with the grand neighbouring buildings.

At Thorbeckeplein, take the bridge to the right, which marks the beginning of Reguliersgracht. Follow the left bank.

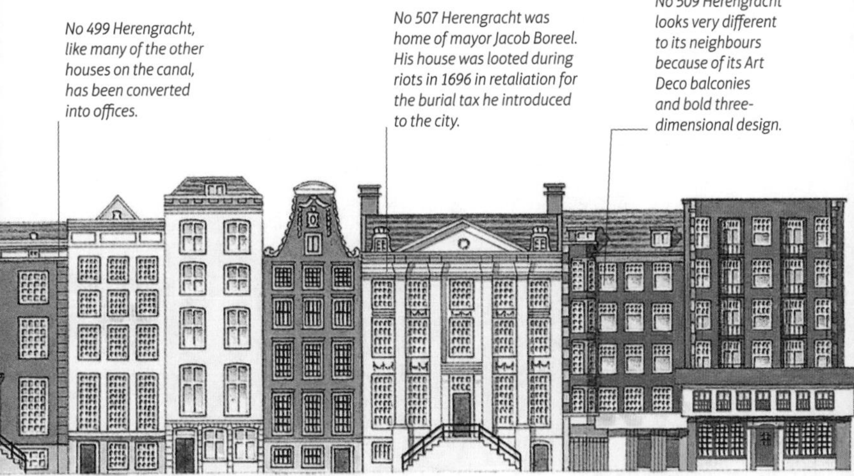

No 499 Herengracht, like many of the other houses on the canal, has been converted into offices.

No 507 Herengracht was home of mayor Jacob Boreel. His house was looted during riots in 1696 in retaliation for the burial tax he introduced to the city.

No 509 Herengracht looks very different to its neighbours because of its Art Deco balconies and bold three-dimensional design.

1

2

A CANAL WALK

REGULIERSGRACHT TO THE AMSTEL

Distance 750 m (820 yards) **Nearest tram** Rembrandtplein **Time** 10 minutes

The final part of the walk takes you along Reguliersgracht – one of the city's most famous canals. Before you begin, pause where the canal crosses Herengracht to see 15 bridges in total, including the one that you're standing on.

Continue past the buildings shown below and then cross Keizersgracht. You'll pass Nos 57, 59 and 63 Reguliersgracht, which have ornate stone, brick and woodwork façades.

Turn left by the church and take the left bank of Prinsengracht. You should be ready

19

Arched stone bridges cross the Reguliersgracht.

The spout-gabled 16th-century warehouses at Nos 11 and 13 Reguliersgracht are called the Sun and the Moon.

Three houses boasting typical neck gables, at Nos 17, 19 and 21 Reguliersgracht, are now much sought-after addresses.

1 With their distinctive red shutters, Nos 11 and 13 Reguliersgracht are identical, hence their nicknames, the Sun and Moon.

2 The seven bridges that cross Reguliersgracht make a great picture.

3 Nos 37 and 39 can be found at the intersection with Keizersgracht.

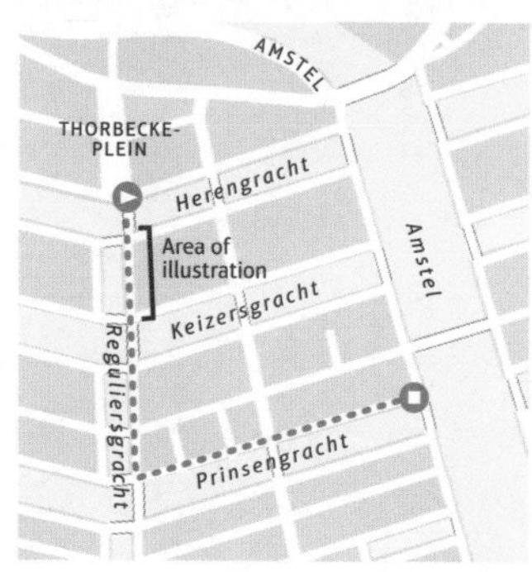

Locator Map

for a break. Stop for lunch at NeL in Amstelkerk *(p145)* or a refreshing beverage at Café Marcella, at No 1047a Prinsengracht, which is a typical local bar with outside seating in the summer. Refreshed, follow the Prinsengracht to the Amstel river.

The Nieuwe Amsterdammer, *a weekly magazine aimed at Amsterdam's Bolshevik intelligentsia, was published at No 19 Reguliersgracht from 1914 to 1920.*

The façades of Nos 37 and 39 Reguliersgracht lean towards the water, showing the danger caused by subsidence when building on marshland.

EXPERIENCE

Tulips in Keukenhof gardens

Munttoren and a canal-side restaurant at dusk

NIEUWE ZIJDE

The western side of medieval Amsterdam was known as the Nieuwe Zijde (New Side). Together with the Oude Zijde it formed the heart of the early maritime settlement. As Amsterdam grew, it expanded eastwards, leaving large sections of the Nieuwe Zijde neglected and in decline. With its many wooden houses, the city was prone to fires and in 1452 much of the area was burned down. Surprisingly, this event reinvigorated the Nieuwe Zijde. During rebuilding, a broad moat, the Singel, was cut, attracting the *nouveaux riches* to the area. Warehouses, rich merchants' homes and fine quays sprang up where once there was poverty.

The area was also rejuvenated during this period by the Miracle of Amsterdam. At a house on Kalverstraat in 1345, a dying man regurgitated the Eucharist. Due to liturgical reasons, the sacramental bread was thrown onto a fire, but it would not burn and was retrieved from the ashes the following day. This event transformed the city into a place of pilgrimage and a chapel was built on the site, bringing commerce to the Nieuwe Zijde as worshippers passed through.

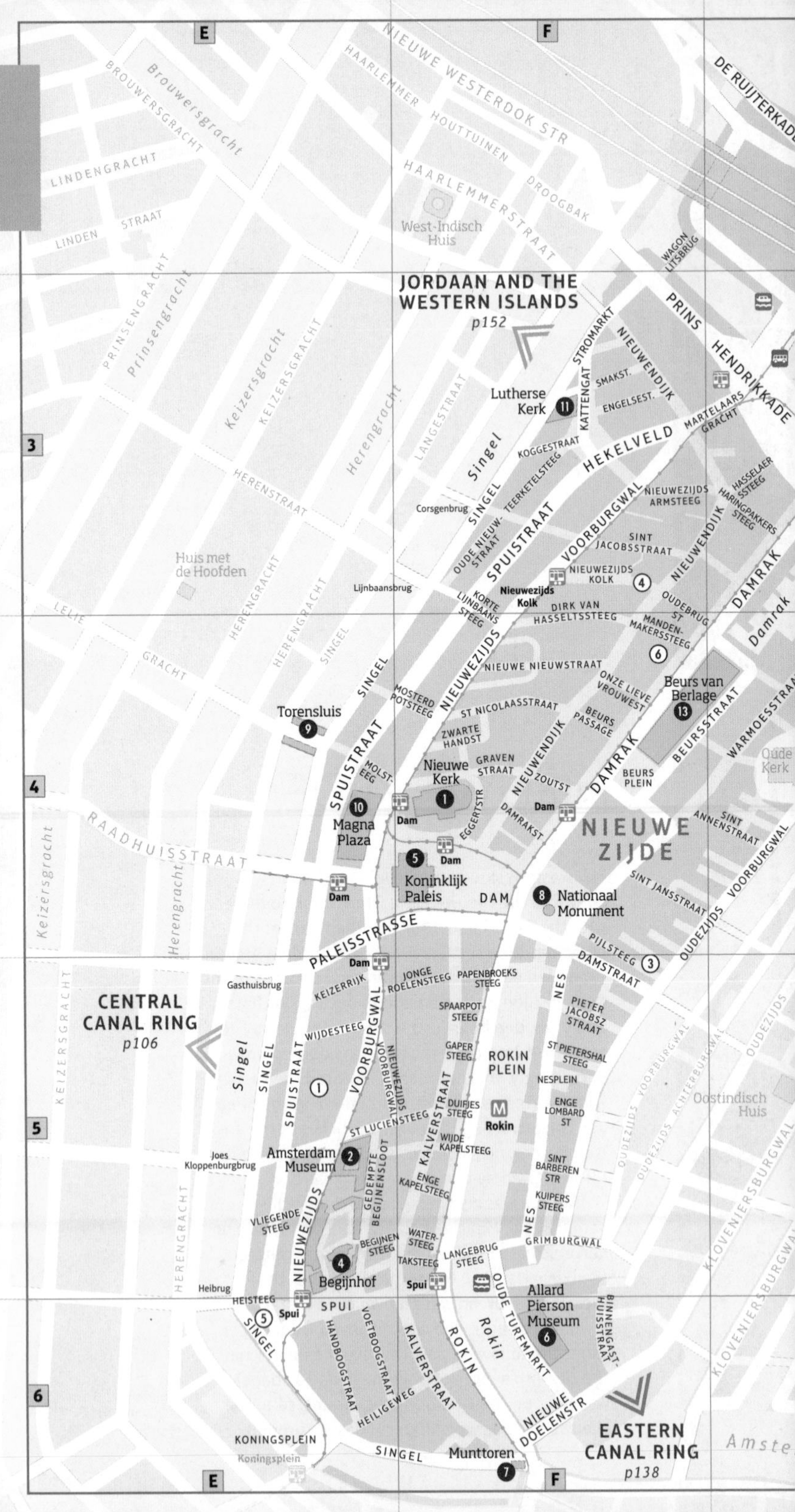

E
F
NIEUWE WESTERDOK STR
HAARLEMMER HOUTTUINEN
DE RUIJTERKADE
Brouwersgracht
BROUWERSGRACHT
LINDENGRACHT
LINDEN STRAAT
HAARLEMMERSTRAAT
DROOGBAK
West-Indisch Huis
WAGON LITSBRUG
JORDAAN AND THE WESTERN ISLANDS
p152
PRINS HENDRIKKADE
PRINSENGRACHT
Prinsengracht
Keizersgracht
KEIZERSGRACHT
Herengracht
LANGESTRAAT
STROMARKT
NIEUWENDIJK
SMAKST.
ENGELSEST.
Lutherse Kerk
11
KATTENGAT
MARTELAARS GRACHT
3
Singel
KOGGESTRAAT
HEKELVELD
HERENSTRAAT
TEERKETELSTEEG
NIEUWEZIJDS ARMSTEEG
HASSELAER SSTEEG
HARINGPAKKERS STEEG
Corsgenbrug
SINGEL
OUDE NIEUW-STRAAT
SPUISTRAAT
VOORBURGWAL
SINT JACOBSSTRAAT
NIEUWENDIJK
DAMRAK
Huis met de Hoofden
NIEUWEZIJDS KOLK
4
Lijnbaansbrug
KORTE LIJNBAANS STEEG
Nieuwezijds Kolk
DIRK VAN HASSELTSSTEEG
OUDEBRUG ST
MANDEN-MAKERSSTEEG
Damrak
LELIE GRACHT
HERENGRACHT
SINGEL
NIEUWEZIJDS
NIEUWE NIEUWSTRAAT
6
ONZE LIEVE VROUWEST
Beurs van Berlage
13
MOSTERD POTSTEEG
ST NICOLAASSTRAAT
BEURS PASSAGE
WARMOESSTRAAT
Torensluis
9
ZWARTE HANDST
BEURSSTRAAT
Oude Kerk
MOLST-EEG
Nieuwe Kerk
1
GRAVEN STRAAT
NIEUWENDIJK
DAMRAK
BEURS PLEIN
4
ZOUTST
SPUISTRAAT
10
Magna Plaza
Dam
EGGERTSTR
Dam
DAMRAKST
NIEUWE ZIJDE
SINT ANNENSTRAAT
Keizersgracht
RAADHUISSTRAAT
Herengracht
5
Dam
Koninklijk Paleis
DAM
8
Nationaal Monument
SINT JANSSTRAAT
OUDEZIJDS VOORBURGWAL
Dam
PALEISSTRASSE
PIJLSTEEG
3
DAMSTRAAT
Dam
Gasthuisbrug
KEIZERRIJK
JONGE ROELENSTEEG
PAPENBROEKS STEEG
NES
PIETER JACOBSZ STRAAT
KEIZERSGRACHT
CENTRAL CANAL RING
p106
SPAARPOT STEEG
WIJDESTEEG
Singel
SINGEL
SPUISTRAAT
1
VOORBURGWAL
NIEUWEZIJDS VOORBURGWAL
GAPER STEEG
ROKIN PLEIN
ST PIETERSHAL STEEG
NESPLEIN
OUDEZIJDS VOORBURGWAL
OUDEZIJDS ACHTERBURGWAL
OUDEZIJDS
Oostindisch Huis
KALVERSTRAAT
DUIFJES STEEG
Rokin
ENGE LOMBARD ST
5
ST LUCIENSTEEG
WIJDE KAPELSTEEG
Joes Kloppenburgbrug
Amsterdam Museum
2
GEDEMPTE BEGIJNENSLOOT
ENGE KAPELSTEEG
SINT BARBEREN STR
KUIPERS STEEG
HERENGRACHT
VLIEGENDE STEEG
NIEUWEZIJDS
BEGIJNEN STEEG
WATER-STEEG
NES
GRIMBURGWAL
KLOVENIERSBURGWAL
4
Begijnhof
TAKSTEEG
LANGEBRUG STEEG
Spui
OUDE TURFMARKT
Allard Pierson Museum
BINNENGAST-HUISSTRAAT
Heibrug
HEISTEEG
5
Spui
SPUI
SINGEL
HANDBOOGSTRAAT
VOETBOOGSTRAAT
KALVERSTRAAT
ROKIN
Rokin
6
6
HEILIGEWEG
NIEUWE DOELENSTR
KONINGSPLEIN
Koningsplein
SINGEL
Munttoren
7
EASTERN CANAL RING
p138
Amster

G
H
J
NDSM
Veer Buiksloterweg
NOORD
p176
Centraal Station
WESTERPLEIN WEST
Centraal Station
Het IJ
MICHIEL DE RUIJTERTUNNEL
NIEUWE ZIJDE
Centraal Station
STATIONS PLEIN
Centraal Station
Open Havenfront
Nieuwe Brug
DE RUIJTERKADE
OOSTERDOKSTRAAT
Sint Nicolaasbasiliek
NIEUWEBRUGSTEEG
OUDEZIJDS KOLK
Oosterdok
Armbrug
HEINTJE HOEKSSTEEG
Museum Ons' Lieve Heer op Solder
L. NIEZEL
GELDERSEKADE
KROMME WAAL
PRINS HENDRIKKADE
Scheepvaarthuis
OUDE ZIJDE
p86
ACHTERBURGWAL
ZEEDIJK
Waag
NIEUWMARKT
Nieuwmarkt
RECHT BOOMSSLOOT
OUDE WAAL
Waalseilandsgracht
BINNENKANT
OUDESCHANS
OUDE ZIJDE
Trippenhuis
Oudeschans
NIEUWE UILENBURGERSTR.
Zuiderkerk
JODENBREESTRAAT
WATERLOOPLEIN
Stadhuis
Nationale Opera and Ballet
0 metres 200
0 yards 200
N
2
3
6
NIEUWE ZIJDE
Must Sees
1 Nieuwe Kerk
2 Amsterdam Museum
3 Museum Ons' Lieve Heer op Solder
4 Begijnhof
Experience More
5 Koninklijk Paleis
6 Allard Pierson Museum
7 Munttoren
8 Nationaal Monument
9 Torensluis
10 Magna Plaza
11 Lutherse Kerk
12 Sint Nicolaasbasiliek
13 Beurs van Berlage
Eat
① Visrestaurant Lucius
② Kam Yin City Centre
Drink
③ Wynand Fockink
④ In de Wildeman
⑤ Café Hoppe
Stay
⑥ Hotel The Exchange

NIEUWE KERK

F4 Dam Square 2, 4, 11, 12, 13, 14, 17, 24 10am-5pm daily (during exhibitions only; check website) nieuwekerk.nl

The medieval "New Church" is both stately and surprising, hosting not only royal coronations but also impressive exhibitions on inspiring individuals, different cultures, contemporary art and photography.

Dating from the 14th century, Amsterdam's second parish church was built as the population outgrew the Oude Kerk *(p90)*. During its turbulent history, the church was destroyed several times by fire, rebuilt and then stripped of its finery after the Alteration *(p53)*. It reached its present size in the 1650s. Highlights of the interior include the Great Organ (1645), which is adorned with marbled-wood cherubs and has shutters painted by Jacob van Campen, Rombout Verhulst's tomb of Michiel de Ruyter (1607–76) – the heroic admiral who died in battle against the French at Messina – and the carved pulpit (1664). Since 1814, all the Dutch monarchs have been crowned here.

← Dominating Dam Square, the church, with its huge stained-glass windows

Carved pulpit

Ornate blind windows

Great Organ

Baptistry

Rood screen by Johannes Lutma (c 1650)

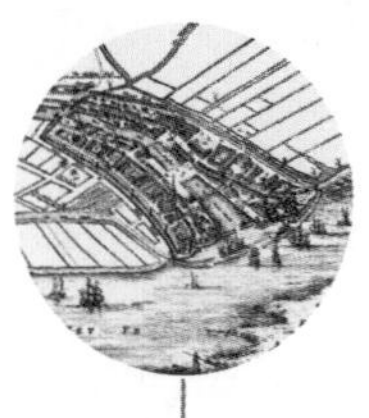

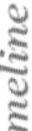

Timeline

1380
▲ Estimated date of the earliest church on this site. The original building was destroyed in 1421

1578
▼ Church plundered following the Alteration, when it became Protestant

1645
▲ Fire destroys all but the façade and walls, and restoration work begins soon after

1814
▼ First royal investiture in Nieuwe Kerk of William I

↑ The Nieuwe Kerk's magnificent interior

Did You Know?

Joost van den Vondel *(p133)* was buried here in an unmarked grave.

↑ The flamboyant pulpit, which took Dutch sculptor Albert Vinckenbrinck 15 years to carve

↑ Colourful stained-glass window depicting Prince William of Orange *(p53)* surrounded by his courtiers

2

AMSTERDAM MUSEUM

E5 Kalverstraat 92, St Luciensteeg 27 2, 4, 11, 12, 14, 24 Rokin 10am-5pm daily 27 April, 25 Dec amsterdammuseum.nl

The city's historical museum explores Amsterdam's dramatic evolution from marshland to modern times, as well as the city's future. The setting tells a story just as varied as the one told by the main collection. The red-brick building began life as the Convent of St Lucien, before it was turned into a civic orphanage two years after the Alteration *(p53)*.

An interior courtyard of the red-brick Amsterdam Museum

The Collection

At the museum's heart is the Amsterdam DNA exhibition, which offers a multimedia introduction to the development of Amsterdam, from its humble origins as a small fishing village at the mouth of the Amstel in the Middle Ages to today's cosmopolitan city. Visitors can then explore the other rooms, where aspects of Amsterdam's history are dealt with in more detail, including the city's Golden Age in the 17th century. The Amsterdam Gallery also covers both the past and the present with exhibits ranging from 16th-century portraits to modern-day graffiti. Meanwhile, the Regents' Chamber and The Little Orphanage unlock the building's history.

Did You Know?

Boys and girls played in separate courtyards when the building was an orphanage.

The globe, crafted by Willem Blaeu (cartographer of the Dutch East India Company), on display in Amsterdam DNA to emphasize the city's history of overseas trade and colonial expansion

Exhibits from the 20th century on display in Amsterdam DNA

Gallery Rooms

Amsterdam DNA

This one-hour, historical tour of the city explores Amsterdam's main cultural characteristics, including the spirit of enterprise, freedom of thought, civic virtue and creativity. Touch-sensitive screens and archival film footage are used to great effect.

Amsterdam Gallery

Leading from Begijnensteeg to the museum, this is the world's only "museum street" and it does not have an admission charge. Don't miss Albert Jansz Vinckenbrinck's wooden statue of *David, Goliath and His Shield-Bearer* (1648–50).

Regents' Chamber

Built in 1634, this room was the meeting place of the orphanage's directors (regents). Its fine ceiling, added in 1656, shows the orphans receiving charity. Portraits of the regents hang on the walls. The long table and cabinets are 17th century.

The Little Orphanage

This exhibition gives children and parents the opportunity to experience life in a 17th-century orphanage. Along with authentically arranged classrooms, kitchens and animal sheds are talking exhibits and pop-up characters who tell visitors about their day-to-day lives.

3

MUSEUM ONS' LIEVE HEER OP SOLDER

G4 Oudezijds Voorburgwal 38
4, 14, 24 10am-6pm Mon-Sat, 1-6pm Sun and public hols 27 Apr opsolder.nl

Tucked away on the edge of the Red Light District is a restored 17th-century canal house, with two smaller houses to the rear. The upper storeys conceal a secret Catholic church known as Our Lord in the Attic (Ons' Lieve Heer op Solder).

Our Lord in the Attic

After the Alteration *(p53)*, when Amsterdam officially became Protestant, many hidden churches were built throughout the city. Bourgeois merchant Jan Hartman added this chapel to his house in 1663. It was extended in around 1735 to create more seating space.

The building became a museum in 1888, and displays fine church silver, religious artifacts and paintings. Next door to the church is an exhibition space, café and shop.

Simple spout gable on the first house
Canal room
Main entrance
A chaplain's tiny box bedroom is hidden off a bend in the stairs. There was a resident chaplain in the church from 1663.

↑ Hartman's house on the canal, concealing the two smaller houses behind

↑ The three houses that make up the Museum Ons' Lieve Heer Op Solder

Wooden viewing gallery of the church

Sacristy, where vestments were kept

Did You Know?

The church is painted *caput mortuum*, or "dead head" pink.

Our Lord in the Attic served the Catholic community until Sint Nicolaasbasiliek (p82) was finished in 1887.

The landing where the tiny wooden confessional stands was the living room of the rear house.

The 17th-century kitchen was originally part of the priest's living quarters.

The parlour

1 Restored to its former opulence, the parlour is furnished in the Dutch Classical style of the 17th century.

2 Unlike the rest of the house, Our Lord in the Attic has been restored to its 19th-century appearance, when it was last used by worshippers.

3 The canal room is where 17th-century residents would have spent the day.

4 BEGIJNHOF

E5 Spui (entrance at Gedempte Begijnensloot)
2, 4, 11, 12, 14, 24 Gates: 9am-5pm daily

With its beautiful rows of houses overlooking a well-kept green, the Begijnhof is the perfect place for some respite from the frenetic energy of the Nieuwe Zijde.

The Begijnhof was originally built in 1346 as a sanctuary for the Begijntjes, a lay Catholic sisterhood who lived like nuns, although they took no monastic vows. In return for lodgings within the complex, these worthy women undertook to educate the poor and care for the city's sick. Nothing survives of the earliest dwellings, but the Begijnhof still retains a sanctified atmosphere. No groups are allowed and visitors should respect the residents' privacy.

No 19 has a plaque depicting the exodus of the Jews from Egypt.

Engelse Kerk

Het Houten Huis

The Begijnhof Chapel, a clandestine church (Nos 29–30), was completed in 1680.

Main entrance from Gedempte Begijnensloot

Spui entrance

Did You Know?

The houses in the Begijnhof are still occupied by single women.

↑ A statue of Jesus stands in the middle of Begijnhof's green

↓ The houses in the Begijnhof, encircling the green

PICTURE PERFECT
Het Houten Huis

Behind Het Houten Huis (No 34) - one of the oldest houses in Amsterdam - is a white wall adorned with biblical plaques. Capture the wooden-fronted house - one of only two left in the city - and the plaques in one frame for the perfect shot.

↑ The Engelse Kerk's stark interior reflects its Presbyterian past

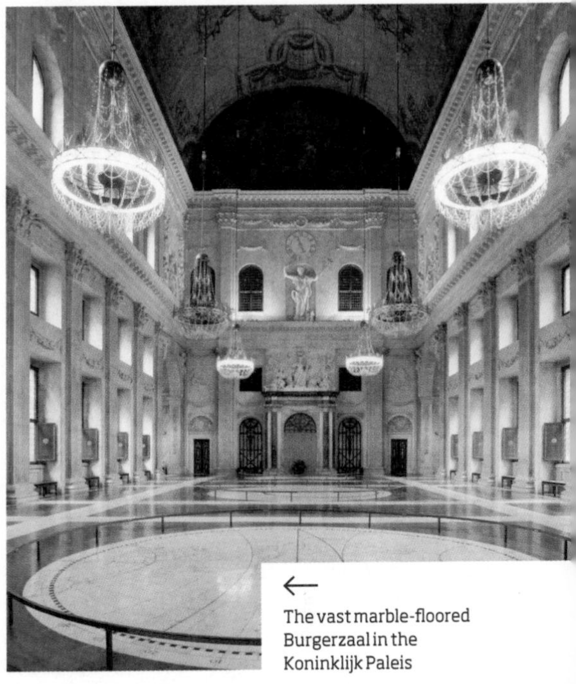

← The vast marble-floored Burgerzaal in the Koninklijk Paleis

EXPERIENCE MORE

5 

Koninklijk Paleis

F4 Dam Square
2, 4, 11, 12, 13, 14, 17, 24
Check website for details
paleisamsterdam.nl

The Koninklijk Paleis, still used by the king for official events, was built as the Stadhuis (town hall). Work began in 1648, after the end of the Eighty Years' War with Spain *(p53)*. Dominating its surroundings, the Classically inspired design by Jacob van Campen (1595–1657) reflects the city's mood of confidence after the Dutch victory. Civic pride is also shown in the mythological sculptures by Artus Quellien (1609–68), which decorate the pediments, and in the carrillon by François Hemony (1609–67). The full magnificence is best seen in the Burgerzaal (citizens' hall). Based on the assembly halls of ancient Rome, this 30-m- (95-ft-) high room boasts a marble floor inlaid with a celestial map flanked by the two terrestrial hemispheres.

STAY

Hotel The Exchange

Centrally located, this quirky hotel has rooms designed by graduates of the Amsterdam Fashion Institute.

F4
Damrak 50
hotelthe exchange.com

Allard Pierson Museum

F6 Oude Turfmarkt 127 4, 14, 24 Rokin 10am-5pm Tue-Fri, 1-5pm Sat & Sun 1 Jan, 27 Apr, 25 Dec allardpiersonmuseum.nl

Amsterdam's only specialist archaeological collection is named after Allard Pierson (1831–96), a humanist and scholar. Part of the University of Amsterdam and housed in a former bank, this museum is not just a dusty collection of ancient relics. Although small, it interestingly links vanished civilizations with the modern world through its collection of thousands of objects from the ancient worlds of Greece, Rome, Egypt and beyond. Look out for a case of rather gruesome Egyptian mummy remains and a film showing the process of mummification, a computer that enables you to write your name in hieroglyphics, a jointed Greek doll from 300 BC and some fine Roman jewellery. The Greek pottery collection has examples of black-figure and red-figure pottery produced in the 5th and 6th centuries BC. The museum also hosts challenging themed exhibitions that shed new light on European history. Located next door to the museum is Amsterdam University's special collections department.

Munttoren

F6 Muntplein 4, 14, 24 Rokin Shop: Apr-Oct: 9:30am-9pm daily; Nov-Mar till 6pm

The polygonal base of the Munttoren (mint tower) was part of the Regulierspoort – the southern gateway in Amsterdam's medieval city wall. The gate was destroyed by fire in 1618, but the base survived. In the following year, Hendrick de Keyser *(p37)* added the clock tower (closed to the public), capped with a steeple and openwork orb. The carillon was designed by François Hemony in 1699, and rings every 15 minutes. The tower acquired its name in 1673, during the French occupation, when the former city mint was temporarily housed here.

The ground floor is home to a shop that sells delftware still made by hand at the Royal Delft factory.

Nationaal Monument

F4 Dam Square 4, 9, 14, 16, 24

Sculpted by John Rädecker (1885–1956) and designed by architect J J P Oud (1890–1963), the 22-m (70-ft) obelisk that looms over Dam Square commemorates Dutch World War II casualties. It was unveiled in 1956, and is fronted by two lions – heraldic symbols of the Netherlands. Embedded in the wall behind are urns containing earth from all the Dutch provinces and the former colonies of Indonesia, the Antilles and Surinam.

PICTURE PERFECT
Canal View from Torensluis

Spanning the Singel, the Torensluis is the ideal place from which to snap a quintessential Amsterdam image. Capture the canalboats chugging along against a backdrop of high-gabled canal houses. On warm days, take a seat at a café table while you wait for the perfect photo opportunity.

Torensluis

E4 Singel between Torensteeg and Oude Leliestraat 2, 11, 12, 13, 17

The Torensluis is one of the oldest and widest bridges in Amsterdam. Spanning a width

The striking Munttoren sits on the edge of the Singel ↓

Retaining its former opulence, Magna Plaza's colonnaded interior

of 42 m (138 ft), it was built on the site of a 17th-century sluice gate and took its name from a tower that stood on the bridge until it was demolished in 1829 (its outline is marked in the pavement). A jail was built in its foundations and if you look carefully you can see the barred windows and arched entrance leading to the old dungeon below the water line.

The statue dominating the bridge is of the 19th-century Dutch author Eduard Douwes Dekker (1820–87), who wrote under the pseudonym Multatuli. His novel *Max Havelaar,* which was published in 1860, is a polemic against the atrocities committed by Dutch colonialists in the East Indies (modern-day Indonesia). The protagonist, Max Havelaar, battles against the corrupt government of Java. The book was a source of encouragement to reformers, but the Dutch were ultimately evicted from their empire only by force.

Magna Plaza

E4 Nieuwezijds Voorburgwal 182 2, 11, 12, 13, 17 11am-7pm Mon, 10am-7pm Tue, Wed, Fri & Sat, 10am-9pm Thu, noon-7pm Sun magnaplaza.nl

A wall panel on the current building's façade depicts the site's original function. In 1748, it was a *postkantoor* (post office), but it was taken out of service in 1854. The present building was completed in 1899. C H Peters (1847–1932), the architect, was ridiculed for the extravagance of its Neo-Gothic design: critics dubbed the elaborately decorated exterior, with its spindly towers, "post-office Gothic". It was redeveloped in 1992, though the grand dimensions of Peters' design were beautifully preserved, and is now an elegant shopping mall, set over three floors, called the Magna Plaza.

EAT

Visrestaurant Lucius

Lobster and crab are specialities at this long-established seafood restaurant. It has an outstanding set menu.

E5 Spuistraat 247
lucius.nl

Kam Yin City Centre

Traditional Surinamese *roti* (pancakes with either a vegetable or meat filling) are a house speciality.

G3
Warmoesstraat 6
kamyin.nl

11

Lutherse Kerk

F3 Kattengat 2 2, 11, 12, 13, 17 To the public

The Lutherse Kerk, located in Singel, was designed by Adriaan Dortsman (1625–82) and opened in 1671. It is sometimes known as the Ronde Lutherse Kerk, being the first Dutch Reformed church to feature a circular ground plan and two upper galleries, giving the whole congregation a clear view of the pulpit.

In 1882 a fire started by careless plumbers destroyed everything except the exterior walls. When the interior and entrance were rebuilt in 1883, they were made squarer and more ornate, in keeping with ecclesiastical architecture of that time. A vaulted copper dome replaced the earlier ribbed version.

Falling attendances led to the closure and deconsecration of the church in 1935 and, since 1975, it has acted as the Renaissance Amsterdam Hotel's conference centre and banqueting chamber. Take time, however, to admire its unique exterior, which stands out among the canal houses.

12

Sint Nicolaasbasiliek

G3 Prins Hendrikkade 73 2, 11, 12, 13, 14, 17, 24 Centraal Station Noon-3pm Mon & Sat, 11am-4pm Tue-Fri nicolaas-parochie.nl

Sint Nicolaas, the patron saint of seafarers, is an important icon in Holland. Many churches are named after him, and 5 December (Sint Nicolaas Day) is the Netherlands' principal day for the giving of presents. In November, the gift-giving saint arrives at the church, accompanied by a helper, Zwarte Piet (Black Pete) in blackface make-up. This tradition in fact dates only from the 19th century, and has been denounced by anti-racism campaigners.

Amsterdam's biggest Catholic church, the Sint Nicolaasbasiliek was designed by A C Bleys (1842–1912) and completed in 1887. Despite its rather grim and forbidding exterior, with its twin towers looming over Zeedijk and the Oosterdok, Sint Nicolaasbasiliek's completion marked the rehabilitation of the Catholic faith after centuries of clandestine worship during the period when Amsterdam was officially Protestant *(p53)*. The joy and relief of the congregation is reflected in the church's interior, which is brightened by stained-glass windows set in its imposing dome.

Services are held most days (Tuesday in English), and the church occasionally hosts concerts and recitals featuring the magnificently restored 19th-century Sauer organ.

1,281

bridges span the 50 km (31 miles) of canals in Amsterdam.

13   

Beurs van Berlage

F4 Damrak 2 4, 14, 24 Only during exhibitions beursvanberlage.nl

Built in 1903 to a design by Hendrik Petrus Berlage (1856–1934), this is a striking modernist building. The former stock exchange's clean, functional appearance marked a departure from late 19th-century Revivalist architecture. Its curvaceous lines, plain exterior and, above all,

→ The circular copper dome of Lutherse Kerk reflected in the canal

Colourful stained-glass windows adorn Sint Nicolaasbasiliek's impressive dome ↑

Despite its rather grim and forbidding exterior, with its twin towers looming over Zeedijk and the Oosterdok, Sint Nicolaasbasiliek's completion marked the rehabilitation of the Catholic faith.

Berlage's imaginative use of red brick as a decorative construction material inspired the later architects of the Amsterdam School *(p37)*. It has an impressive frieze above the entrance showing the evolution of man from Adam to stockbroker. The building is entered through a 40-m (130-ft) clock tower that gives access to three massive halls once used as trading floors.

Inside, the main hall is decorated with ceramic friezes depicting different labourers, including miners and coffee pickers.

Now used as a conference venue, it also hosts a variety of changing exhibitions and concerts, and there is a good bistro. Guided tours of the building allow you to climb the bell tower for extensive views over Amsterdam.

DRINK

Wynand Fockink
Famous *proeflokaal* with a huge choice of *jenevers* and beers.
F5 Pijlsteeg 31
wynand-fockink.nl

In de Wildeman
This tavern has at least 18 craft beers on tap and 200 more by the bottle.
F3 Kolksteeg 3
Sun
indewildeman.nl

Café Hoppe
A 17th-century *bruin café* (local pub) serving limited-edition craft ales, traditional *jenevers* and liqueurs.
E6 Spui 18
cafehoppe.com

A SHORT WALK
NIEUWE ZIJDE

Distance 1.5 km (1 mile) **Nearest metro** Rokin
Time 15 minutes

Although much of the medieval Nieuwe Zijde has disappeared, the area is still rich in buildings that relate to the city's past. A walk from Dam Square to Spui takes you past examples of architecture from the 15th to the 20th century. You'll stroll along narrow streets and alleys which follow the course of some of the earliest dykes and footpaths. Along the way, pause at traditional gabled houses that have been turned into bustling shops and cafés. Financial institutions on Rokin and Nes have made way for chic department stores and lively cafés. Nes is also known for its alternative theatre venues.

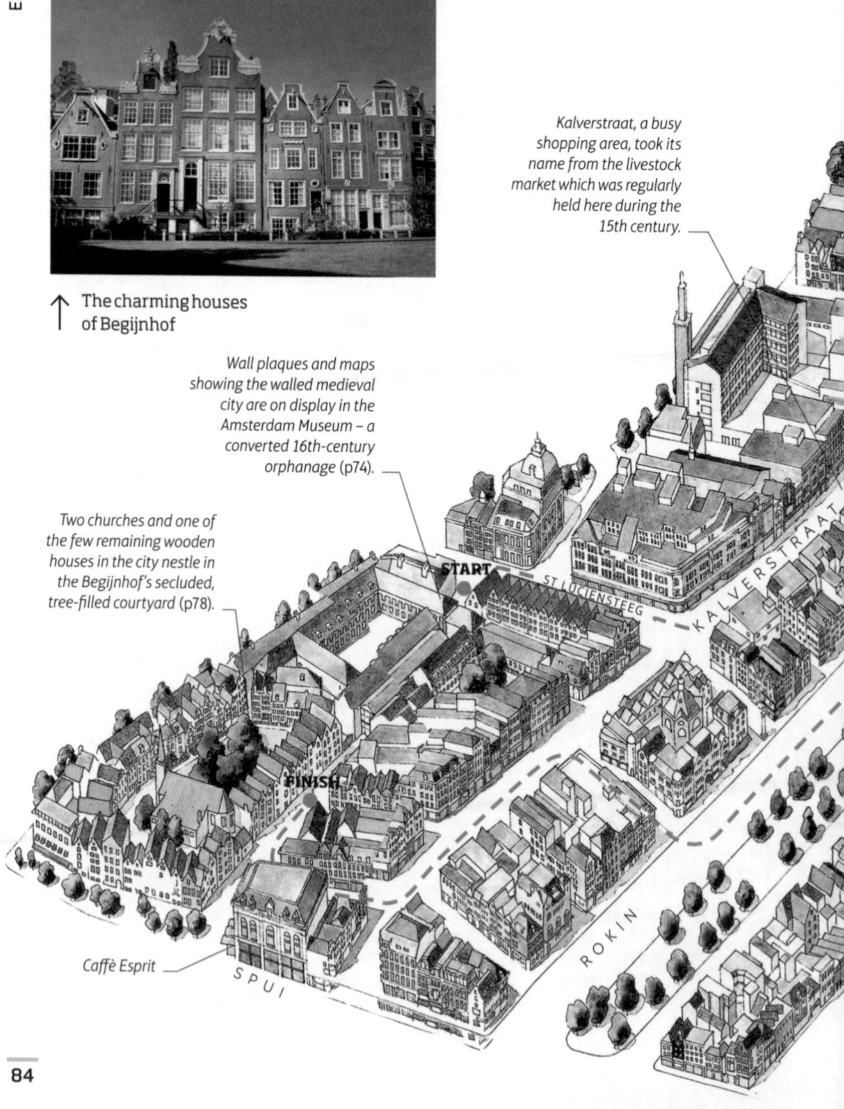
Kalverstraat, a busy shopping area, took its name from the livestock market which was regularly held here during the 15th century.
Wall plaques and maps showing the walled medieval city are on display in the Amsterdam Museum – a converted 16th-century orphanage (p74).
Two churches and one of the few remaining wooden houses in the city nestle in the Begijnhof's secluded, tree-filled courtyard (p78).
Caffè Esprit
START
ST LUCIENSTEEG
KALVERSTRAAT
FINISH
ROKIN
SPUI

↑ The charming houses of Begijnhof

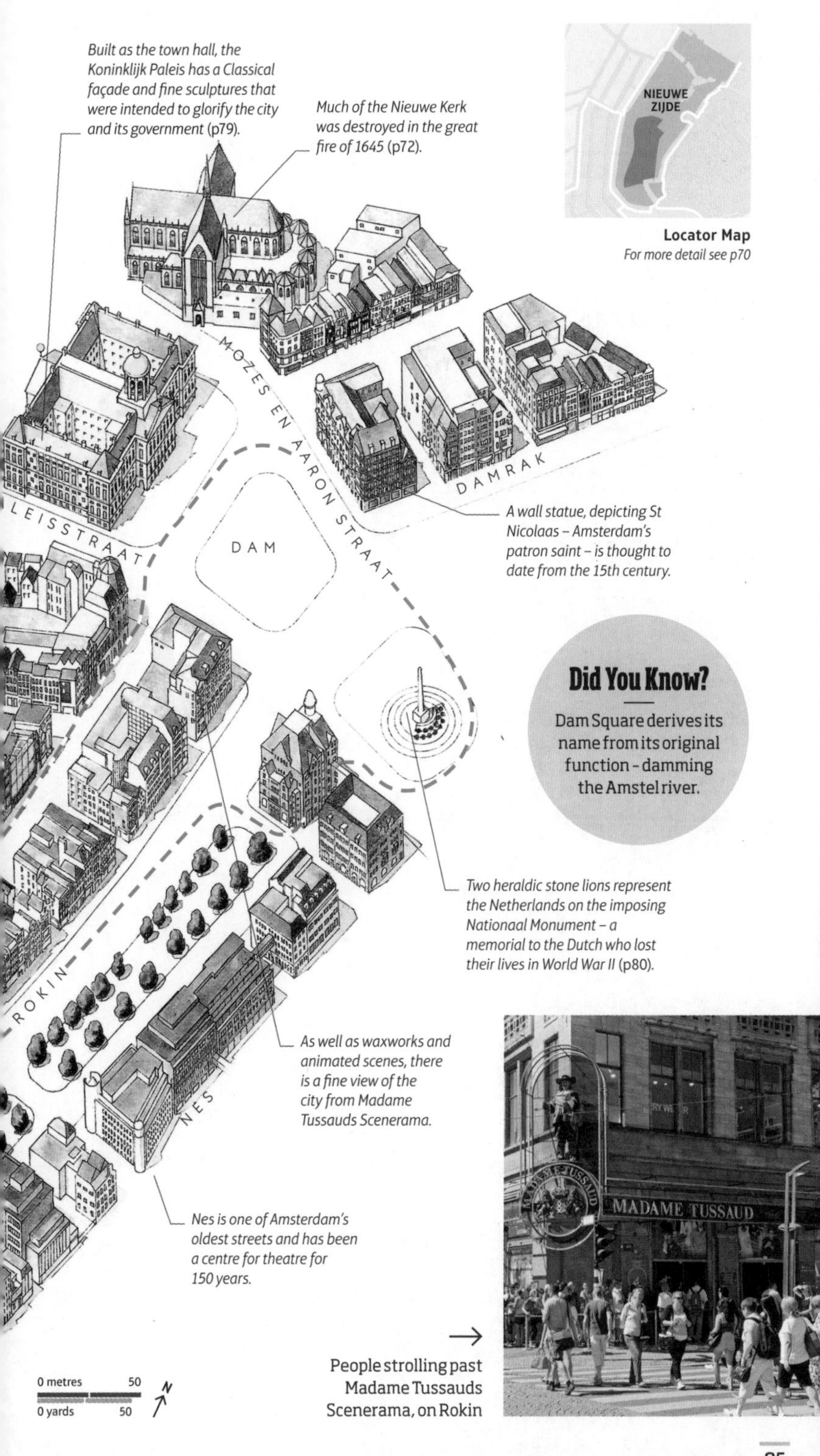

Locator Map
For more detail see p70

Built as the town hall, the Koninklijk Paleis has a Classical façade and fine sculptures that were intended to glorify the city and its government (p79).

Much of the Nieuwe Kerk was destroyed in the great fire of 1645 (p72).

A wall statue, depicting St Nicolaas – Amsterdam's patron saint – is thought to date from the 15th century.

Did You Know?

Dam Square derives its name from its original function - damming the Amstel river.

Two heraldic stone lions represent the Netherlands on the imposing Nationaal Monument – a memorial to the Dutch who lost their lives in World War II (p80).

As well as waxworks and animated scenes, there is a fine view of the city from Madame Tussauds Scenerama.

Nes is one of Amsterdam's oldest streets and has been a centre for theatre for 150 years.

→

People strolling past Madame Tussauds Scenerama, on Rokin

PRIDE
P

The historic buildings lining the Oudezijds Voorburgwal canal

OUDE ZIJDE

As the name – Oude Zijde (Old Side) – suggests, this is where Amsterdam has its roots. Originally Amsterdam occupied a ribbon of land on the east bank of the Amstel river, running between Damrak and the Oudezijds Voorburgwal ("before the city wall") canals. At its heart was the Oude Kerk, the oldest church in the city. In the early 1400s the Oude Zijde began an eastward expansion which continued into the 17th century. This growth was fuelled by an influx of Jewish refugees from Portugal, who were fleeing the Inquisition. Many of these Sephardic Jews were merchants and craftsmen and they brought wealth to their new, tolerant city, building schools and synagogues. The Grote Synagogue, as well as the three other synagogues that make up the Joods Historisch Museum, were central to Jewish life in the city for centuries. During the Golden Age, the Oude Zijde was an important commercial centre. Boats could sail up the Geldersekade to Nieuwmarkt, where goods were weighed at the 15th-century Waag before being sold at the market.

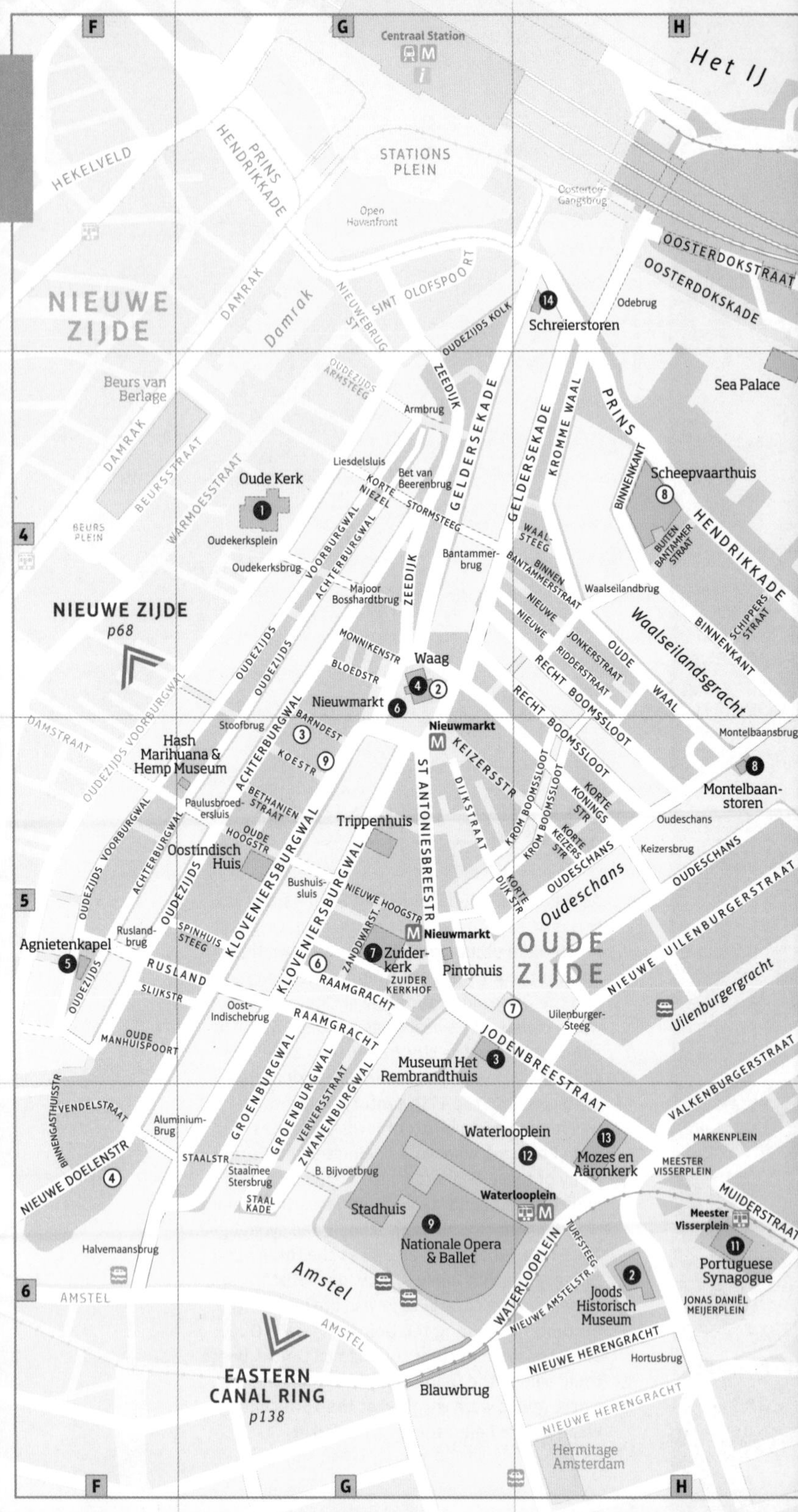

F
G
H
Centraal Station
Het IJ
HEKELVELD
PRINS HENDRIKKADE
STATIONS PLEIN
Open Havenfront
Oostertog-Gangsbrug
OOSTERDOKSTRAAT
OOSTERDOKSKADE
Odebrug
NIEUWE ZIJDE
DAMRAK
Damrak
NIEUWEBRUG ST
SINT OLOFSPOORT
OUDEZIJDS KOLK
Schreierstoren
Beurs van Berlage
OUDEZIJDS ARMSTEEG
Armbrug
ZEEDIJK
GELDERSEKADE
KROMME WAAL
PRINS HENDRIKKADE
Sea Palace
Scheepvaarthuis
BINNENKANT
BUITEN BANTAMMER STRAAT
BEURSSTRAAT
WARMOESSTRAAT
Oude Kerk
Liesdelsluis
Bet van Beerenbrug
KORTE NIEZEL
STORMSTEEG
BEURS PLEIN
Oudekerksplein
Oudekerksbrug
VOORBURGWAL
ACHTERBURGWAL
Bantammer-brug
WAAL-STEEG
BINNEN BANTAMMERSTRAAT
Waalseilandbrug
Majoor Bosshardtbrug
NIEUWE ZIJDE
p68
NIEUWE
JONKERSTRAAT
OUDE WAAL
Waalseilandsgracht
BINNENKANT
SCHIPPERS STRAAT
MONNIKENSTR
Waag
BLOEDSTR
RIDDERSTRAAT
RECHT BOOMSSLOOT
OUDEZIJDS
Nieuwmarkt
DAMSTRAAT
OUDEZIJDS VOORBURGWAL
Stoofbrug
BARNDEST
Nieuwmarkt
KEIZERSSTR
Montelbaansbrug
Hash Marihuana & Hemp Museum
KOESTR
Montelbaan-storen
ACHTERBURGWAL
BETHANIEN STRAAT
Paulusbroed-ersluis
ST ANTONIESBREESTR
DIJKSTRAAT
KROM BOOMSSLOOT
KORTE KONINGS STR
Oudeschans
Trippenhuis
OUDE HOOGSTR
Keizersbrug
Oostindisch Huis
KORTE KEIZERS STR
OUDESCHANS
OUDEZIJDS VOORBURGWAL
KLOVENIERSBURGWAL
Bushuis-sluis
NIEUWE HOOGSTR
KORTE DIJK STR
Oudeschans
NIEUWE ULENBURGERSTRAAT
Rusland-brug
SPINHUIS STEEG
Nieuwmarkt
Agnietenkapel
ZANDDWARST.
Zuider-kerk
OUDE ZIJDE
RUSLAND
SLIJKSTR
RAAMGRACHT
ZUIDER KERKHOF
Pintohuis
Oost-Indischebrug
Uilenburger-Steeg
Uilenburgergracht
OUDE MANHUISPOORT
JODENBREESTRAAT
Museum Het Rembrandthuis
VALKENBURGERSTRAAT
BINNENGASTHUISSTR
VENDELSTRAAT
GROENBURGWAL
VERVERSSTRAAT
ZWANENBURGWAL
Aluminium-Brug
Waterlooplein
MARKENPLEIN
NIEUWE DOELENSTR
STAALSTR
Mozes en Aäronkerk
MEESTER VISSERPLEIN
Staalmee Stersbrug
B. Bijvoetbrug
MUIDERSTRAAT
STAAL KADE
Stadhuis
Waterlooplein
TURFSTEEG
Meester Visserplein
Nationale Opera & Ballet
Portuguese Synagogue
Halvemaansbrug
Amstel
WATERLOOPLEIN
NIEUWE AMSTELSTR.
Joods Historisch Museum
JONAS DANIËL MEIJERPLEIN
AMSTEL
NIEUWE HERENGRACHT
Hortusbrug
EASTERN CANAL RING
p138
Blauwbrug
NIEUWE HERENGRACHT
Hermitage Amsterdam
4
5
6

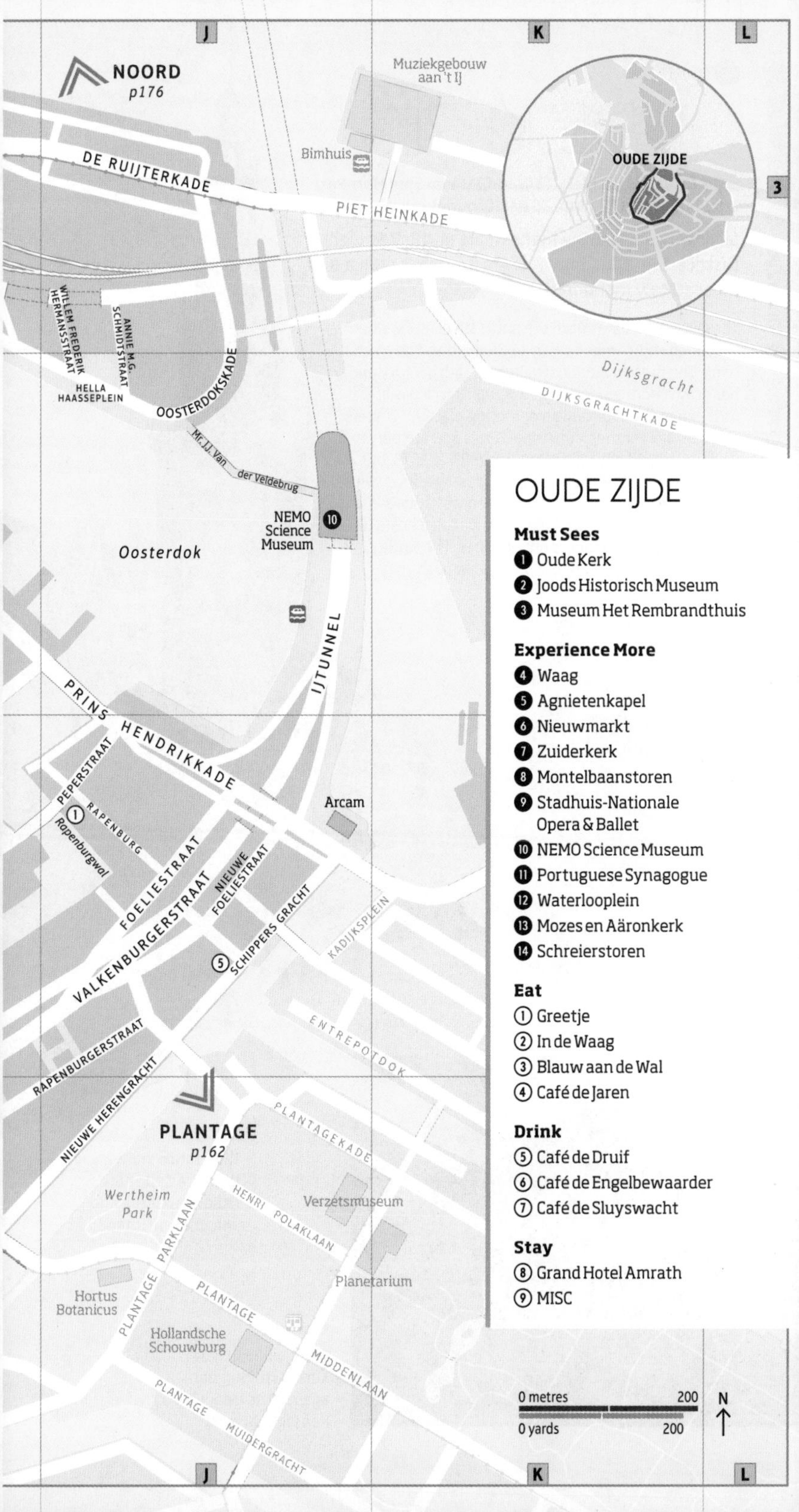
J
K
L
NOORD
p176
Muziekgebouw aan 't IJ
Bimhuis
OUDE ZIJDE
3
DE RUIJTERKADE
PIET HEINKADE
WILLEM FREDERIK HERMANSSTRAAT
ANNIE M.G. SCHMIDTSTRAAT
HELLA HAASSEPLEIN
OOSTERDOKSKADE
Dijksgracht
DIJKSGRACHTKADE
Mr. J.J. Van der Veldebrug
NEMO Science Museum
10
Oosterdok
IJTUNNEL
PRINS HENDRIKKADE
PEPERSTRAAT
1
RAPENBURG
Rapenburgwal
Arcam
FOELIESTRAAT
NIEUWE FOELIESTRAAT
VALKENBURGERSTRAAT
SCHIPPERS GRACHT
5
KADIJKSPLEIN
ENTREPOTDOK
RAPENBURGERSTRAAT
NIEUWE HERENGRACHT
PLANTAGE
p162
PLANTAGEKADE
Wertheim Park
HENRI POLAKLAAN
Verzetsmuseum
PLANTAGE PARKLAAN
Planetarium
Hortus Botanicus
PLANTAGE
Hollandsche Schouwburg
MIDDENLAAN
PLANTAGE MUIDERGRACHT
OUDE ZIJDE
Must Sees
1 Oude Kerk
2 Joods Historisch Museum
3 Museum Het Rembrandthuis
Experience More
4 Waag
5 Agnietenkapel
6 Nieuwmarkt
7 Zuiderkerk
8 Montelbaanstoren
9 Stadhuis-Nationale Opera & Ballet
10 NEMO Science Museum
11 Portuguese Synagogue
12 Waterlooplein
13 Mozes en Aäronkerk
14 Schreierstoren
Eat
① Greetje
② In de Waag
③ Blauw aan de Wal
④ Café de Jaren
Drink
⑤ Café de Druif
⑥ Café de Engelbewaarder
⑦ Café de Sluyswacht
Stay
⑧ Grand Hotel Amrath
⑨ MISC
0 metres 200
0 yards 200
N

OUDE KERK

G4 Oudekerksplein 4, 24 10am-6pm Mon-Sat, 1-5:30pm Sun 27 Apr, 25 Dec oudekerk.nl

Sitting incongruously in the heart of the Red Light District, the "Old Church" is Amsterdam's oldest and most stately monument.

The Oude Kerk dates from the mid-13th century, when a wooden church was built in a burial ground on a sand bank. The present Gothic structure is 14th century and has grown from a single-aisled church into a basilica. As it expanded, it became a gathering place for traders and a refuge for the poor. Its paintings and statuary were destroyed after the Alteration *(p53)* in 1578, but the rare gilded ceiling and stained-glass windows were undamaged. The world-famous organ was added in 1724. The church still holds services, but also hosts art exhibitions, performances and debates. The Oude Kerk is dedicated to St Nicholas, patron saint of the city.

The spire of the bell tower was built in 1565, but the 47-bell carillon was added in 1658.

Great Organ

2,500

tombstones are found in the church floor.

Tomb of Admiral Abraham van der Hulst, hero of the Second Anglo-Dutch War

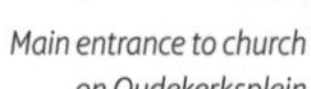

Main entrance to church on Oudekerksplein

Illustration showing both the Oude Kerk's medieval exterior and its magnificent interior ↑

The medieval Oude Kerk, a striking sight against the frenetic Red Light District

1

2

3

1 Contemporary art exhibitions, such as Christian Boltanski's *NA*, juxtapose with the Oude Kerk's medieval interior.

2 The Lady Chapel (1552) has three restored stained-glass windows, including *The Death of the Virgin Mary* by Dirk Crabeth.

3 Delicate 15th-century gilded vault paintings decorate the ceiling of the nave. They were hidden under layers of blue paint in 1755 and not revealed until 1955.

Timeline

1250
First wooden chapel built

1330
Church dedicated to St Nicholas

1578
Calvinists triumph in the Alteration and iconoclasts destroy many of the statues in the church

1724
▶ Christian Vater's oak-encased Great Organ, with its 4,000 pipes, is installed in the nave

2

JOODS HISTORISCH MUSEUM

H6 Nieuwe Amstelstraat 1 14 Nationale Opera & Ballet Waterlooplein 11am-5pm daily 27 Apr, Yom Kippur and Jewish New Year jck.nl/en

From the first Jews to arrive in Amsterdam to the preservation of Jewish identity today, this museum tells the turbulent history of the Jewish community in the Netherlands.

The Collection

This remarkable museum of Jewish heritage is housed in four monumental synagogues – the Grote Synagoge, Nieuwe Synagoge, Obbene Shul and Dritt Shul. Three permanent multimedia exhibitions present the history and culture of the Jewish people in the Netherlands through paintings, drawings, artifacts, photographs, films and 3D displays. In addition, there are temporary exhibitions and a Children's Museum. This museum, the Portuguese Synagogue *(p102)* and the Hollandsche Schouwburg *(p170)*, form the Jewish Cultural Quarter.

The Nieuwe Synagoge (1752)

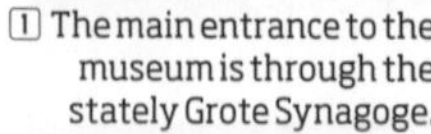

1 The main entrance to the museum is through the stately Grote Synagoge.

2 This Festival Prayer Book was presented to the city's Jewish community by printer Uri Phoebus ha-Levi in 1669.

3 The side galleries of the Nieuwe Synagoge house part of the permanent collection. Photographs and artifacts tell emotive stories.

JEWS IN AMSTERDAM

The first Jew to gain Dutch citizenship was a member of the Portuguese Sephardic community in 1597. The Ashkenazi Jews from eastern Europe came to Amsterdam later, in the 1630s. They were restricted to working in certain trades, but were granted full civil equality in 1796. With the rise of Zionism in the 19th century, Jewish identity re-emerged, but the Nazi occupation almost obliterated the community *(p55)*.

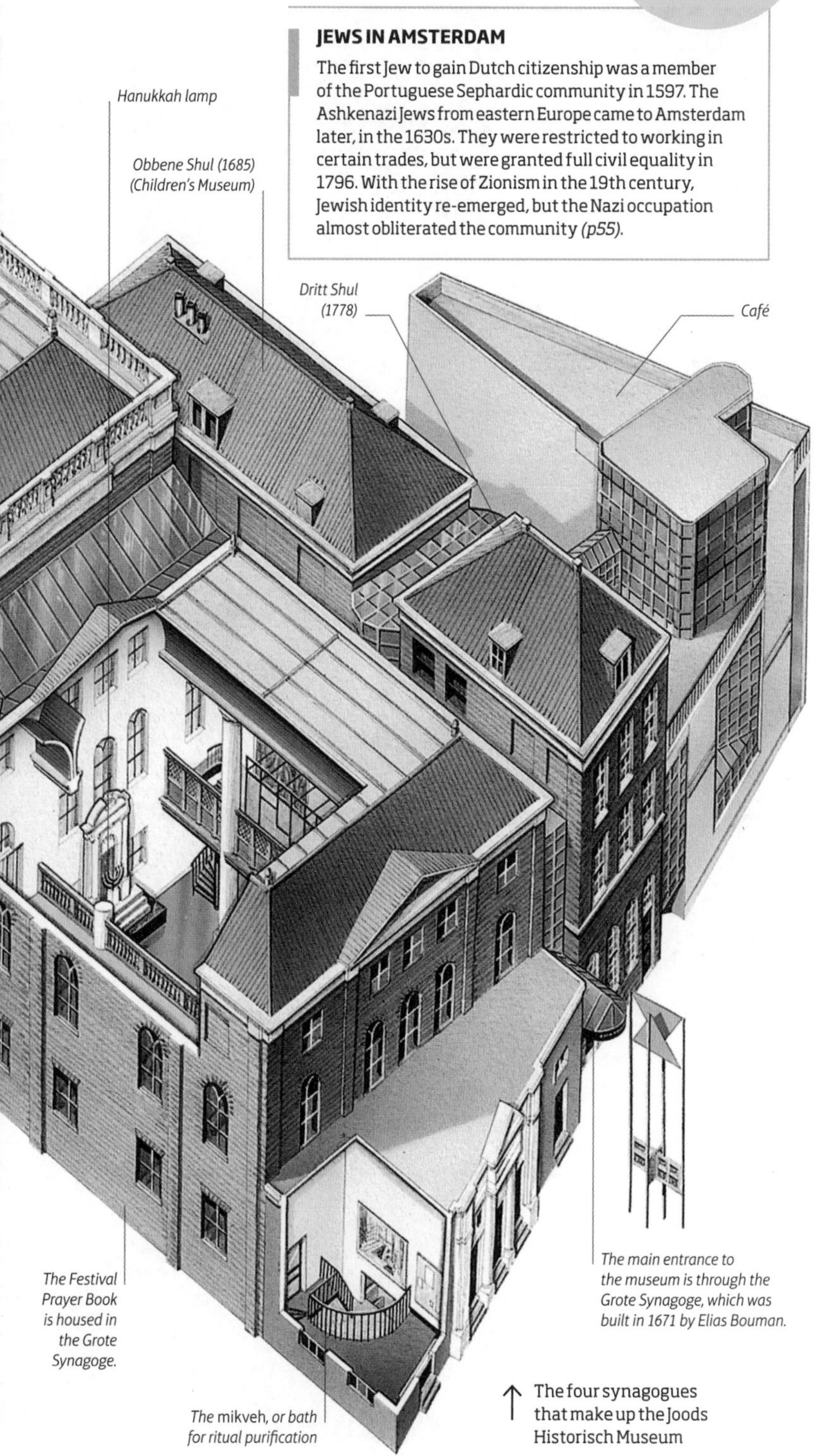
Hanukkah lamp
Obbene Shul (1685) (Children's Museum)
Dritt Shul (1778)
Café
The Festival Prayer Book is housed in the Grote Synagoge.
The mikveh, or bath for ritual purification
The main entrance to the museum is through the Grote Synagoge, which was built in 1671 by Elias Bouman.

↑ The four synagogues that make up the Joods Historisch Museum

Did You Know?

Rembrandt painted himself into many of his works as a spectator.

A canvas set up in the artist's former studio

3

MUSEUM HET REMBRANDTHUIS

G5 Jodenbreestraat 4 14 Nieuwmarkt 10am-6pm daily 27 Apr, 25 Dec rembrandthuis.nl

The former home of Amsterdam's most famous artist – creator of *The Nightwatch*, *The Anatomy Lesson of Dr Nicolaes Tulp* and over 300 other works – has been transformed into a sensitive museum allowing an intimate glimpse into the life and times of Rembrandt Harmenszoon van Rijn.

Rembrandt was an established portraitist, married to the daughter of a wealthy bourgeois family, when he bought this red-shuttered house on the edge of the Jewish district in 1639. By 1656, however, his fortunes had changed. No longer an artistic star, he was forced to sell his home.

Furnished according to the 1656 inventory, the house is now a museum dedicated to the artist. On the first floor is the studio where Rembrandt created many of his most famous works. A room on the mezzanine floor has some of his superb etchings on display, and the exhibition wing next door shows work by his contemporaries. Younger visitors will love the cabinet of curiosities on the second floor, with its stuffed crocodiles, narwhal tusks, skulls and fossils. Daily 17th-century etching and paint-mixing demonstrations – at no extra cost – enhance the experience.

The exterior of Rembrandt's home looking much as it did when he lived here in the Golden Age

A visitor admiring an exhibition of Rembrandt's works alongside paintings by artists he inspired

REMBRANDT'S SITTERS

Sephardi Jews fleeing the Spanish Inquisition began to arrive in Amsterdam in the early 17th century. They settled on the eastern fringes of the Oude Zijde. Many Sephardim were already wealthy when they arrived in Amsterdam, and in Rembrandt's day this part of town was an up-and-coming neighbourhood. Its exotic, striking young women and craggy elders were the perfect models for Rembrandt's series of paintings inspired by Old Testament myths.

EXPERIENCE MORE

Waag

G4 Nieuwmarkt 4
Nieuwmarkt waag.org

The multi-turreted Waag is Amsterdam's oldest surviving gatehouse. Built in 1488, it was then called St Antoniespoort. Public executions were held here, and prisoners awaited their fate in the "little gallows room". In 1617, the building became the public weigh house *(waaggebouw)*; peasants had their produce weighed here and paid tax accordingly. Various guilds moved into the upper rooms of each tower, including the Guild of Surgeons, who from 1619 had their meeting room and anatomy theatre here. They added the central octagonal tower in 1691. Rembrandt's *Anatomy Lesson of Dr Nicolaes Tulp*, now in the Mauritshuis *(p204)*, and *The Anatomy Lesson of Dr Jan Deijman*, in the Amsterdam Museum *(p74)*, were commissioned by the guild.

After the weigh house closed in the early 1800s, the Waag served as a fire station and two city museums. But even into the first half of the 19th century, punishments were carried out in front of the building. The ground floor is home to the café-restaurant In de Waag *(p102)*. Upstairs is the Waag Society, a research collective focusing on science, technology and the arts.

Agnietenkapel

F5 Oudezijds Voorburgwal 231 4, 14, 24 To the public

The Agnietenkapel, which dates from 1470, was part of the convent of St Agnes until 1578, when it was closed after the Alteration *(p53)*. It is one of the few Gothic chapels to have survived this period of turmoil. In 1632, the Athenaeum Illustre, the precursor of the University of Amsterdam, took it over and by the mid-17th century it was a centre of scientific learning. It also housed the municipal

Café de Druif

Fragrant with four centuries of tobacco smoke and rum, Café de Druif may be the city's oldest tavern.

J5
Rapenburgerplein 83
624 4530

Café de Engelbewaarder

Drop in to this traditional tavern on a Sunday for live jazz. Its arty habitués are lubricated by 15 brands of tasty beer from its taps.

G5
Kloveniersburgwal 59
cafe-de-engelbewaarder.nl

Café de Sluyswacht

Perched beside the Oude Schans, Café de Sluyswacht greets visitors with appetizing smells from the kitchen. In summer, watch the canalboats puttering past from the terrace.

G5
Jodenbreestraat 1
D Sun
sluyswacht.nl

The imposing 15th-century Waag lit up at dusk

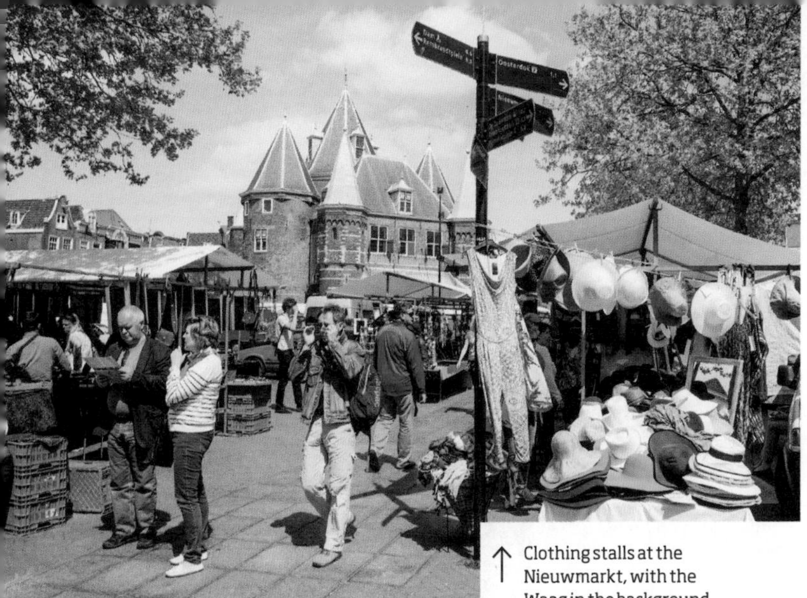

Clothing stalls at the Nieuwmarkt, with the Waag in the background

library until the 1830s. During restoration from 1919 to 1921, elements of Amsterdam School architecture were introduced to the building *(p37)*. Despite these changes and long periods of secular use, the building still has the feel of a Franciscan chapel.

The large auditorium on the first floor is the city's oldest, and is used for university lectures. It has a lovely ceiling, painted with Renaissance motifs and a portrait of Minerva. A series of portraits of scholars – a gift from local merchant Gerardus van Papenbroeck in 1743 – also adorns the walls.

From 1921 until 2007, the chapel was home to the University Museum. It is now used as a conference centre and is not open to the public.

Nieuwmarkt

G4 Nieuwmarkt Antiques market: May-Sep: 9am-5pm Sun; Organic market: 9am-4pm Sat

An open, paved square, the Nieuwmarkt is flanked to the west by the Red Light District. Along with the top end of the Geldersekade, it forms Amsterdam's Chinatown. The Waag dominates the square, and construction of this gateway led to the site's development in the 15th century as a marketplace.

When the city expanded in the 17th century, the square took on its present dimensions and was named the Nieuwmarkt. It retains an array of 17th- and 18th-century gabled houses and, true to tradition, antiques and organic markets are still held here.

The old Jewish Quarter leads off the square down St Antoniesbreestraat. In the 1970s, many houses in this area were demolished to make way for the metro, sparking clashes between protesters and police. The action of conservationists persuaded the city council to renovate rather than redevelop old buildings. In tribute to them, photographs of their protests decorate the metro.

RED LIGHT DISTRICT

Barely clad prostitutes bathed in a red neon glow and touting for business at their windows is one of the defining images of Amsterdam. The city's Red Light District, referred to locally as de Walletjes (the little walls), is concentrated around the Oude Kerk, although it extends as far as Warmoesstraat to the west, the Zeedijk to the north, the Kloveniersburgwal to the east and then along the line of Damstraat to the south.

Prostitution in Amsterdam dates back to the city's emergence as a port in the 13th century. By 1478, prostitution had become so widespread, with increasing numbers of sea-weary sailors flooding into the city, that attempts were made to contain it.

Today, hordes of visitors generate a buzz, and despite the sleaze, the council is making this area more culturally attractive, promoting the bars, eateries and beautiful canal-side houses that punctuate the streets.

7 Zuiderkerk

G5 Zuiderkerkhof 72 14 Nieuwmarkt Concerts only, check website; tower: closed for renovations, check website zuiderkerkamsterdam.nl

The Renaissance-style Zuiderkerk, designed by Hendrick de Keyser in 1603 *(p37)*, was the first Calvinist church in Amsterdam after the Alteration *(p53)*. The spire, with its columns, decorative clocks and onion dome, is a prominent city landmark.

The Zuiderkerk ceased to function as a church in 1929 and it is now a meeting and congress centre. You can attend one of the venue's concerts, but the main reason to visit the Zuiderkerk is to climb the tower, which overlooks olive-green canals.

↑ The medieval Montelbaanstoren, with its decorative timber steeple

8 Montelbaanstoren

H5 Oudeschans 2 Nieuwmarkt To the public

The lower portion of the Montelbaanstoren was built in 1512 and formed part of Amsterdam's medieval fortifications. It lay just beyond the city wall, protecting the city's wharves on the newly built St Antoniesdijk (now the Oudeschans) from the neighbouring Gelderlanders.

The octagonal structure and open-work timber steeple were both added by Hendrick de Keyser in 1606. His decorative addition bears a close resemblance to the spire of the Oude Kerk, designed by Joost Bilhamer, which was built 40 years earlier *(p90)*. In 1611, the tower began to list, prompting Amsterdammers to attach ropes to the top and pull it right again.

Sailors from the VOC *(p54)* would gather at the Montelbaanstoren before being ferried in small boats down the IJ to the massive East Indies-bound sailing ships, anchored further out in deep water to the north.

The building, now housing Amsterdam's water authority, appears in a number of etchings by Rembrandt, and is still a popular subject for artists.

MARIJUANA AND HEMP

Cannabis, or marijuana, has played a large part in Amsterdam's history. Around 8,000 years ago, early Asiatic civilizations used the plant for medicines and clothing. It was first prescribed in the Netherlands, according to a herbal manual of 1554, as a cure for earache. The Hash Marihuana & Hemp Museum *(www.hashmuseum.com)* explores the plant's historic links to Amsterdam and explains its place in the city today.

HASH MARIHUANA & HEMP MUSEUM SIGN

9 Stadhuis-Nationale Opera & Ballet

G6 Waterlooplein 22 Stadhuis: 625 5455 14 Waterlooplein Offices: 8:30am-8pm Mon-Fri operaballet.nl

Few buildings in Amsterdam caused as much controversy

as the Stadhuis (town hall) and Nationale Opera & Ballet (opera house). Nicknamed the "Stopera" by protesters, the scheme required the destruction of dozens of medieval houses, which were virtually all that remained of the original Jewish quarter. This led to running battles between squatters and police.

Completed in 1986, the Nationale Opera & Ballet has the largest auditorium in the country, seating 1,689 people, and is home to the Netherlands' national opera and ballet companies. Book a ticket for a performance, take a backstage tour or, better yet, attend one of the free concerts at 12:30pm on Tuesdays from September to May.

NEMO Science Museum

J4 Oosterdok 2 22, 48 2, 4, 11, 12, 13, 14, 17, 24 Centraal Station 10am-5:30pm Tue-Sun (daily during school hols & Feb-Aug) 27 Apr nemosciencemuseum.nl

In June 1997 the Netherlands' national science museum moved to this dazzling curved building, desiged by Renzo Piano, which protrudes 30 m (98 ft) over water. NEMO is the largest science museum in the Netherlands, with five floors filled with interactive exhibits, presenting technological innovations in a manner that allows both adults' and children's creativity full expression.

You can interact with virtual reality, operate the latest industrial equipment under expert supervision and harness science to produce your own art. Visitors – who in this setting might equally be termed explorers – can participate in experiments, demonstrations, games and workshops, or take in lectures, films and even educational stage shows.

The five floors are crammed full of fascinating exhibitions and fun activities. Discover new ways to enjoy mathematics in the World of Shapes; go on a voyage into space to learn more about the stars and the planets in Life in the Universe; or awaken a fascination for physics in Sensational Science.

NEMO Science Museum has the largest roof terrace in Amsterdam, with great views of the city. Piano designed the roof to resemble an Italian piazza and it provides the perfect spot to relax. Here you will also find an open-air exhibition and a restaurant. Access the roof via the lift from the central hall, or the stairs from street level, for free. Check the website for special events, including live music and film screenings, held on the roof in spring and summer.

STAY

Grand Hotel Amrath

Redolent of another era, rooms here combine Art Deco with 21st-century style.

H4 Prins Hendrikkade 108 amrathamsterdam.com

MISC

This boutique hotel is in a 17th-century canal house.

G5 Kloveniersburgwal 20 misceatdrinksleep.com

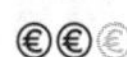

The futuristic copper hull of NEMO Science Museum

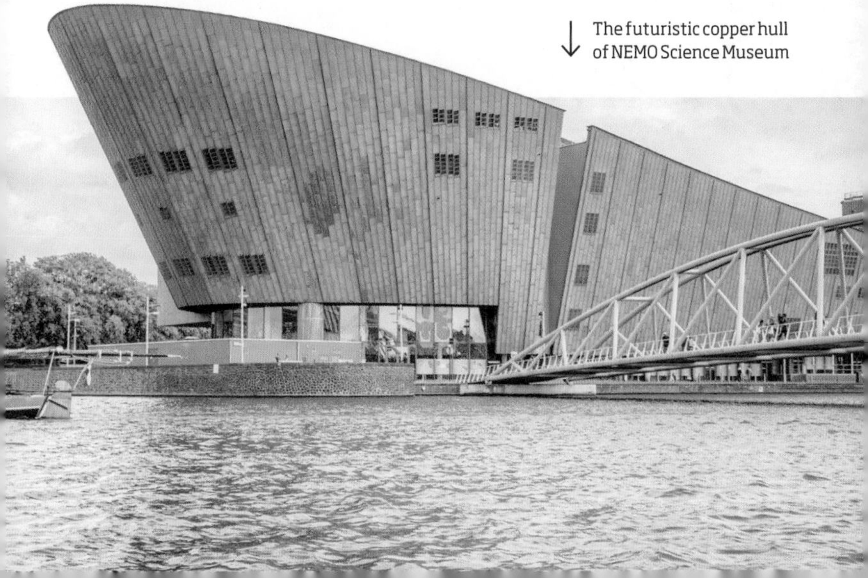

A bike leans against a tree in a square near the Oude Kerk

11  

Portuguese Synagogue

H6 Mr Visserplein 3 14 Waterlooplein Feb-Nov: 10am-5pm Sun-Thu (to 4pm Fri Sep, Oct, Mar & Apr, to 2pm Fri Nov & Feb); Dec & Jan: 10am-4pm Sun-Thu (to 2pm Fri) Jewish hols jck.nl/en

The design for this synagogue, by Elias Bouman (1636–86), was inspired by the architecture of the Temple of Solomon in Jerusalem. Built for the Portuguese Sephardic community of Amsterdam *(p93)* and inaugurated in 1675, the huge building has a rectangular ground plan with the Holy Ark in the southeast corner facing Jerusalem, and the *tebah* (the podium from which the service is led) at the opposite end.

The wooden, barrel-vaulted ceiling is supported by four Ionic columns. The interior of the synagogue is illuminated by more than 1,000 candles. Treasure chambers in the basement contain a sumptuous collection of ceremonial objects made of silver, gold and silk brocades, and rare manuscripts. The synagogue is part of the city's Jewish Cultural Quarter.

Did You Know?

Amsterdam's nickname - "Mokum" - means "place of refuge" in Yiddish.

EAT

Greetje

Come here for elegant Dutch cuisine - stewed rabbit with sweet potato purée and *trekdrop* (liquorice) crème brûlée.

J5 Peperstraat 23 L daily restaurantgreetje.nl

Blauw aan de Wal

The eclectic menu features razor clams, oysters, buffalo ricotta and North Sea fish.

G5 Oudezijds Achterburgwal 99 Mon & Sun blauwaandewal.com

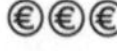

In de Waag

This candlelit room in a 15th-century gatehouse is beautiful. The menu lists classic dishes.

G4 Nieuwmarkt 4 indewaag.nl

Café de Jaren

The restaurant's biggest selling point is its terrace overlooking the Amstel.

F6 Nieuwe Doelenstraat 20 cafedejaren.nl

12

Waterlooplein

H6 14 Waterlooplein Market: 9am-5pm Mon-Fri, 8:30am-5pm Sat

The Waterlooplein dates from 1882, when two canals were filled in to create a large market square. The site was originally called Vlooyenburg, an artificial island built in the 17th century to house the Jewish settlers.

The original market disappeared during World War II when most of the Jewish residents of Amsterdam were transported by the Nazis to concentration camps *(p55)*. After the war, a popular flea market grew up in its place.

Despite encroachment by the Stadhuis-Nationale Opera & Ballet, the northern

← Decorated stalls awaiting opening time at Waterlooplein's flea market

end of the Waterlooplein still operates a lively and interesting market, selling anything from bric-a-brac and army-surplus clothing to Balinese carvings.

13 Mozes en Aäronkerk

H6 Waterlooplein 205 14 Waterlooplein Prayer services: 8pm Tue & Fri; Holy Mass: 5pm Sun santegidio.nl

Designed by the Flemish architect T Suys the Elder in 1841, Mozes en Aäronkerk was built on the site of a hidden Catholic church. The later church, with its two towers, took its name from the Old Testament figures of Moses and Aaron depicted on the gable stones of the original building. These are now set into the rear wall.

The church was restored in 1990, when its twin wooden towers were painted to look like sandstone. After years of hosting events, it is again a place of worship.

14 Schreierstoren

H3 Prins Hendrikkade 94-95 Centraal Station 10am-11pm daily weepingtower.nl

Dating from 1480, the Schreierstoren (Weepers' Tower) was a defensive structure forming part of the medieval city walls. It was one of the few fortifications not to be demolished as the city expanded beyond its medieval boundaries in the 17th century. The building now houses the VOC café. Popular legend states that the tower derived its name from the weeping (*schreien* in the original Dutch) of women who came here to wave their men off to sea. It is more likely, however, that the title comes from the tower's position on a sharp (*screye* or *scherpe*) 90-degree bend in the old town walls. A wall plaque, dated 1569, adds considerably to the confusion by depicting a weeping woman alongside the inscription *scrayer hovck*, which means "sharp corner".

In 1609, Henry Hudson set sail from here in an attempt to discover a new and faster trading route to the East Indies. Instead, he unintentionally "discovered" the river in North America that bears his name. A bronze plaque, laid in 1927, commemorates his voyage.

The Schreierstoren standing out from the canal houses ↓

A SHORT WALK UNIVERSITY DISTRICT

Distance 1.5 km (1 mile) **Nearest metro** Nieuwmarkt **Time** 15 minutes

The University of Amsterdam, founded in 1877, is predominantly located in the peaceful, southwestern part of the Oude Zijde. A walk around the university district from Nieuwmarkt to the Agnietenkapel – where the university has its roots – takes in everything from the bustling Red Light District, where Damstraat meets the Nieuwmarkt, to the 15th-century Waag, which evokes a medieval air. As you head south of the Nieuwmarkt, stop off at Museum Het Rembrandthuis for a fascinating insight into the life of the city's most famous artist.

↑ The exterior of the Hash Marihuana & Hemp Museum

Marijuana through the ages is explored at the Hash Marihuana & Hemp Museum (p98).

Originally part of a convent, the Agnietenkapel survived destruction during the Alteration, and got a new lease of life serving as the University of Amsterdam's first lecture hall (p96).

This house, which was built in 1610, unusually faces three canals.

The large Oudemanhuispoort was built in the 18th century to function as an almshouse for elderly men.

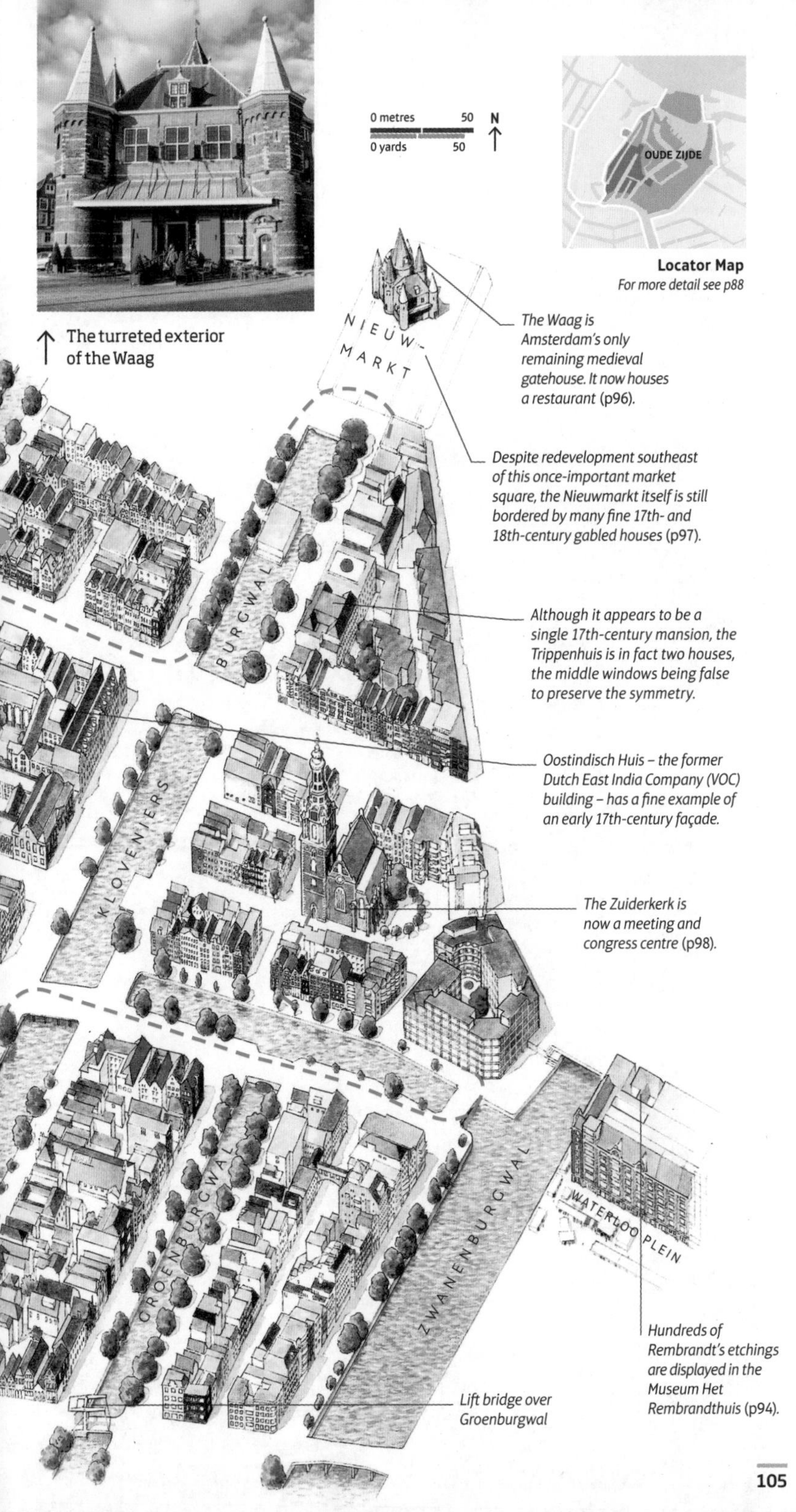

The turreted exterior of the Waag

Locator Map
For more detail see p88

The Waag is Amsterdam's only remaining medieval gatehouse. It now houses a restaurant (p96).

Despite redevelopment southeast of this once-important market square, the Nieuwmarkt itself is still bordered by many fine 17th- and 18th-century gabled houses (p97).

Although it appears to be a single 17th-century mansion, the Trippenhuis is in fact two houses, the middle windows being false to preserve the symmetry.

Oostindisch Huis – the former Dutch East India Company (VOC) building – has a fine example of an early 17th-century façade.

The Zuiderkerk is now a meeting and congress centre (p98).

Lift bridge over Groenburgwal

Hundreds of Rembrandt's etchings are displayed in the Museum Het Rembrandthuis (p94).

Art Deco interior of Café Americain

CENTRAL CANAL RING

The extension of Amsterdam's three major canals continued from the early 17th century, as the merchant classes, rich from booming maritime trade, sought to escape the overcrowding and industrial squalor in the old city, around the Amstel. They bought plots of land along the new extensions to the Herengracht, Keizersgracht and Prinsengracht canals, and in the 1660s the wealthiest built opulent houses on a stretch of Herengracht known as the Golden Bend. Designed and decorated by the best architects of the day, such as Philips Vingboons (1607–1678), the mansions built here were often twice the width of standard canal houses, demonstrating the wealth of their occupants. The area's most famous building, however, is the Anne Frank House. Together with the Homomonument, these sites attest to Amsterdam's characteristic tolerance, as well as serving as reminders of the realities of the Nazi occupation during World War II.

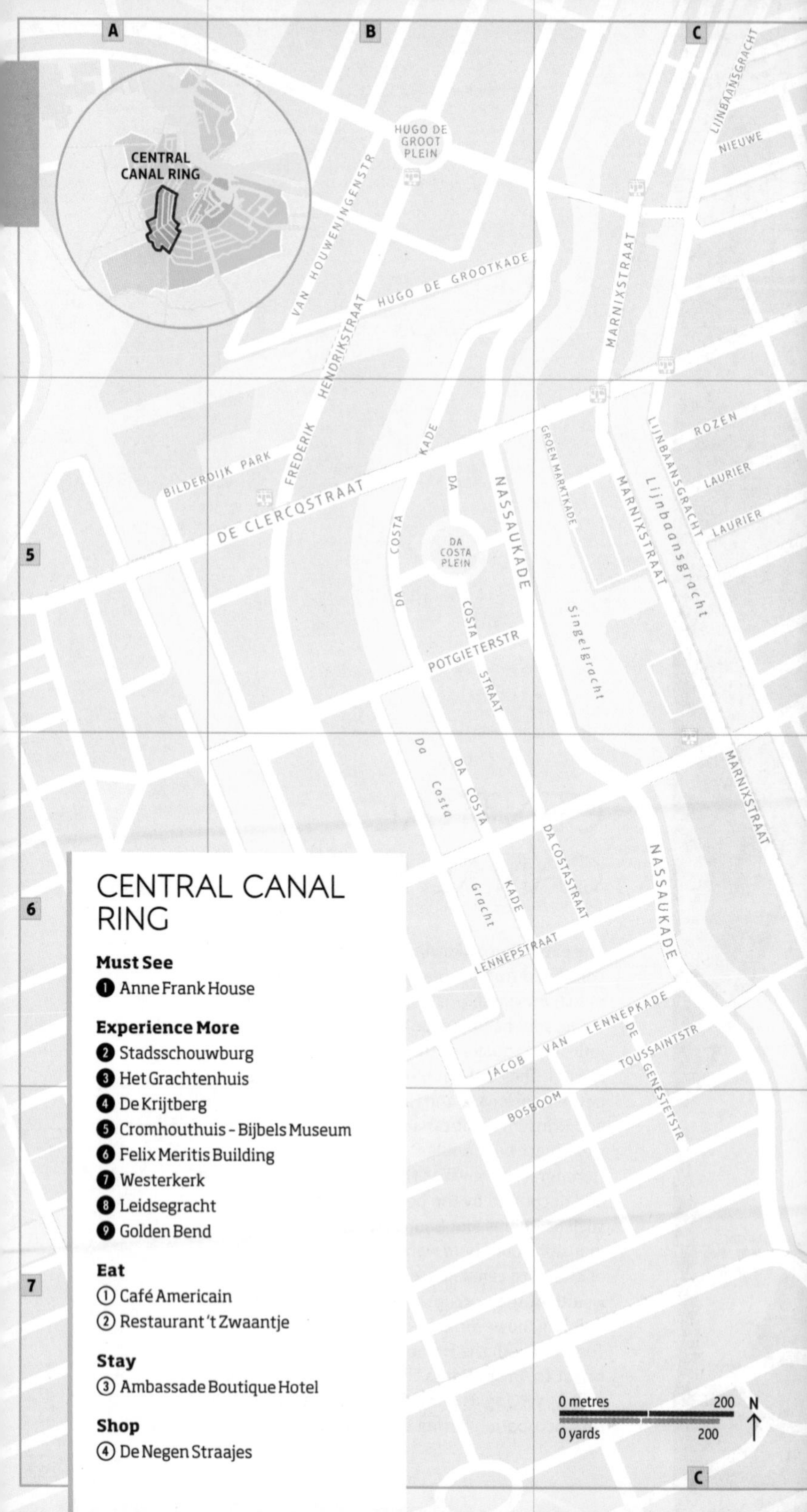

CENTRAL CANAL RING

Must See

❶ Anne Frank House

Experience More

❷ Stadsschouwburg
❸ Het Grachtenhuis
❹ De Krijtberg
❺ Cromhouthuis – Bijbels Museum
❻ Felix Meritis Building
❼ Westerkerk
❽ Leidsegracht
❾ Golden Bend

Eat

① Café Americain
② Restaurant 't Zwaantje

Stay

③ Ambassade Boutique Hotel

Shop

④ De Negen Straajes

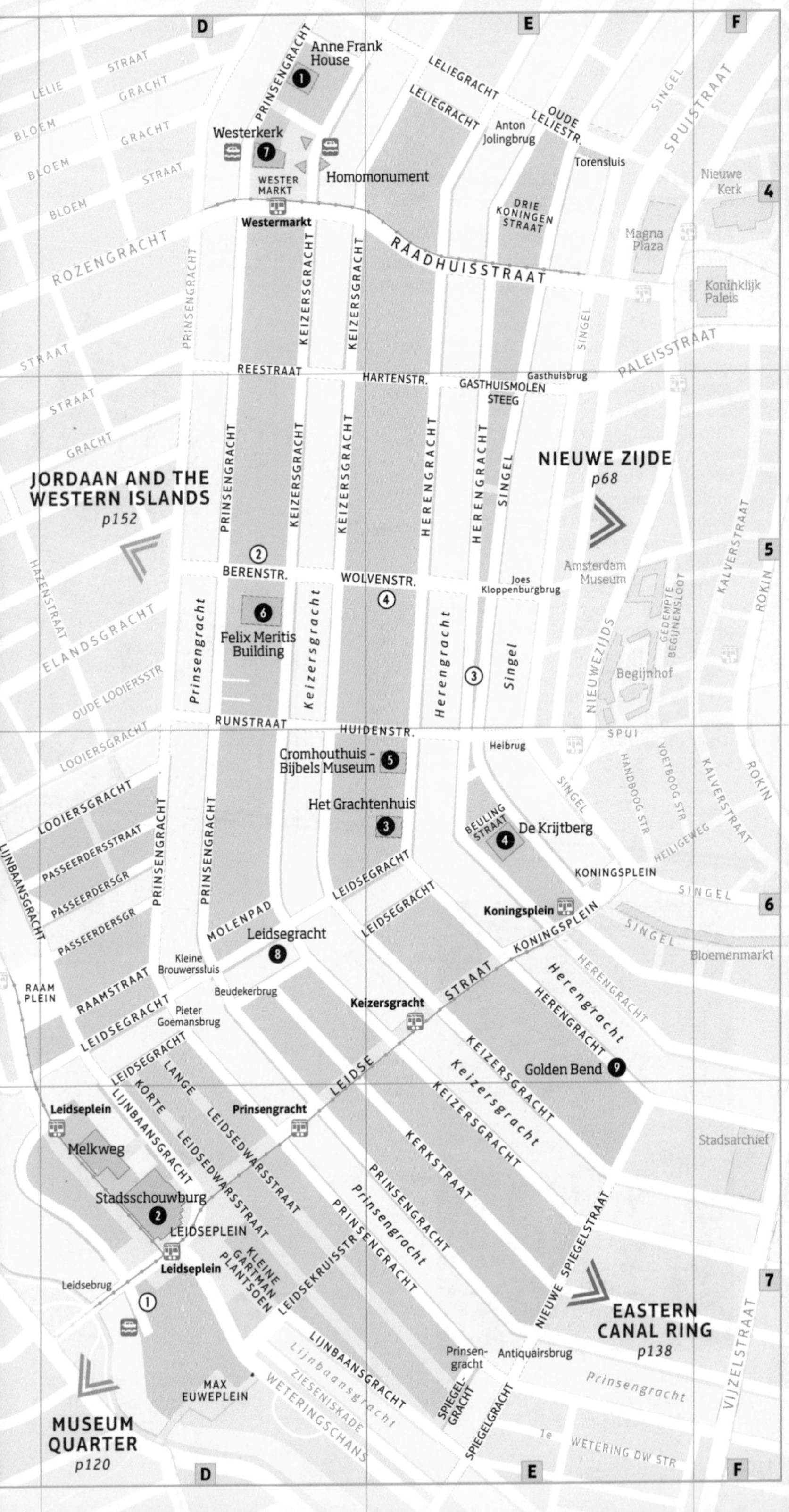
Anne Frank House
Westerkerk
Homomonument
Westermarkt
Felix Meritis Building
Cromhouthuis - Bijbels Museum
Het Grachtenhuis
De Krijtberg
Leidsegracht
Golden Bend
Melkweg
Stadsschouwburg
Leidseplein
JORDAAN AND THE WESTERN ISLANDS
p152
NIEUWE ZIJDE
p68
EASTERN CANAL RING
p138
MUSEUM QUARTER
p120
Amsterdam Museum
Begijnhof
Nieuwe Kerk
Magna Plaza
Koninklijk Paleis
Stadsarchief
Bloemenmarkt
Koningsplein
Keizersgracht
Prinsengracht
MAX EUWEPLEIN
RAAMPLEIN
Anton Jolingbrug
Torensluis
Gasthuisbrug
Joes Kloppenburgbrug
Heibrug
Kleine Brouwersluis
Beudekerbrug
Pieter Goemansbrug
Leidsebrug
Antiquairsbrug
RAADHUISSTRAAT
PRINSENGRACHT
KEIZERSGRACHT
HERENGRACHT
SINGEL
REESTRAAT
HARTENSTR.
GASTHUISMOLEN STEEG
BERENSTR.
WOLVENSTR.
RUNSTRAAT
HUIDENSTR.
LEIDSEGRACHT
LEIDSESTRAAT
KONINGSPLEIN
NIEUWE SPIEGELSTRAAT
SPIEGELGRACHT
KERKSTRAAT
LIJNBAANSGRACHT
VIJZELSTRAAT
KALVERSTRAAT
ROKIN
SPUI
SPUISTRAAT
PALEISSTRAAT
ROZENGRACHT
ELANDSGRACHT
LOOIERSGRACHT
RAAMSTRAAT
MOLENPAD
WETERINGSCHANS
ZIESENISKADE
LELIEGRACHT
OUDE LELIESTR.
DRIE KONINGEN STRAAT
NIEUWEZIJDS
D
E
F
4
5
6
7

ANNE FRANK HOUSE

D4 Westermarkt 58 13, 17 Apr-Oct: 9am-10pm daily; Nov-Mar: 9am-7pm daily (to 9pm Sat) Yom Kippur annefrank.org

Anne Frank's diary is a moving portrait of a little girl growing up in times of oppression. Even those who have not read her diary will be moved by the annexe where she and her family hid.

On 6 July 1942, to avoid their Nazi persecutors, the Jewish Frank family moved from Merwedeplein to the rear annexe of the warehouse at Prinsengracht 263. Anne, her mother Edith, her father Otto and her older sister Margot lived here, along with the Van Pels family and dentist Fritz Pfeffer. It was here that Anne wrote her famous diary. On 4 August 1944, the annexe was raided by the Gestapo. All those hiding were arrested and taken to different Nazi concentration camps.

The building beside Anne Frank House holds exhibitions exploring all forms of persecution and discrimination, as well as explaining Anne's story. It is the almost empty annexe, however, which conveys the realities of persecution.

Tickets are only available online; it is advisable to book well in advance.

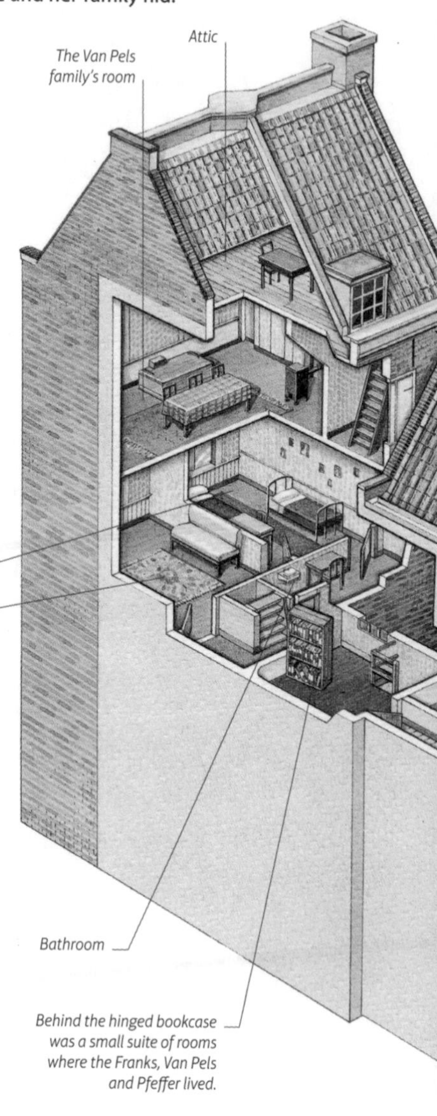

↑ The plain façade offering no clues to the secret annexe found inside

Illustration showing the Anne Frank House's secret annexe ↑

1 Photographs of Anne - happy and carefree - before she went into hiding are displayed in the building beside the annexe.

2 Anne and Fritz shared a room on the first floor of the annexe. On Anne's bedroom walls were photos of film stars, which she collected. Anne wrote most of her diary at the table here.

3 Visitors to the Anne Frank House enter the annexe via the revolving bookcase that hid its entrance.

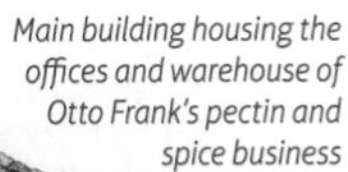

Main building housing the offices and warehouse of Otto Frank's pectin and spice business

THE DIARY OF ANNE FRANK

Otto Frank returned to Amsterdam in 1945 to discover that his entire family had perished: his wife, Edith, in Auschwitz and his daughters, Anne and Margot, in Bergen-Belsen. Miep Gies, one of the family's helpers while they were in hiding, had kept Anne's diary. First published in 1947, it has since been translated into 70 languages, with some 35 million copies sold. For many, Anne symbolizes the six million Jews murdered by the Nazis in World War II.

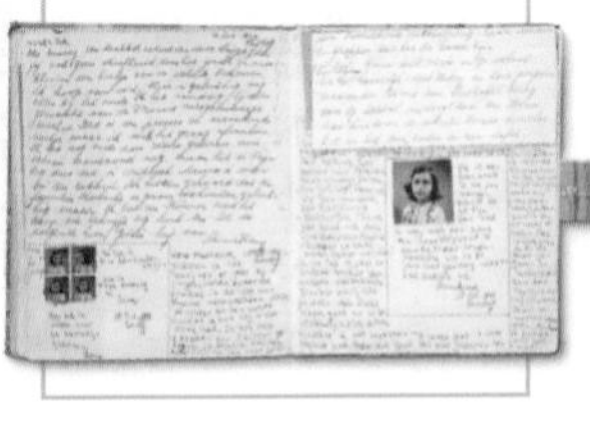

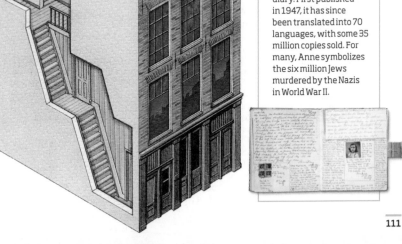

EXPERIENCE MORE

2 

Stadsschouwburg

D7 Leidseplein 26 1, 2, 5, 7, 11, 12, 19 Box office: noon-6pm Mon-Sat; two hours before performance Sun ssba.nl

This Neo-Renaissance building, dating from 1894, is the most recent of three successive municipal theatres in the city, its predecessors having burned down. The theatre was designed by Jan Springer (1850–1915), whose other credits include the Frascati building on Oxford Street in London, and A L van Gendt (1835–1901), who was also responsible for the Concertgebouw *(p132)* and for part of Centraal Station. The planned ornamentation of the theatre's red-brick exterior was never carried out because of budget cuts. This, combined with a hostile public reaction to his theatre, forced a disillusioned Springer into virtual retirement. Public disgust was due, however, to the theatre management's policy of restricting use of the front door to patrons who had bought expensive tickets. The whole building has since been given a face-lift.

Until the Nationale Opera & Ballet was completed in 1986 *(p98)*, the Stadsschouwburg was home to the Dutch national ballet and opera companies. Today, the theatre stages plays from local artistic groups such as the resident Toneelgroep Amsterdam, and international companies, including some English-language productions.

An auditorium, located between the Melkweg *(p41)* and the Stadsschouwburg, is used by both centres for large-scale performances.

SHOP

De Negen Straajes

The Singel bounds this rectangle of nine small shopping streets to the east and the Prinsengracht borders it to the west. The "Nine Streets" are filled with designer boutiques and vintage stores. Be sure to check out Laura Dols at Wolvenstraat 7, which specializes in the 1950s, and I Love Vintage at Prinsengracht 201.

E5

3   

Het Grachtenhuis

E6 Herengracht 386 2, 11, 12 10am-5pm Tue-Sun (daily Jun-Aug) 27 Apr, 25 Dec hetgrachtenhuis.nl

This ornate canal house was designed in 1663 and 1665 by Philips Vingboons (1607–78), the architect of the Cromhouthuis – Bijbels Museum *(p114)*.

Once the former home of merchants and bankers, the house is now the Museum of the Canals. Using fun interactive displays, it tells the story of town planning and engineering for the creation of Amsterdam's triple canal ring. The ground floor has been restored to its 18th-century splendour, complete with original wall paintings. The museum's upper rooms showcase detailed models, films and 3D animation on the construction of the canals, along with the stately mansions that line the route.

25,000

bicycles end up in Amsterdam's canals every year.

4 

De Krijtberg

E6 Singel 448 2, 11, 12 Noon-1:15pm & 5-6:15pm Mon & Fri, noon-6:15pm Tue-Thu & Sat, 9am-6:30pm Sun krijtberg.nl

An impressive Neo-Gothic church, the Krijtberg (chalk hill) replaced a clandestine Jesuit chapel in 1884. It is officially known as Franciscus Xaveriuskerk, after St Francis Xavier, one of the founding Jesuit priests.

Designed by Alfred Tepe (1840–1920), the church was constructed on the site of three houses; the presbytery beside the church is on the site of two other houses, one of which had belonged to a chalk merchant – hence the church's nickname. The back of the church is wider than the front. The narrowness of the façade is redeemed by its two magnificent, steepled towers, which soar to 17 m (55 ft).

The ornate interior of the building has spectacular lighting and contains some good examples of Neo-Gothic design. The stained-glass windows, walls painted in bright colours and liberal use of gold are in striking contrast to the city's austere Protestant churches. A statue of St Francis Xavier stands to the front left of the high altar; one of St Ignatius, founder of the Jesuits, stands to the right.

The colourful interior of De Krijtberg

5 Cromhouthuis - Bijbels Museum

E6 Herengracht 366-368 2, 11, 12 Herengracht/ Leidsegracht 10am-5pm daily 27 Apr cromhouthuis.nl

This canal house, and the one next door, were owned by the Cromhout family, eminent Amsterdam citizens in the 17th and 18th centuries. They were avid art collectors, and the houses have been restored to recreate their eclectic collection of portraits and curiosities. Two of the salons have fine ceiling paintings by Jacob de Wit, and other features include two well-preserved 17th-century kitchens. The top floors house the Biblical Museum, which is packed with artifacts that aim to give historical weight to biblical stories. Displays have models of historical sites, and highlights include a copy of the Book of Isaiah from the Dead Sea Scrolls and the Delft Bible, dating from 1477. The museum has a lovely garden.

6 Felix Meritis Building

D5 Keizersgracht 324 2, 11, 12, 13, 17 For renovation until late 2019 felixmeritis.nl

This Neo-Classical building is best viewed from the opposite side of the canal. Designed by Jacob Otten Husly, it opened in 1787 as a science and arts centre set up by the Felix Meritis society. The name means "happiness through merit". An association of wealthy citizens, the society was founded by the watchmaker Willem Writs in 1777, at the time of the Dutch Enlightenment *(p54)*.

Five reliefs on the façade proclaim the society's interest in natural science and art. The building was fitted out with an observatory, library, laboratories and a small concert hall. Mozart, Grieg, Brahms and Saint-Saëns are among the many distinguished musicians who have given performances in the society's hall.

In the 19th century, it became Amsterdam's main cultural centre, and its concert hall inspired the design of the Concertgebouw *(p132)*.

The Dutch Communist Party (CPN) occupied the premises from 1946, but cultural prominence was restored in the 1970s when the Shaffy Theatre Company

HIDDEN GEM
Homomonument

The pink triangle used to "brand" homosexual men during World War II influenced Karin Daan's 1987 design of this memorial to oppressed gay men and women. The seating provides a quiet place of contemplation amid the bustle of Westermarkt.

→ The Palladian façade of the 18th-century Felix Meritis Building

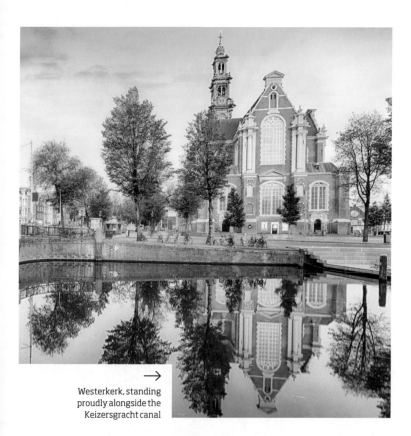

Westerkerk, standing proudly alongside the Keizersgracht canal

used the building as a theatre and won acclaim for its avant-garde productions.

In 1988 the building housed the European Centre for Arts and Sciences. It is undergoing extensive renovation and will reopen once more as a cultural centre in 2019.

Westerkerk

D4 Prinsengracht 281 13, 17 Church: Nov-Mar: 10am-3pm Mon-Fri; Apr-Oct: 10am-3pm Mon-Sat; tower tours: Apr-Oct: 10am-7:30pm Mon-Sat westerkerk.nl

This is the most beautiful of the four churches built to the north, south, east and west of the city's core in the 17th century as part of the development of the Canal Ring. It has the tallest tower in the city at 85 m (272 ft) high, and the largest nave of any Dutch Protestant church. It was designed by Hendrick de Keyser, who died in 1621, a year after work began *(p37)*.

Rembrandt was buried here, though his grave has never been found. The shutters of the huge organ (1686) were painted, by Gérard de Lairesse, with scenes showing King David, the Queen of Sheba and the Evangelists.

The spire of the Westerkerk, which is built in tapering sections, is topped by the Imperial Crown of Maximilian. The panoramic views of Amsterdam from the top of the tower justify the rather gruelling climb.

The church is undergoing restoration and sections may be closed during this time.

EAT

Café Americain

Stained glass illuminates the Art Deco interior of this café.

D7 Leidsekade 97
cafeamericain.nl

Restaurant 't Zwaantje

The walls of this pub are covered with prints and theatre posters.

D5 Berenstraat 12
zwaantje-restaurant.nl

8

Leidsegracht

D6 1, 2, 5, 7, 11, 12, 19

The Leidsegracht was for a few years the main route for barges from Amsterdam to Leiden. It was cut in 1664 to a plan by city architect Daniel Stalpaert, and stretches for only four blocks between the grand Herengracht and the long Singelgracht, the outermost of Amsterdam's canal rings. Despite its small size, it is now one of the city's most desirable addresses. Townhouses for sale here start at around €2 million.

Cornelis Lely, who drew up the original plans for draining the Zuiderzee *(p190)*, was born at No 39 in 1854. A wall plaque shows Lely poised between the Zuiderzee and the newly created IJsselmeer.

Golden Bend

E6 2, 11, 12, 24
Kattenkabinet: 10am-5pm Mon-Fri, noon-5pm Sat & Sun 1 Jan, 27 Apr, 25 Dec

The stretch of the Herengracht between Leidsestraat and Vijzelstraat was first called the Golden Bend in the 17th century, because of the great wealth of the shipbuilders, merchants and politicians who originally lived along here. Most of the mansions have been converted into offices, but their former elegance remains. The majority of the buildings are faced with sandstone, which was more expensive than brick.

The earliest mansions date from the 1660s. One very fine example of the Classicist style, designed by Philips Vingboons in 1664, stands at No 412. Building continued into the 18th century, with the Louis XIV style predominating; built in 1730, No 475 is typical

STAY

Ambassade Boutique Hotel

Ten canal houses have been merged to create this stunning and spacious boutique.

E5
Herengracht 341
ambassade-hotel.nl

Grand mansions lining the Leidsegracht

of this trend and it is often called the jewel of canal houses. Two sculpted female figures over the front door adorn its sandstone façade. The ornate mansion at No 452 is a good example of a 19th-century conversion.

The Kattenkabinet (Cat Museum) at No 497 Herengracht is one of the few houses on the Golden Bend that is accessible to the public and is a must-visit for fans of all things feline.

Did You Know?

Canal houses tilt to allow goods to be winched to the attic without crashing into the windows.

CANAL-HOUSE ARCHITECTURE

Amsterdam has been called a city of "well-mannered" architecture because its charms lie in intimate details rather than in grand effects. From the 15th century on, planning laws, plot sizes and the instability of the topsoil dictated that façades were largely uniform in size and built of lightweight brick or sandstone, with large windows to reduce the weight. As a result of this, owners stamped their own individuality on the buildings mainly through the use of decorative gables and cornices, ornate doorcases and varying window shapes. Carved and painted wall plaques were used to identify houses before street numbering was introduced in the 19th century.

A SHORT WALK
LEIDSEBUURT

Distance 2 km (1.5 miles) **Nearest tram** 2, 11, 12 (Koningsplein) **Time** 20 minutes

The area around Leidseplein is one of Amsterdam's busiest nightspots. There are plays to be seen at the Stadsschouwburg and music to be heard at Melkweg. But this area also has plenty to offer on a daytime walk. There is fine architecture to admire around the Canal Ring, such as the Former City Orphanage on Prinsengracht, the lavish De Krijtberg on the Singel and scores of grand houses on the Golden Bend.

↑ Buzzy open-air cafés on Leidseplein

In addition to bibles, there are several archaeological finds from Egypt and the Middle East on display at the Cromhouthuis – Bijbels Museum (p114).

Located in an old merchant house, Het Grachtenhuis is a museum that tells the story of Amsterdam's canal ring (p112).

Cut in 1664, the Leidsegracht was the main waterway for barges heading for Leiden (p116).

This building at one time and another housed Amsterdam's orphans and the Court of Appeal.

Young people flock to Leidseplein to watch street performances and enjoy the vibrant nightlife (p35).

This converted milk-processing factory and former hippy hangout survives as Melkweg, one of Amsterdam's key venues for alternative entertainment (p41).

A historic theatre, Stadsschouwburg was built in 1894. It is one of the venue for Amsterdam's Holland Festival in June (p112).

The American Hotel's Café Americain has a fine Art Deco interior and is a popular place to while away an afternoon (p115).

De Krijtberg – an impressive Neo-Gothic church – houses an ornate wooden carving of the Immaculate Conception (p112).
SINGEL
CENTRAL CANAL RING
HERENGRACHT
Classical columns and façades on the Herengracht's Golden Bend powerfully recall the city's wealth (p116).
KEIZERSGRACHT
LEIDSESTRAAT
LEIDSEDWARSSTRAAT
0 metres 50
0 yards 50
N

Locator Map
For more detail see p108

De Krijtberg rising above its neighbouring gabled canal houses

Cyclists pause in the Rijksmuseum's bike tunnel

MUSEUM QUARTER

Until the late 1800s, this land was little more than farms and smallholdings, then the city council designated it an area of art and culture. It was decided that it would be the new home of the ever-expanding Rijksmuseum, whose growing collection was at the time split between the Trippenhuis in Amsterdam, the Mauritshuis in Den Haag and a gallery in Haarlem. A design competition for the Rijksmuseum was held in 1876 and the building was completed in 1885. Further development of the area was driven by the International Colonial and Export Exhibition of 1883. By 1895 the Museumplein was home to Amsterdam's great cultural monuments: the Rijksmuseum, the Stedelijk Museum and the Concertgebouw. The Van Gogh Museum followed in 1973, its striking extension added in 1999.

The area fast became a central space in the city and was used for national celebrations and commemorations. The Museumplein has two memorials to the victims of World War II. The park is still used as a site for political demonstrations as it is seen as the spiritual home of freethinkers in the city. To the north and south are turn-of-the-century houses, where the streets are named after artists and intellectuals such as the 17th-century poet Roemer Visscher.

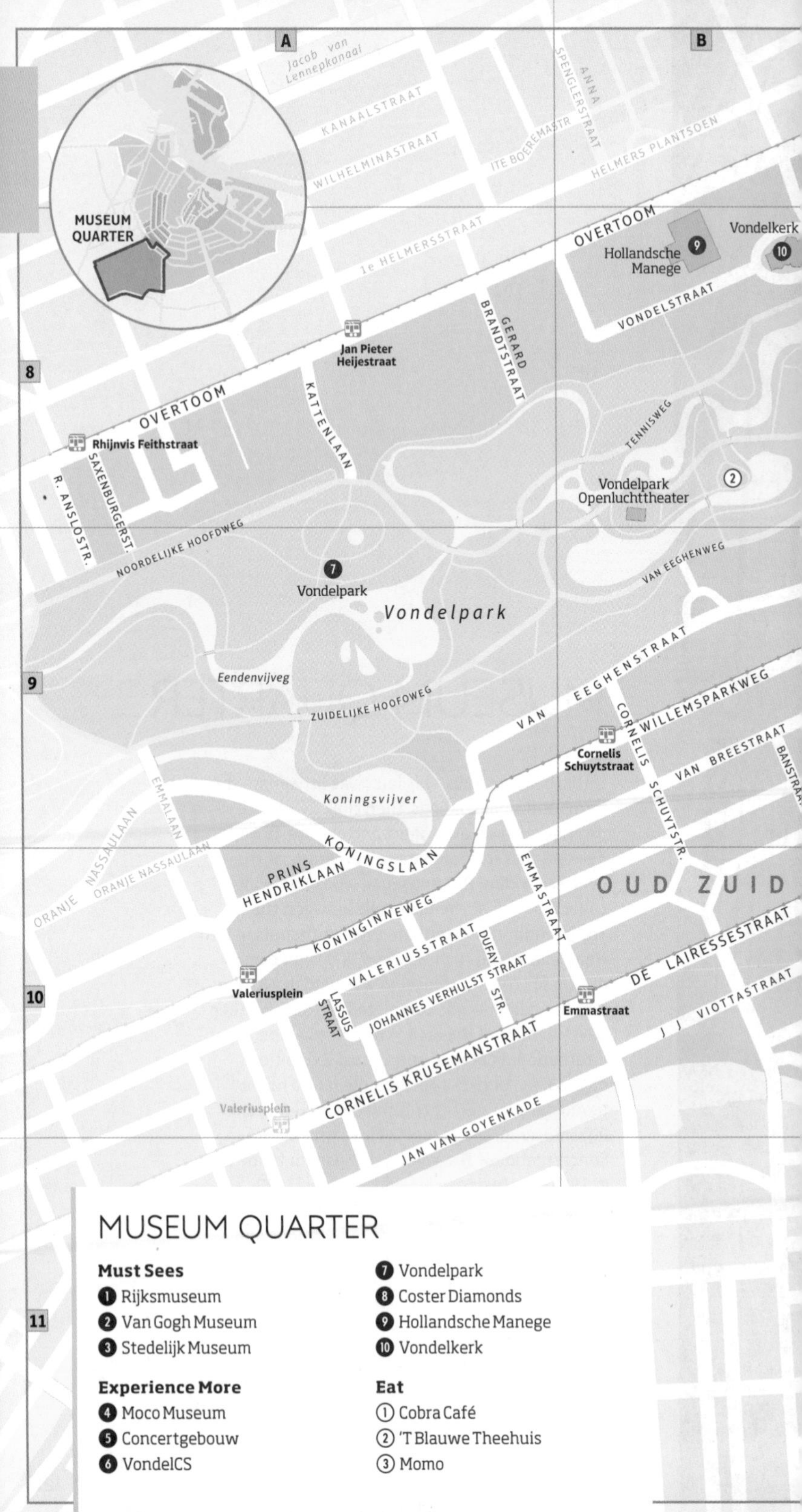

A
B
8
9
10
11
MUSEUM QUARTER
Jacob van Lennepkanaal
KANAALSTRAAT
WILHELMINASTRAAT
ITE BOEREMASTR
ANNA SPENGLERSTRAAT
HELMERS PLANTSOEN
1e HELMERSSTRAAT
OVERTOOM
Hollandsche Manege
Vondelkerk
VONDELSTRAAT
GERARD BRANDTSTRAAT
Jan Pieter Heijestraat
KATTENLAAN
Rhijnvis Feithstraat
SAXENBURGERST.
R. ANSLOSTR.
TENNISWEG
Vondelpark Openluchttheater
NOORDELIJKE HOOFDWEG
Vondelpark
Vondelpark
VAN EEGHENWEG
Eendenvijveg
ZUIDELIJKE HOOFDWEG
VAN EEGHENSTRAAT
CORNELIS SCHUYTSTR.
WILLEMSPARKWEG
Cornelis Schuytstraat
VAN BREESTRAAT
BANSTRAAT
Koningsvijver
EMMALAAN
ORANJE NASSAULAAN
KONINGSLAAN
PRINS HENDRIKLAAN
EMMASTRAAT
OUD ZUID
KONINGINNEWEG
VALERIUSSTRAAT
DUFAY STR.
DE LAIRESSESTRAAT
Valeriusplein
LASSUS STRAAT
JOHANNES VERHULST STRAAT
Emmastraat
J J VIOTTASTRAAT
CORNELIS KRUSEMANSTRAAT
Valeriusplein
JAN VAN GOYENKADE
MUSEUM QUARTER
Must Sees
1 Rijksmuseum
2 Van Gogh Museum
3 Stedelijk Museum
Experience More
4 Moco Museum
5 Concertgebouw
6 VondelCS
7 Vondelpark
8 Coster Diamonds
9 Hollandsche Manege
10 Vondelkerk
Eat
① Cobra Café
② 'T Blauwe Theehuis
③ Momo

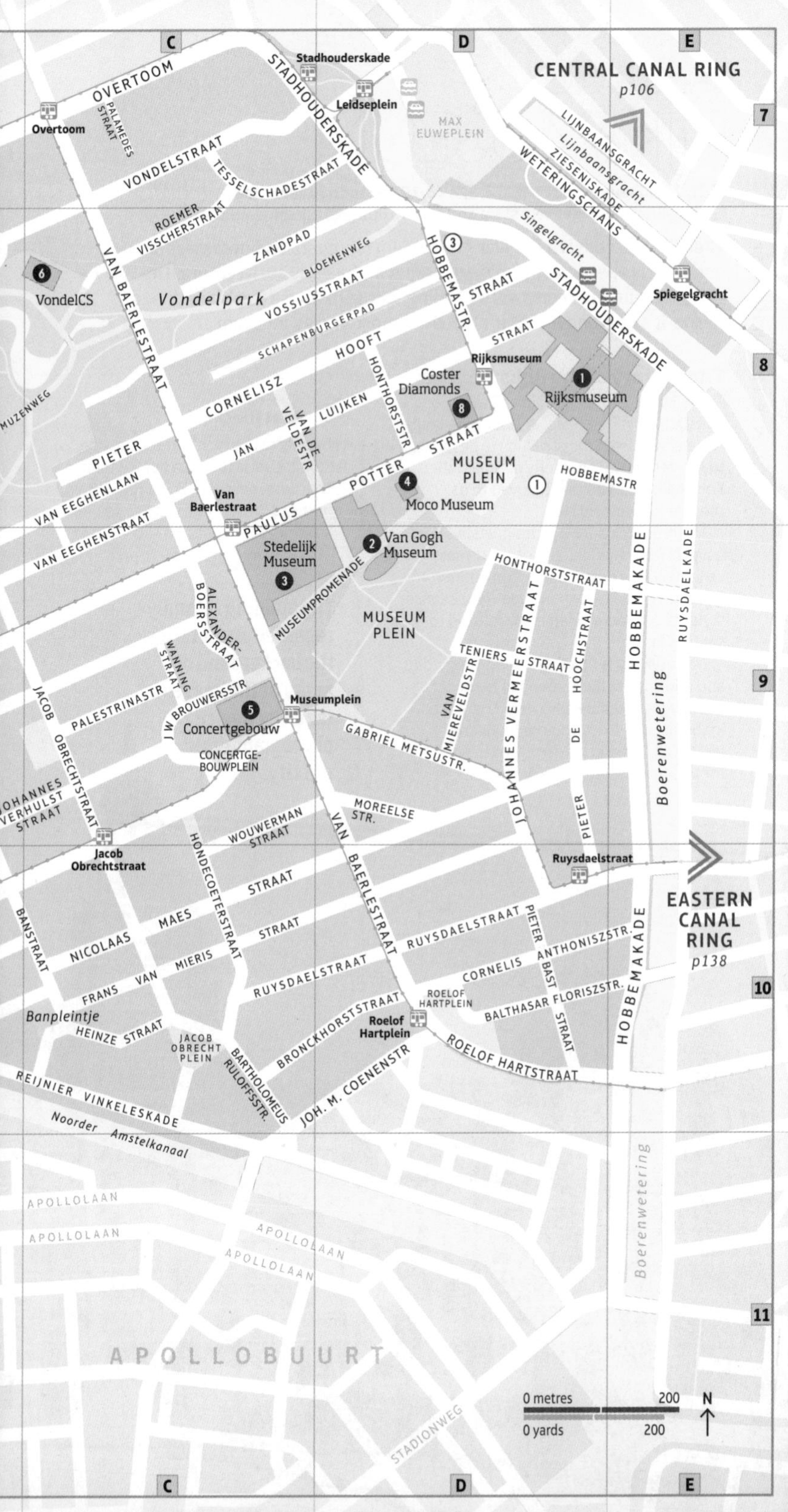

CENTRAL CANAL RING
p106
EASTERN CANAL RING
p138
Rijksmuseum
Van Gogh Museum
Stedelijk Museum
Moco Museum
Concertgebouw
VondelCS
Coster Diamonds
Vondelpark
MUSEUM PLEIN
APOLLOBUURT
Stadhouderskade
Leidseplein
Overtoom
Van Baerlestraat
Museumplein
Jacob Obrechtstraat
Roelof Hartplein
Ruysdaelstraat
Spiegelgracht
0 metres
200
0 yards
200
N

1

RIJKSMUSEUM

D8 Museumstraat 1 1, 2, 5, 7, 12, 19 Stadhouderskade
9am-5pm daily (garden, shop and café to 6pm) rijksmuseum.nl

The Rijksmuseum is a familiar Amsterdam landmark and possesses an unrivalled collection of Dutch art, begun in the early 19th century. The vast museum can seem overwhelming, but with such a wealth of things to see, it's no wonder that it's the city's most-visited museum.

The History of the Rijksmuseum

The Rijksmuseum began life as the Nationale Kunstgalerij in Den Haag. In 1808, King Louis Napoleon ordered the collection to be moved to Amsterdam and it briefly occupied the Koninklijk Paleis before it moved to its present location in 1885.

The red-brick building, designed by P J H Cuypers *(p36)*, was initially criticized, most vehemently by Amsterdam's Protestant community for its Catholic Neo-Renaissance style. King William III famously refused to set foot inside.

Nowadays, the building is fondly regarded and it forms the background of many of the images taken by novice photographers in the city due to its iconic exterior and beautifully tended gardens, which make for the perfect shot in every season.

INSIDER TIP
Beat the Queue

The only way to walk straight inside the museum is to book a guided tour. Otherwise, get there at 9am or 3:30pm, and avoid Fridays and weekends.

The building is fondly regarded and it forms the background of many of the images taken by novice photographers in the city.

↑ Rembrandt's *The Night Watch* is the museum's most-prized possession and its most-visited piece

→ A huge 17th-century model of the *William Rex*, housed in the Rijksmuseum

TOP 5 UNMISSABLE EXHIBITS

The Night Watch (1642)
This vast canvas was commissioned by an Amsterdam militia.

The Kitchen Maid (1658)
The stillness and light are typical of Vermeer.

St Elizabeth's Day Flood (1500)
An unknown artist painted a flood in 1421.

The Square Man (1951)
This painting is typical of Appel's CoBrA work.

Shiva Nataraja (c 1100-1200)
This bronze statue shows the god dancing.

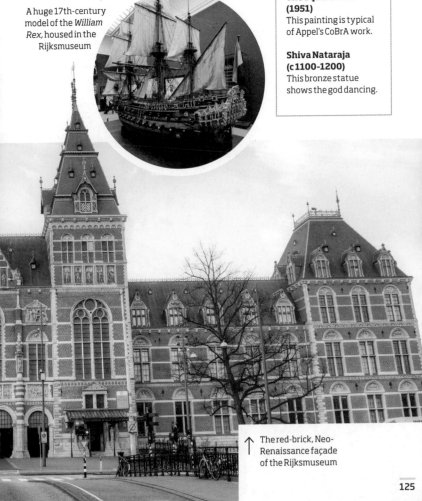

↑ The red-brick, Neo-Renaissance façade of the Rijksmuseum

↑ Visitors admiring the art, and taking a break, in one of the galleries

Exploring the Rijksmuseum

The Rijksmuseum is almost too vast to be seen in a single visit. If time is short, visit the Gallery of Honour, taking in Frans Hals, Vermeer and scores of other Old Masters, to finally arrive at Rembrandt's *The Night Watch* at the centre of the building.

Visitors with more time shouldn't miss the museum's other collections, which span the 11th century to the present day. Paintings, sculpture, historical objects and applied arts are shown side by side, emphasizing contrasts and connections. A pavilion houses the Asiatic Collection.

8,000

pieces are displayed in the Rijksmuseum's 80 galleries.

The Gallery of Honour is lined with Golden Age masterpieces ↓

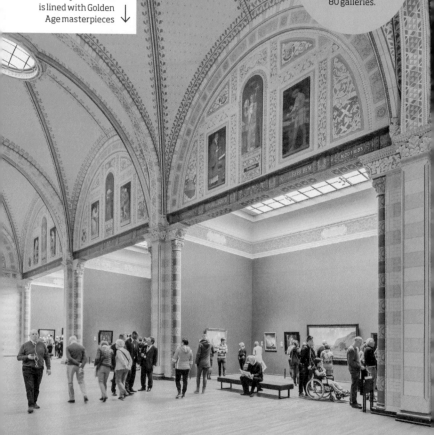

GENRE PAINTING

For the contemporaries of Jan Steen (1625-79), the everyday scene depicted in *Woman at her Toilet* (c 1660) was full of symbols that are obscure to the modern viewer. The dog on the pillow may represent fidelity, and the red stockings suggest the woman's sexuality.

Gallery Guide

Medieval and Renaissance

The first specifically "Dutch" paintings. These works are mostly religious, such as *The Seven Works of Charity* (1504) by the Master of Alkmaar. As the 16th century progressed, religious themes were superseded by pastoral subjects; by 1552, paintings like Pieter Aertsen's *The Egg Dance* were full of realism.

Golden Age

By the Alteration in 1578 *(p53)*, Dutch art had moved away completely from religious to secular themes. Artists turned to realistic portraiture, landscapes, still lifes, seascapes, domestic interiors, including genre work, and animal portraits. Don't miss Rembrandt's paintings.

18th-century Art

The still lifes of the 17th century turned into satirical "conversation pieces". *The Art Gallery of Jan Gildemeester Jansz* (1794), by Adriaan de Lelie (1755-1820), shows an 18th-century salon crowded with 17th-century works.

↑ Vermeer's *The Kitchen Maid*, a highlight of the Dutch Golden Age

19th-century Art

The early 19th century is represented by the Dutch romantics, who all reinterpreted the art of landscape painting but in contrasting styles. Artists such as Johannes Tavenraat and Wijnand Nuijen excelled in painting stormy and dramatic scenes, while Andreas Schelfhout preferred to paint more temperate and serene landscapes.

20th-century Art

A small collection of 20th-century works are found under the museum's roof. Along with clothing, photography and sculpture, works by artists Le Corbusier and Karel Appel are on display. The FK 23 Bantam biplane, designed by Koolhoven for the British Aerial Transport Company, is a highlight of this section.

Asiatic Art

The pavilion between the main building and the Philips Wing is testament to the skill of artists and artisans in early Eastern cultures. Some of the earliest artifacts are the most unusual, such as tiny bronze Tang dynasty figurines from 7th-century China. Later exhibits include an extremely explicit Hindu statue entitled *Heavenly Beauty*.

Special Collections and Philips Wing

The Special Collections gallery in the basement is a treasure trove of delftware, porcelain and much more. Temporary exhibitions are held in the Philips Wing.

← A temporary exhibition of Rembrandt's works in the Philips Wing

2

VAN GOGH MUSEUM

D9 Museumplein 6 2, 3, 5, 12 Jan, Feb, Nov & Dec: 9am-9pm Fri, 9am-5pm Sat-Thu; Mar-Jun, Sep & Oct: 9am-9pm Fri, 9am-6pm Sat-Thu; Jul & Aug: 9am-9pm Fri & Sat, 9am-7pm Sun-Thu vangoghmuseum.com

When Van Gogh died in 1890, he was on the verge of stardom. His brother Theo, an art dealer, amassed a collection of 200 of his paintings and 500 drawings. These, with around 850 letters by the artist, form the core of the world's largest Van Gogh collection.

Museum Guide

The Van Gogh Museum is based on a design by De Stijl architect Gerrit Rietveld (1888–1964) and opened in 1973. A freestanding wing, designed by Kisho Kurokawa, was added in 1999.

The ground floor shows Van Gogh's self-portraits chronologically. Paintings from his Dutch and French periods are on the first floor, along with works by other 19th-century artists. The second floor focuses on Van Gogh's personal life, with a selection of letters. Works from his last year are shown on the third floor, as well as works by later artists who were influenced by him. The main entrance is through the Exhibition Wing, which houses temporary exhibitions. Every Friday night the central hall is turned into a bar with lounge chairs and DJs.

→ The curvaceous Van Gogh Museum sitting on the manicured Museumplein

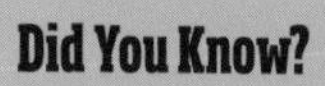

Did You Know?

Van Gogh claimed that all his work was "based to some extent on Japanese art".

One of Van Gogh's most famous works, *Vincent's Bedroom in Arles* (1888), painted to celebrate his domestic stability at the Yellow House in the south of France

AN ARTIST'S LIFE

Vincent van Gogh (1853–90), born in Zundert, began painting in 1880. He worked in the Netherlands for five years before moving to Paris, later settling in the south of France. After an argument with Gauguin, he cut off part of his own ear and his mental instability forced him into an asylum in Saint-Rémy. He sought help in Auvers, where he shot himself, dying two days later.

↑ Visitors milling around the entrance hall of the Van Gogh Museum

3 

STEDELIJK MUSEUM

C9 Museumplein 10 2, 3, 5, 12 10am-6pm daily (to 10pm Fri) stedelijk.nl

Built to house a collection left to the city by Sophia de Bruyn in 1890, the Stedelijk Museum became the national museum of modern art and design in 1938, displaying works by artists such as Picasso, Matisse, Mondriaan, Chagall and Cézanne, and designers including Rietveld, Wirkkala and Sottsass.

The museum is housed in two contrasting spaces. The Neo-Renaissance main building was designed by A W Weissman (1858–1923) in 1895. The façade is adorned with turrets and gables and with niches containing statues of artists and architects, including Hendrick de Keyser *(p37)* and Jacob van Campen, architect of the Koninklijk Paleis *(p79)*. The Stedelijk's modern addition – the Benthem Crouwel Wing – opened in 2012. The giant "bathtub" appears to float, given its continuous glass walls at ground level; it remains a love-it-or-loathe-it addition to the city's architecture.

Inside, both spaces are ultramodern, providing the perfect backdrop for the museum's 90,000 modern and contemporary artworks. The collection represents virtually every artistic movement of the 20th and 21st centuries, including examples of the De Stijl,

The futuristic Benthem Crouwel Wing - or the "bathtub" - illuminated in the evening

1988

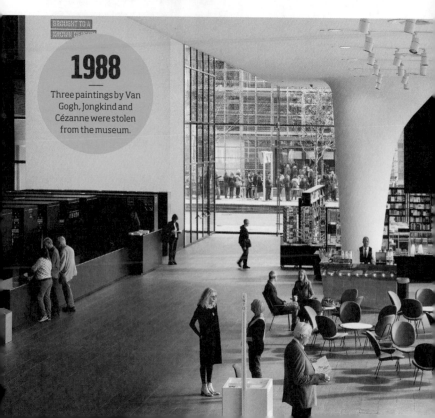

Three paintings by Van Gogh, Jongkind and Cézanne were stolen from the museum.

↑ *The Fiddler* (1912-13), by Marc Chagall (1887-1985), was isnpired by the artist's memories of St Petersburg and his new surroundings in Paris

Pop Art and CoBrA groups. It also houses a small group of works by Post-Impressionists, including Van Gogh and Cézanne, to highlight the late 19th century.

The museum holds collections from present-day artists in a larger exhibition space, with a restaurant and a terrace overlooking Museumplein. The museum also stages performances and film screenings.

TOP 5 PERMANENT ARTISTS ON DISPLAY

Willem de Kooning (1904-97)
This Dutch abstract expressionist often focused on the female figure.

Kazimir Malevich (1878-1935)
Russian founder of Suprematism, an abstract movement which experimented with colour.

Jean Tinguely (1925-1991)
The swiss sculptor crafted humorous, moving sculptures.

Karel Appel (1921-2006)
A Dutch member of the short-lived, experimental CoBrA movement.

Ernst Ludwig Kirchner (1880-1938)
The German Expressionist was inspired by the art of early African and Asian cultures.

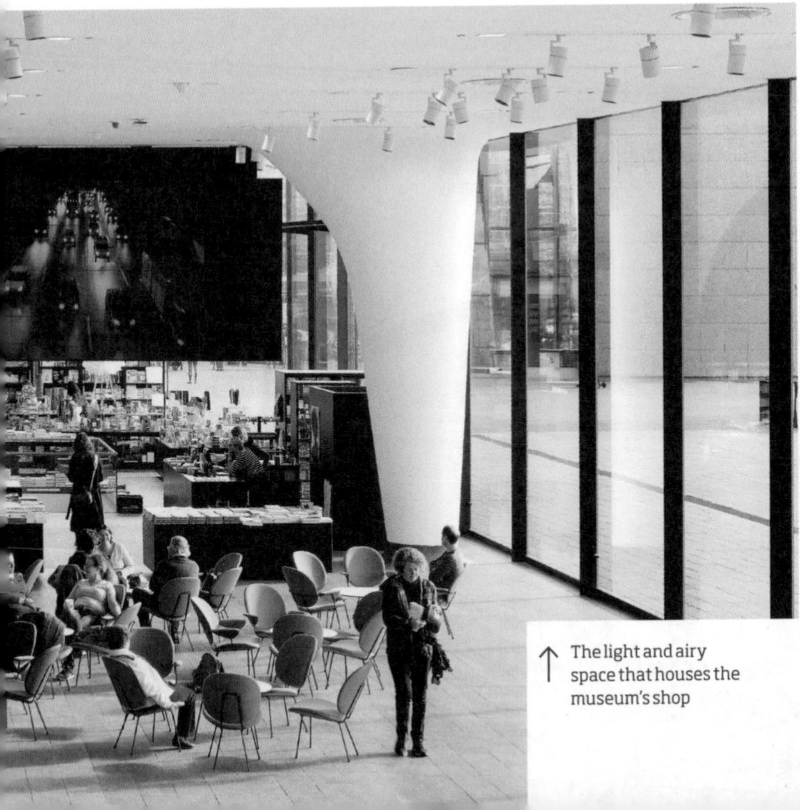

↑ The light and airy space that houses the museum's shop

EXPERIENCE MORE

Moco Museum

D8 Honthorststraat 20 1, 2, 5, 7, 12, 19 Stadhouderskade 10am-6pm daily; check website for later openings mocomuseum.com

The exterior of this beautiful 20th-century mansion, designed by Eduard Cuypers, the nephew of P J H Cuypers *(p36)*, belies the groundbreaking collection housed inside.

Carefully curated by private collectors, the groundbreaking Modern Contemporary (Moco) Museum displays pieces by artists who expose the irony at work in modern society. The museum aims to show visitors what cannot be seen anywhere else.

The collection includes Roy Lichtenstein's pop art and more than 90 original works by the street artist Banksy *(p34)*. The British activist's indoor pieces are far less exposed than his usual murals and make for an interesting contrast when compared to the few works rescued from buildings that are also on display here.

Concertgebouw

C9 Concertgebouwplein 10 2, 3, 5, 12 Box office: 1-7pm Mon-Fri, 10am-7pm Sat & Sun concertgebouw.nl

Following an open architectural competition held in 1881, A L van Gendt (1835–1901) was chosen to design a vast new concert hall for Amsterdam. The resulting Neo-Renaissance building boasts an elaborate pediment and colonnaded façade, and houses two concert halls. Despite Van Gendt's lack of musical knowledge, he managed to produce near-perfect acoustics in the Grote Zaal (main concert hall), which is renowned the world over.

The inaugural concert at the Concertgebouw was held on 11 April 1888, complete with an orchestra of 120 musicians and a choir of 600.

Though primarily designed to hold concerts, the building has become multifunctional; it has played host to exhibitions, political meetings and occasional boxing matches.

INSIDER TIP
Rollerblading in Vondelpark

Don rollerblades for a different way of exploring Vondelpark's network of cycle paths. Rent wheels or book a training session with Skate Dokter *(www.skatedokter.nl)*.

Take a guided tour at 5pm on Friday or 12:30pm on Sunday to hear about the secret history of the building. For the best experience, visit on a Wednesday and take the 1:30pm tour after enjoying a free concert (not available in July and August).

VondelCS

C8 Vondelpark 3 1, 3, 5, 11, 12 vondelpark3.nl

Vondelpark's pavilion opened in 1881 as a restaurant and café. A flamboyant, Neo-Renaissance-style building, it was the favourite haunt of

Concertgebouw façade sparkling after dark

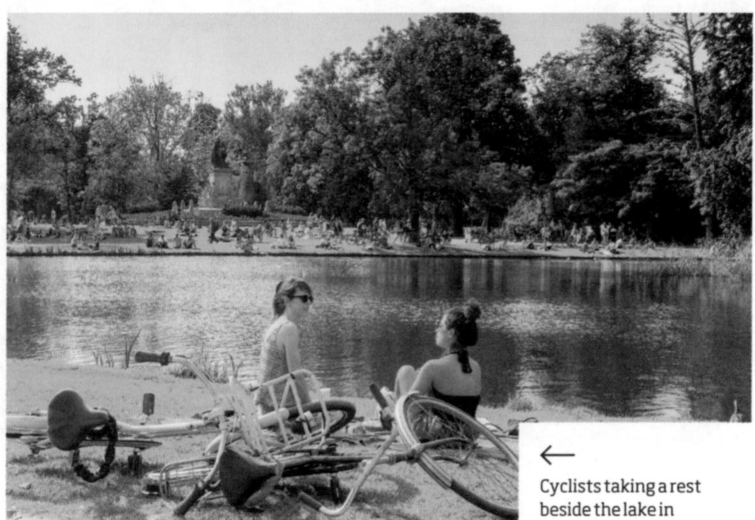

←

Cyclists taking a rest beside the lake in Vondelpark

Amsterdam's bohemian crowd, and its salons often featured contemporary art exhibitions. After World War II, the pavilion became a cultural centre and from 1972 it was the home of the Filmmuseum, which became the EYE *(p183)*.

The pavilion reopened in 2014 as VondelCS, and is now home to AVROTROS, one of the Netherlands' public broadcasting corporations. It hosts talk shows, concerts and debates on culture and current affairs. The ground floor of the pavilion is a café-restaurant called Vondelpark3.

7

Vondelpark

A9 Stadhouderskade 1, 2, 3, 5, 11, 12 Open-air theatre: Jun-last week Aug: Wed-Sun openluchttheater.nl

In 1864, a group consisting of prominent Amsterdammers formed a committee with the aim of founding a public park, and they raised enough money to buy 8 ha (20 acres) of land. J D and L P Zocher, a father-and-son team of landscape architects, were then commissioned to design the park. They used vistas, pathways and ponds to create the illusion of a large natural area, which was opened on 15 June 1865 as the Nieuwe Park.

The park's present name was adopted in 1867, when a statue of Dutch poet Joost van den Vondel was erected here. The committee soon began to raise money to enlarge the park, and by June 1877 it had reached its current dimensions of 47 ha (116 acres). The park now supports around 100 plant species and 127 types of tree. Squirrels, hedgehogs, ducks and garden birds mix with a huge colony of greedy, bright-green parakeets, which gather in front of the pavilion every morning to be fed. Herds of cows, sheep, goats and even a lone llama graze in the pastures.

Vondelpark welcomes more than ten million visitors a year. Free concerts are given by *openluchttheater* (open-air theatre), and musicians play at the bandstand in the summer.

JOOST VAN DEN VONDEL

Joost van den Vondel (1587-1679) was to Dutch poetry and drama what Rembrandt was to painting. Many of his history plays, like *Gijsbrecht van Amstel*, first performed in 1638, and *Joannes de Boetgezant* (1662), were hailed as masterpieces. After converting to his wife's Catholic faith, he became an advocate of religious tolerance. That made him unpopular with hardline Calvinists and, despite his fame, he died an impoverished man.

→ Café tables on Museumplein in front of Coster Diamonds

8  

Coster Diamonds

D8 Paulus Potterstraat 2-6 2, 5, 12 9am-5pm daily coster diamonds.com

Coster was founded in 1840. Twelve years later, Queen Victoria's consort, Prince Albert, gave the company the task of repolishing the enormous Koh-i-Noor (mountain of light) diamond. This blue-white stone is one of the treasures of the British crown jewels and weighs in at 108.8 carats. A replica of the coronation crown, with a copy of the fabulous stone, is found in Coster's entrance hall.

More than 6,000 people visit the factory each week to witness the processes of grading, cutting and polishing the stones. Goldsmiths and diamond-cutters work together to produce customized items of jewellery, which are available over the counter. For serious diamond-buyers, such as the jewellers who come to Amsterdam from all over the world, there is a series of private sales rooms where discretion is assured. A few doors down is a small museum, in which the history of the diamond is traced.

AMSTERDAM'S MILITIA COMPANIES

The Dutch *schutterij* (militia companies) were formed in medieval times. Armed with bows, the forces' purpose was to protect towns from attack and revolts. By the 17th century, they carried muskets, but their role had become ceremonial. Captains had to be wealthy, as they equipped volunteers out of their own purse. They commissioned portraits and Rembrandt's *The Guard Company of Captain Frans Banning Cocq and Lieutenant Willem Ruytenburch* - known as *The Night Watch* - is the most famous. A statue of the painting is found in Rembrandtplein.

9  

Hollandsche Manege

B8 Vondelstraat 140 2 10am-5pm daily 2 weeks in Aug (see website for details) levend paardenmuseum.nl

The Dutch Riding School was originally situated on the Leidsegracht *(p116)*, but in 1882 it moved to a new building on Vondelstraat. Designed by A L van Gendt, it was based on the Spanish Riding School in Vienna.

The Hollandsche Manege was threatened with demolition in the 1980s, but fortunately it was saved after a public outcry. Reopened in 1986 by Prince Bernhard, it has been restored to its former glory.

The Neo-Classical indoor arena boasts gilded mirrors and moulded horses' heads on its elaborate plasterwork walls. Some of the wrought-iron stalls remain and sound is muffled by sawdust. At the top of the staircase, one door leads to a balcony overlooking the arena, another to the café.

10

Vondelkerk

B8 Vondelstraat 120
2

The Vondelkerk was the largest church designed by P J H Cuypers *(p36)*. Work began on the building in 1872, but funds ran out by the following year. Money from public donations and lotteries allowed it to be completed by 1880.

When fire broke out in 1904, firefighters saved the nave of the church by forcing the burning tower to fall away into Vondelpark. A new tower was added later by the architect's son, J T Cuypers. The church was deconsecrated in 1979 and converted into offices in 1985. It hosts concerts and events.

EAT

Cobra Café
Famous for its apple pie, Cobra also serves pancakes and other snacks, such as croquettes.

D8 Hobbemastraat 18 cobracafe.nl

'T Blauwe Theehuis
This Vondelpark landmark serves drinks and toasted sandwiches.

B8 Vondelpark 5 blauwetheehuis.nl

Momo
This stylish bar-cum-restaurant offers sushi or set menus of ten dishes.

D8 Hobbemastraat 1 momo-amsterdam.com

The fairy-tale Vondelkerk, which stands at the edge of Vondelpark ↑

A SHORT WALK MUSEUM QUARTER

Distance 1.5 km (1 mile) **Nearest tram** 2, 3, 5, 12 (Rijksmuseum) **Time** 15 minutes

The green expanse of Museumplein was once bisected by a busy main road known locally as the "shortest motorway in Europe". Dramatic renovation between 1996 and 1999 transformed it into a stately park, fringed by Amsterdam's major cultural centres. Traverse one of the wealthiest districts in the city, with wide streets lined with grand houses. After the heady delights of the museums, why not window-shop at the upmarket boutiques along the exclusive PC Hooftstraat and Van Baerlestraat, or watch the diamond polishers at work in Coster Diamonds?

↑ The modern exterior of the Van Gogh Museum

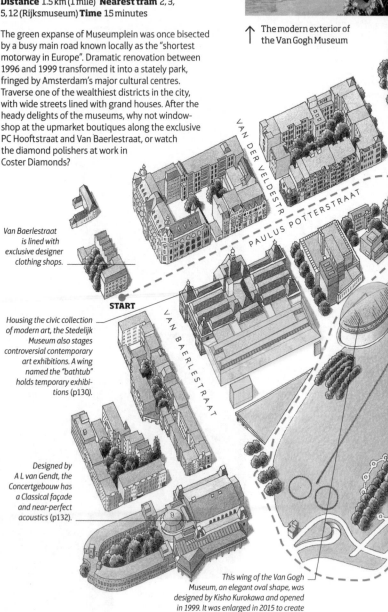

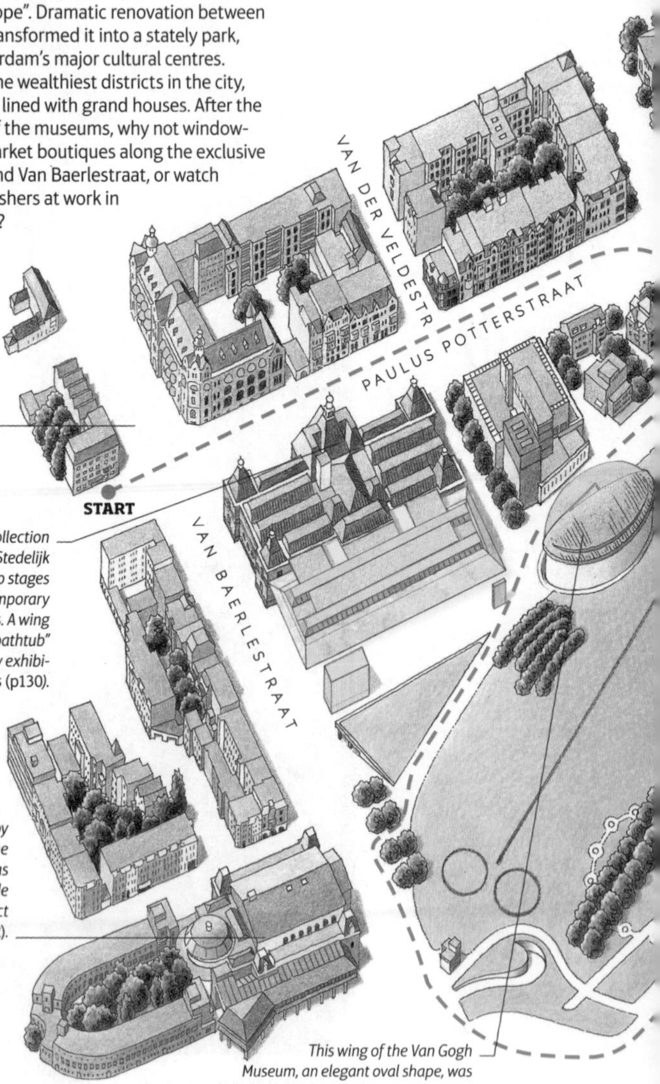

Van Baerlestraat is lined with exclusive designer clothing shops.

Housing the civic collection of modern art, the Stedelijk Museum also stages controversial contemporary art exhibitions. A wing named the "bathtub" holds temporary exhibitions (p130).

Designed by A L van Gendt, the Concertgebouw has a Classical façade and near-perfect acoustics (p132).

This wing of the Van Gogh Museum, an elegant oval shape, was designed by Kisho Kurokawa and opened in 1999. It was enlarged in 2015 to create a new entrance hall (p128).

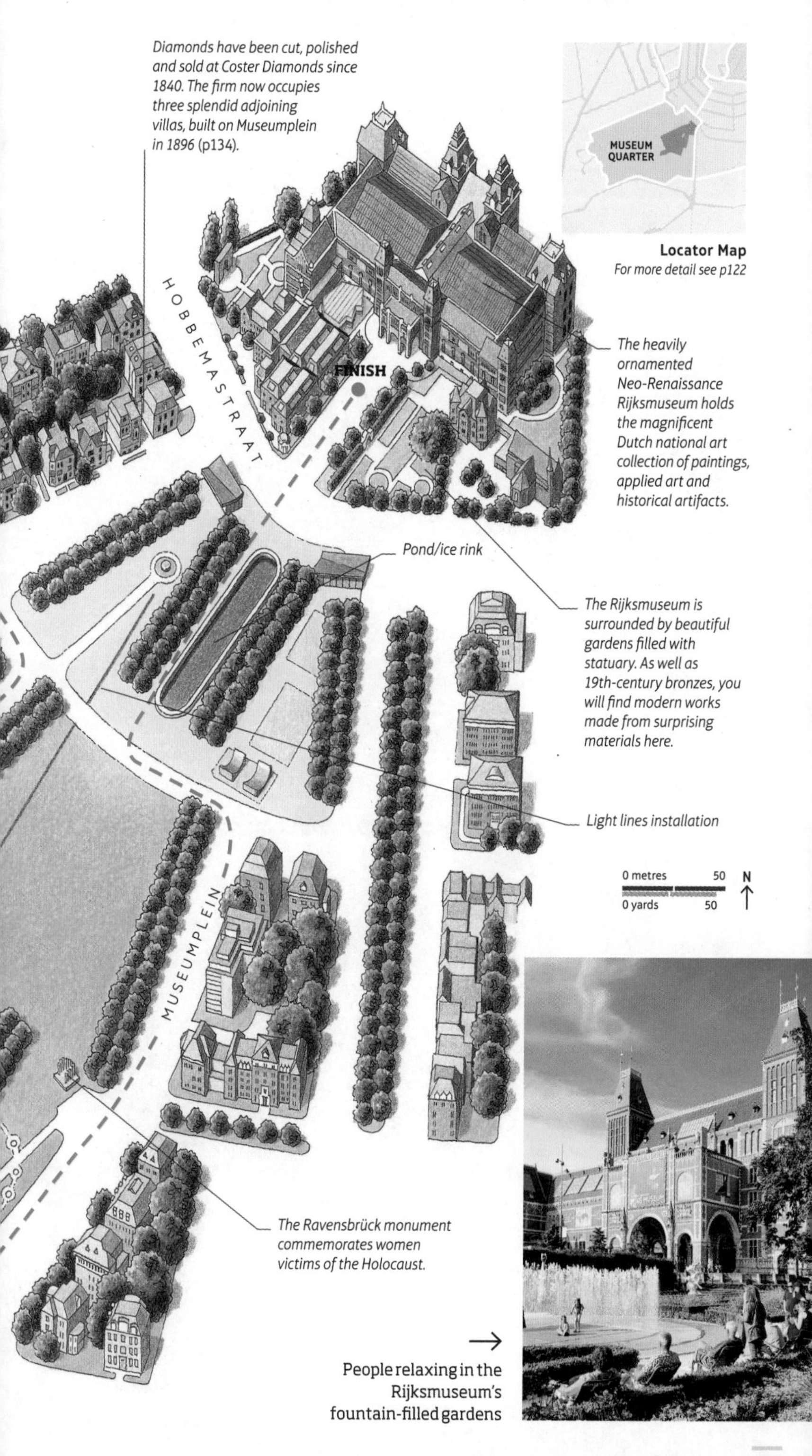
Diamonds have been cut, polished and sold at Coster Diamonds since 1840. The firm now occupies three splendid adjoining villas, built on Museumplein in 1896 (p134).
MUSEUM QUARTER
Locator Map
For more detail see p122
HOBBEMASTRAAT
FINISH
The heavily ornamented Neo-Renaissance Rijksmuseum holds the magnificent Dutch national art collection of paintings, applied art and historical artifacts.
Pond/ice rink
The Rijksmuseum is surrounded by beautiful gardens filled with statuary. As well as 19th-century bronzes, you will find modern works made from surprising materials here.
Light lines installation
0 metres 50
0 yards 50
N
MUSEUMPLEIN
The Ravensbrück monument commemorates women victims of the Holocaust.

People relaxing in the Rijksmuseum's fountain-filled gardens

1 for € 3,50
3 for € 10,00

Flowers hanging in the Bloemenmarkt

EASTERN CANAL RING

Stretching to the south and west of the Amstel river, this area lies wholly beyond the line of the medieval city wall. From the 1660s, the Grachtengordel was extended further east towards the Amstel, and Reguliersgracht, one of Amsterdam's prettiest canals with its seven bridges, was cut at this time. These new stretches of canal became lined with merchants' mansions in the Golden Age *(p54)*, such as the Museum Van Loon. Beyond this 17th-century canal-side façade is the 19th-century De Pijp, a working-class district built to relieve the overcrowded Jordaan. De Pijp was constructed as quickly and cheaply as possible, resulting in almost identical four-storey houses, each with three windows and capped with a white roof and lifting bar. The affordability of the area attracted students, immigrants and artists – including Mondriaan. This population brought with it different cultures and exotic foods, lending the Eastern Canal Ring a lively, bohemian vibe.

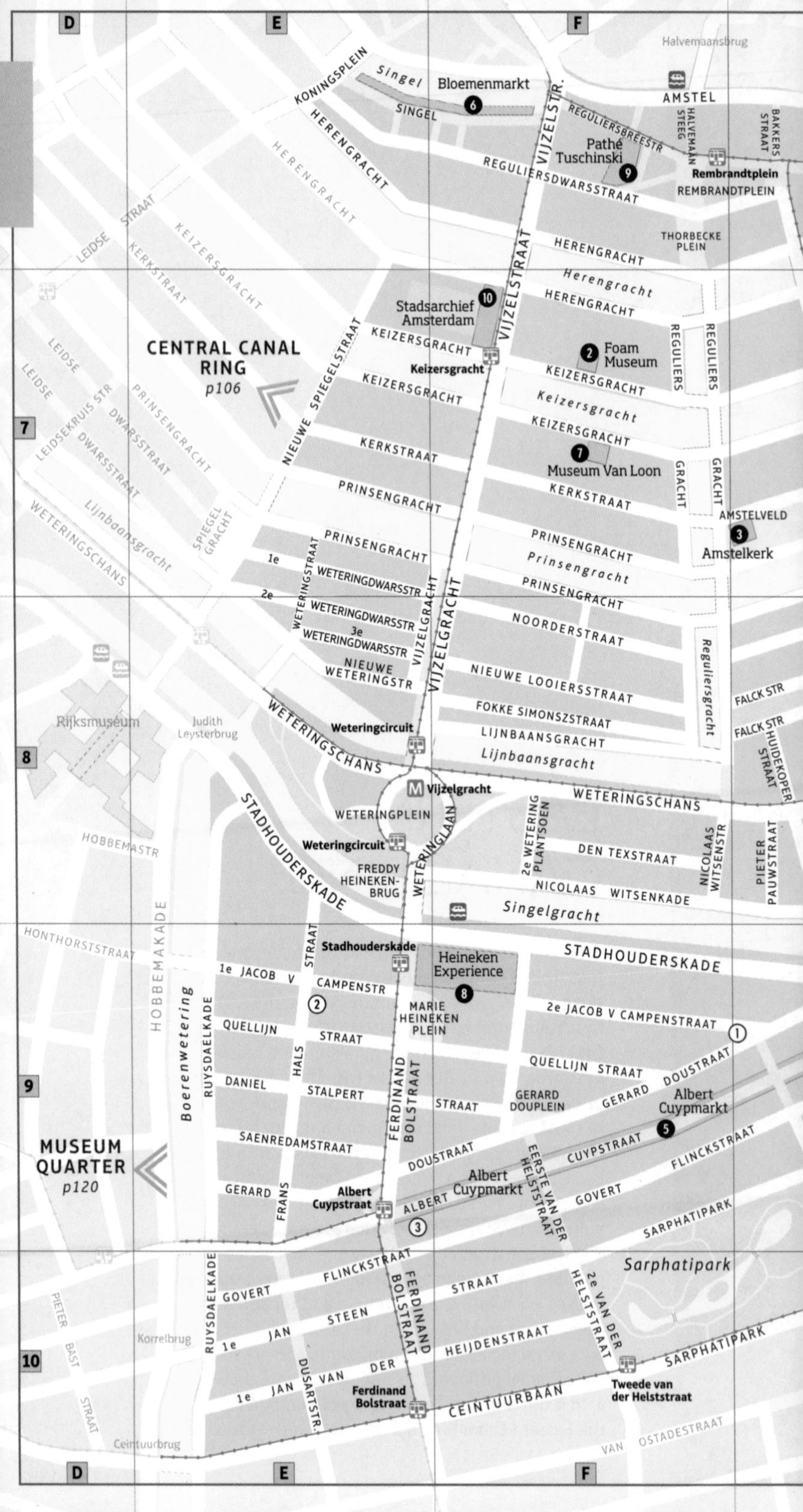

D
E
F
Halvemaansbrug
Singel
Bloemenmarkt
6
SINGEL
KONINGSPLEIN
HERENGRACHT
AMSTEL
REGULIERSBREESTR
HALVEMAN STEEG
BAKKERS STRAAT
Pathé Tuschinski
9
Rembrandtplein
REMBRANDTPLEIN
REGULIERSDWARSSTRAAT
THORBECKE PLEIN
VIJZELSTR.
VIJZELSTRAAT
HERENGRACHT
Herengracht
HERENGRACHT
LEIDSE STRAAT
KERKSTRAAT
KEIZERSGRACHT
Stadsarchief Amsterdam
10
Foam Museum
2
KEIZERSGRACHT
Keizersgracht
KEIZERSGRACHT
Keizersgracht
KEIZERSGRACHT
KEIZERSGRACHT
REGULIERS
REGULIERS
CENTRAL CANAL RING
p106
7
NIEUWE SPIEGELSTRAAT
LEIDSE
LEIDSE
LEIDSEKRUIS STR
PRINSENGRACHT
DWARSSTRAAT
DWARSSTRAAT
KERKSTRAAT
Museum Van Loon
7
GRACHT
GRACHT
PRINSENGRACHT
KERKSTRAAT
AMSTELVELD
3
Amstelkerk
WETERINGSCHANS
Lijnbaansgracht
SPIEGEL GRACHT
PRINSENGRACHT
PRINSENGRACHT
Prinsengracht
PRINSENGRACHT
1e
WETERINGSTRAAT
WETERINGDWARSSTR
2e
WETERINGDWARSSTR
3e
WETERINGDWARSSTR
VIJZELGRACHT
VIJZELGRACHT
NOORDERSTRAAT
NIEUWE WETERINGSTR
NIEUWE LOOIERSSTRAAT
Reguliersgracht
FALCK STR
FOKKE SIMONSZSTRAAT
FALCK STR
Rijksmuseum
Judith Leysterbrug
WETERINGSCHANS
Weteringcircuit
LIJNBAANSGRACHT
Lijnbaansgracht
HUIDEKOPER STRAAT
8
Vijzelgracht
WETERINGSCHANS
STADHOUDERSKADE
WETERINGPLEIN
2e WETERING PLANTSOEN
HOBBEMASTR
Weteringcircuit
DEN TEXSTRAAT
NICOLAAS WITSENSTR
PIETER PAUWSTRAAT
FREDDY HEINEKEN-BRUG
WETERINGLAAN
NICOLAAS WITSENKADE
HOBBEMAKADE
Singelgracht
HONTHORSTSTRAAT
Stadhouderskade
Heineken Experience
STADHOUDERSKADE
1e JACOB V
STRAAT
CAMPENSTR
8
2
MARIE HEINEKEN PLEIN
2e JACOB V CAMPENSTRAAT
1
Boerenwetering
RUYSDAELKADE
QUELLIJN
STRAAT
QUELLIJN STRAAT
HALS
FERDINAND BOLSTRAAT
DOUSTRAAT
9
DANIEL
STALPERT
STRAAT
GERARD DOUPLEIN
GERARD
Albert Cuypmarkt
5
SAENREDAMSTRAAT
CUYPSTRAAT
FLINCKSTRAAT
MUSEUM QUARTER
p120
DOUSTRAAT
Albert Cuypmarkt
EERSTE VAN DER HELSTSTRAAT
GERARD
FRANS
Albert Cuypstraat
ALBERT
GOVERT
3
SARPHATIPARK
Sarphatipark
FLINCKSTRAAT
FERDINAND BOLSTRAAT
STRAAT
2e VAN DER HELSTSTRAAT
RUYSDAELKADE
GOVERT
PIETER
BAST
STEEN
1e
JAN
HEIJDENSTRAAT
Korrelbrug
10
DUSARTSTR.
VAN
DER
SARPHATIPARK
STRAAT
1e
JAN
Ferdinand Bolstraat
CEINTUURBAAN
Tweede van der Helststraat
Ceintuurbrug
VAN
OSTADESTRAAT
D
E
F

EASTERN CANAL RING

Must See

1 Museum Willet-Holthuysen

Experience More

2 Foam Museum
3 Amstelkerk
4 Blauwbrug
5 Albert Cuypmarkt
6 Bloemenmarkt
7 Museum Van Loon
8 Heineken Experience
9 Pathé Tuschinski
10 Stadsarchief Amsterdam
11 Magere Brug

Eat

① Café de Punt
② Restaurant de Waaghals
③ Vlaardingse Haringhandel

Stay

④ Hotel Dwars
⑤ Hotel V Frederiksplein

1

MUSEUM WILLET-HOLTHUYSEN

G6 Herengracht 605 4, 14 10am-5pm daily 27 Apr willetholthuysen.nl

A visit to Amsterdam wouldn't be complete without exploring one of the city's iconic canal houses. Named after its last residents, the Museum Willet-Holthuysen allows the visitor a glimpse into the lives of the emerging merchant class who lived in luxury along the Grachtengordel (Canal Ring) in the 17th century. Three floors, and the formal garden, are open to the public.

The house was built in 1685 for Jacob Hop, mayor of Amsterdam. It became the property of coal magnate Pieter Holthuysen (1788–1858) in 1855. It then passed to his daughter Louisa (1824–95) and her husband, Abraham Willet (1825–88), who were both fervent collectors of paintings, glass, silver and ceramics. When Louisa died childless and a widow in 1895, the house and its many treasures were left to the city on the condition that it became a museum bearing their names. Room by room, the house is being restored and brought back to the time Abraham and Louisa lived here.

Arguably, the most interesting part of the house is found below stairs. Special exhibits illuminating the lives of the Willet-Holthuysens' servants are displayed on the lower floor.

When Louisa died childless and a widow in 1895, the house and its many treasures were left to the city on the condition that it became a museum bearing their names.

↑ The grand façade of the Museum Willet-Holthuysen

↑ The dining room decorated with a copy of the 18th-century silk wallpaper

← The gentlemen's parlour, hung with opulent, heavy blue damask

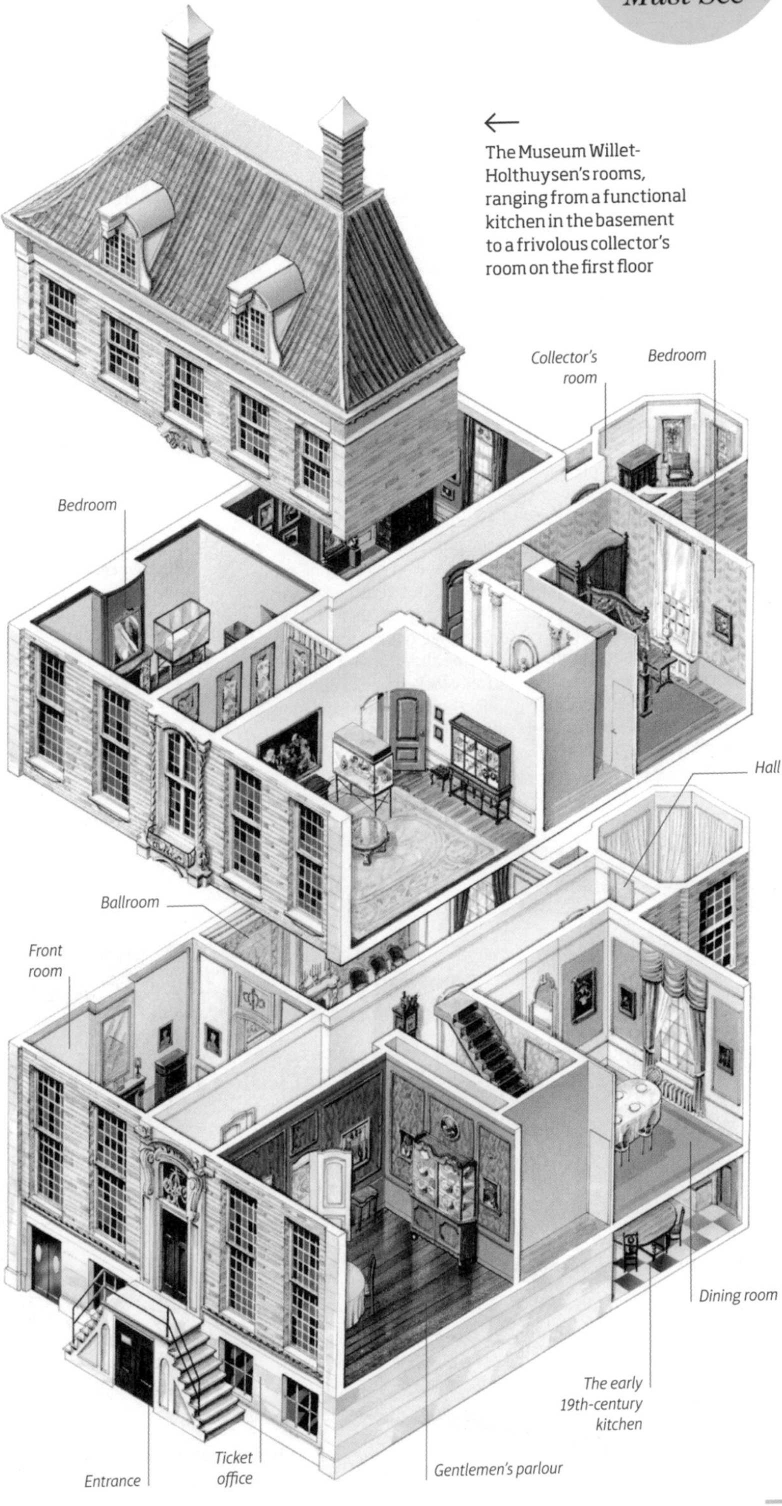

←

The Museum Willet-Holthuysen's rooms, ranging from a functional kitchen in the basement to a frivolous collector's room on the first floor

EXPERIENCE MORE

2 Foam Museum

F7 Keizersgracht 609 24 Vijzelgracht 10am-6pm Sat-Wed, 10am-9pm Thu & Fri 27 Apr foam.org

Three elegant 17th-century canal houses on the Keizersgracht have been joined together and beautifully renovated to create this labyrinth of modern rooms filled with photographs. Over 20,000 visitors flock here annually, making it the most-visited photography museum in the Netherlands by far.

Foam (Fotografiemuseum Amsterdam) is dedicated to exhibiting and celebrating every form of photography, from historical to journalistic, cutting-edge to artistic. The museum has an international outlook – photographs exhibited here are taken all over the world by photographers from a variety of cultures and ethnic backgrounds.

The museum holds four major exhibitions a year and 15 smaller ones, showcasing both established figures of the art form and emerging local talent. Exhibitions at Foam have included Annie Leibovitz's "American Music", a retrospective on Henri Cartier-Bresson and "50 Years of World Press Photo".

More than just a museum, though, Foam prides itself on being an interactive centre for photography, a place where amateurs can learn more about the art by meeting professionals, attending lectures and taking part in discussion evenings, or just stop for a coffee and a browse of the well-stocked bookshop. Foam also hosts pop-up exhibitions in different neighbourhoods to make photography accessible to all.

EAT

Café de Punt

Come here for sandwiches made with local cheeses and ham.

G9 Tweede Jacob van Campenstraat 150 cafe-depunt.nl

Restaurant de Waaghals

This organic vegetarian restaurant serves imaginative dishes.

E9 Franshalsstraat 29 L waaghals.nl

Vlaardingse Haringhandel

Locals rate the creamy raw herring served here, in a bun with pickles and onions.

E9 Albert Cuypstraat 89 Sun & D

€€€

↑ Outdoor exhibition organized by the Foam Museum

Colourful canal houses look over the Blauwbrug

Amstelkerk

G7 Amstelveld 10 520 0060 4 9am-5pm Mon-Fri Public hols

Designed by Daniel Stalpaert in 1668, the squat and wooden Amstelkerk was originally built as a temporary structure, while in the meantime money was going to be raised for a large new church that would be located on the Botermarkt (now Rembrandtplein). Unfortunately, the necessary funds for the grand scheme were never forthcoming, and so the temporary Amstelkerk had to be kept and maintained.

In 1825, the Protestant church authorities attempted to raise money to at least renovate the Amstelkerk's plain interior in a Neo-Gothic style. It was not until 1840, however, when Frederica Elisabeth Cramer donated 25,000 guilders to the project, that work could begin.

During the late 1980s, the Amstelkerk underwent a substantial conversion, which cost some 4 million guilders. Glass-walled offices were installed inside the building and it was closed to the public. However, concerts are still held in the nave, which was preserved in all its Neo-Gothic magnificence. The top-class brasserie NeL is housed in a side building.

Blauwbrug

G6 Amstel 14 Waterlooplein

The Blauwbrug (Blue Bridge) is thought to have taken its name from the colour of the wooden bridge that originally crossed this particular stretch of the Amstel river in the 17th century. Made of stone, the present light-grey bridge was built in preparation for the 1883 World Colonial Exhibition, which attracted thousands of visitors to Amsterdam. Exhibitors came from 28 different nations.

The Blauwbrug is decorated with sculptures of medieval boats, fish and the imperial crown of Amsterdam and is surmounted by ornate lamps. The design was inspired by the plans for the elaborate Alexander III bridge in Paris.

Albert Cuypmarkt

F9 Albert Cuypstraat 3, 4, 12, 24 De Pijp 9:30am-5pm Mon-Sat albertcuyp-markt.amsterdam

The market running along De Pijp's Albert Cuypstraat began trading in 1904, shortly after the expansion of the city. The wide street, once a canal, is named after the Dutch landscape painter Albert Cuyp (1620–91).

This wide street is lined with colour-popping stalls. Described by the stallholders as "the best-known market in Europe", it attracts some 20,000 visitors on weekdays and often twice as many on Saturdays. Vendors sell everything you would expect from a Dutch market – fresh fish, poultry, cheese, fruit and clothes – but the real reason to head to Albert Cuypstraat is for its mouthwatering street food. The sound of frying fills the air and your nose will be assaulted by the scents of dishes from around the globe.

The real reason to head to Albert Cuypstraat is for its mouthwatering street food. The sound of frying fills the air and your nose will be assaulted by the scents of dishes from around the globe.

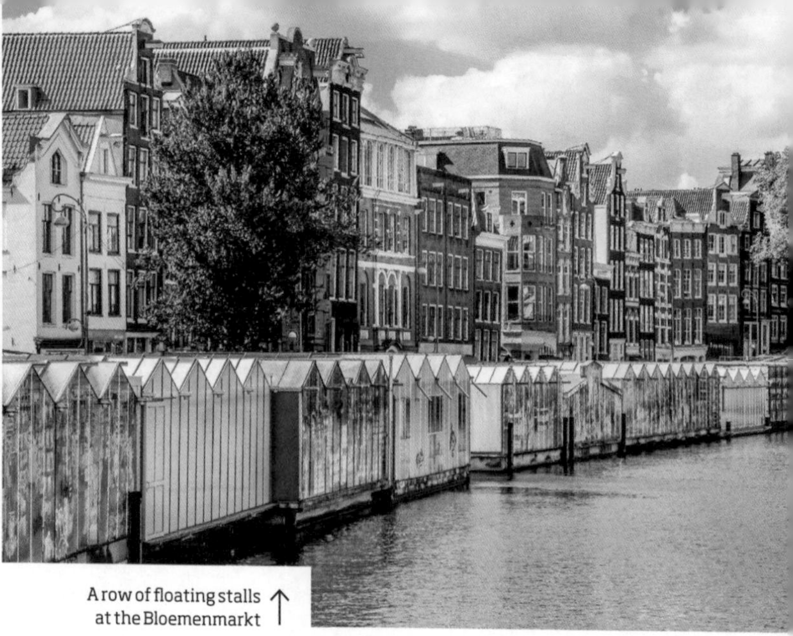

A row of floating stalls at the Bloemenmarkt

Bloemenmarkt

F6 Singel 4, 14, 24 Rokin 9:30am-5pm daily

On the Singel, west of Muntplein, is the last of the city's floating markets. In the past, nurserymen sailed up the Amstel from their smallholdings and moored here to sell cut flowers and plants directly from their boats.

Today, the stalls are still floating but are now a permanent fixture. Despite the sellers' tendency to cater purely for tourists, with prices reflecting this, the displays of fragrant seasonal flowers and bright spring bedding plants are always beautiful to look at.

Museum Van Loon

F7 Keizersgracht 672 24 Vijzelgracht 10am-5pm daily 1 Jan, 27 Apr, 25 Dec museumvanloon.nl

Designed by Adriaan Dortsman, No 672 Keizersgracht is one of a pair of symmetrical houses built in 1672. The first resident was the painter Ferdinand Bol, a pupil of Rembrandt. In 1884, the Van Loon family moved into the house. The Van Loons were one of Amsterdam's foremost families in the 17th century.

The house was opened as a museum in 1973, after many years of restoration, retaining the original charming character of the house. It contains a collection of Van Loon family portraits, stretching back to the early 1600s. The period rooms are adorned with fine pieces of furniture, porcelain and sculpture. Some of the upstairs rooms contain sumptuous illusionistic wall paintings, popular in the 17th and 18th centuries. Four were painted by the Classicist artist Gérard de Lairesse (1641–1711). Outside, in the formal rose garden, is the 18th-century coach house, housing the Van Loon family coaches and livery worn by the servants.

TULIP MANIA

Tulip mania seized Amsterdam in the 1630s. The exotic Asian bulbs tempted investors and their value soared. At the height of the craze, a single rare bulb could cost more than 10,000 guilders - as much as a grand canal-side townhouse. Tempted by the chance to get rich quick, even ordinary folk invested their savings in the flowers, only to lose them when the bubble inevitably burst and prices collapsed in 1637.

Heineken Experience

F9 Stadhouderskade 78 1, 7, 19, 24 Vijzelgracht Sep-Jun: 10:30am-7:30pm Mon-Thu, to 9pm Fri-Sun; Jul & Aug: 10:30am-9pm daily; last tickets 2 hours before closing heinekenexperience.com

Gerard Adriaan Heineken founded the Heineken company in 1864 when he bought

the 16th-century Hooiberg (haystack) brewery on the Nieuwezijds Voorburgwal. The original Stadhouderskade building was erected in 1867. His readiness to adapt to new methods and bring in foreign brewers established him as a major force in Amsterdam's profitable beer industry. In 1988, the company finally stopped producing beer in its massive brick brewery on Stadhouderskade, as it was unable to keep up with the demand. Production is now concentrated in two breweries, one in Zoeterwoude, near Den Haag, another in Den Bosch. Today, Heineken produces around half of the beer sold in Amsterdam, has production facilities in dozens of countries and exports all over the world.

The Stadhouderskade building now houses the Heineken Experience, where visitors can learn about the history of the company and beer-making in general, and enjoy a free tasting. Extensive renovations accommodate the increasing number of visitors. There is also a tasting bar, mini brewery and a stable offering the opportunity to view Heineken's splendid dray horses – you may be lucky enough to see them trotting around Amsterdam. Visitors under the age of 18 must be accompanied by an adult.

STAY

Hotel Dwars

This hotel's nine characterful, cosy rooms are decorated with modern and vintage furniture. It's great value for money.

G7
Utrechtsedwarsstraat 79 **hoteldwars.com**

Hotel V Frederiksplein

A choice of hotel rooms and self-catering loft apartments are offered at this extremely hip hotel.

G8
Weteringschans 136 **hotelv frederiksplein.nl**

↑ Beer wagon displayed at the Heineken Experience

Magere Brug is illuminated at night by strings of lights

9 Pathé Tuschinski

F6 Reguliersbreestraat 26-28 0900 1458 14, 24 Rokin Box office: 12:15-10pm daily

Abraham Tuschinski's cinema and variety theatre caused a sensation when it opened in 1921. Until then, Amsterdam's cinemas had been sombre places, but this building was an exotic blend of Art Deco and Amsterdam School architecture *(p37)*. Its twin towers are 26 m (85 ft) in height. Built in a slum area known as the Duivelshoek (Devil's Corner), the theatre was designed by Heyman Louis de Jong and decorated by Chris Bartels, Jaap Gidding and Pieter den Besten. In its heyday, Marlene Dietrich and Judy Garland performed here.

Now converted into a six-screen cinema, the building has been meticulously restored, both inside and out. The carpet in the entrance hall, replaced in 1984, is an exact copy of the original. For just a few extra euros, you can take a seat in one of the exotic boxes that make up the back row of the huge semicircular, 1,472-seater main auditorium.

INSIDER TIP

Watch a Film at Pathé Tuschinski

A guided tour of the theatre is certainly recommended, but the best way to appreciate the full opulence of the Pathé Tuschinski is to go to see a film.

The ornate façade of the Pathé Tuschinski

10 Stadsarchief Amsterdam

F7 Vijzelstraat 32 24 10am-5pm Tue-Fri, noon-5pm Sat & Sun Public hols amsterdam.nl/stadsarchief

The Stadsarchief, which houses the city's municipal archives, has moved from its former location in Amsteldijk to this monumental building. Designed by K P C de Bazel, who was one of the principal representatives of the Amsterdam School, the edifice was completed in 1926 for the Netherlands Trading Company. In spite of multiple renovation works, the building retains many attractive original features, such as the colourful floor mosaics (designed by De Bazel himself) and the wooden panelling in the boardrooms on the second floor. There is a permanent display of treasures from the archives in the building's monumental vaults.

In 1991 the building, which is affectionately known as "The Bazel", was declared a national monument. Guided tours take place at 2pm on weekends.

Magere Brug

G7 Amstel 4

Of Amsterdam's 1,200 or so bridges, the Magere Brug (Skinny Bridge) is undoubtedly the city's best known. The original drawbridge was constructed in about 1670. The traditional story has it that it was named after two sisters called Mager, who lived on either side of the Amstel. However, it appears more likely that the bridge acquired the name from its narrow *(mager)* design. At night many lights illuminate the bridge.

The drawbridge was widened in 1871 and most recently rebuilt in 1934, though it still conforms to the traditional double-leaf style. The bridge is made from African azobe wood, and was intended to last for at least 50 years. In 1929, the city council considered whether to demolish the old frame, which had rotted. After huge outcry, it was decided to keep the original.

Since 2003 traffic has been limited to bicycles and pedestrians. Several times a day, the bridge master lets boats through the Magere Brug, then jumps on his bicycle and opens up the Nieuwe Herengracht bridge.

HOW THE MAGERE BRUG WORKS

The Magere Brug is a double-leaf-style drawbridge. This means that it continuously balances its span of 5 m (16 ft) on each side throughout its swing. The balance is made up of two counterweighted beams. The arched wooden portal provides a pivot for the balance and a mechanical chain drive operates the steel cables that cause the bridge to lift up.

→ The Magere Brug when open for boats

A SHORT WALK AMSTELVELD

Distance 2 km (1.5 miles) **Nearest metro** Waterlooplein
Time 20 minutes

The eastern end of the Grachtengordel is quiet and largely residential, especially around the Amstelveld, with its pretty wooden church and houseboats. A short walk will take you past shops and numerous cafés, particularly on the bustling Rembrandtplein. As you wander down the broad sweep of the Amstel river, Amsterdam suddenly loses its village atmosphere and begins to feel like a city.

AMSTEL

FINISH

START

REMBRANDTPLEIN

Looking on to the former Botermarkt (butter market) and the cast-iron statue of Rembrandt in Rembrandtplein are dozens of cafés dating from the 19th century, including the De Kroon at No 17.

Café Schiller

HERENGRACHT

REGULIERSGRACHT

KEIZERSGRACHT

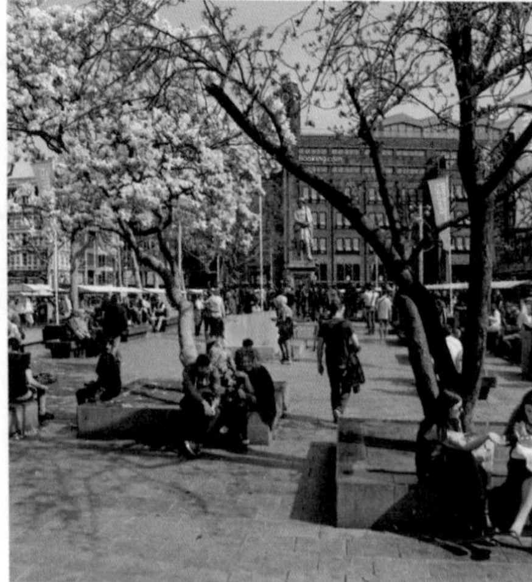

↑ Catching up with friends under cherry blossom in Rembrandtplein

The wooden Amstelkerk was meant to be a temporary structure while money was raised to build a big new church on Rembrandtplein, but the grand scheme fell through and this building became a permanent fixture. Today, the church houses offices and a restaurant (p145).

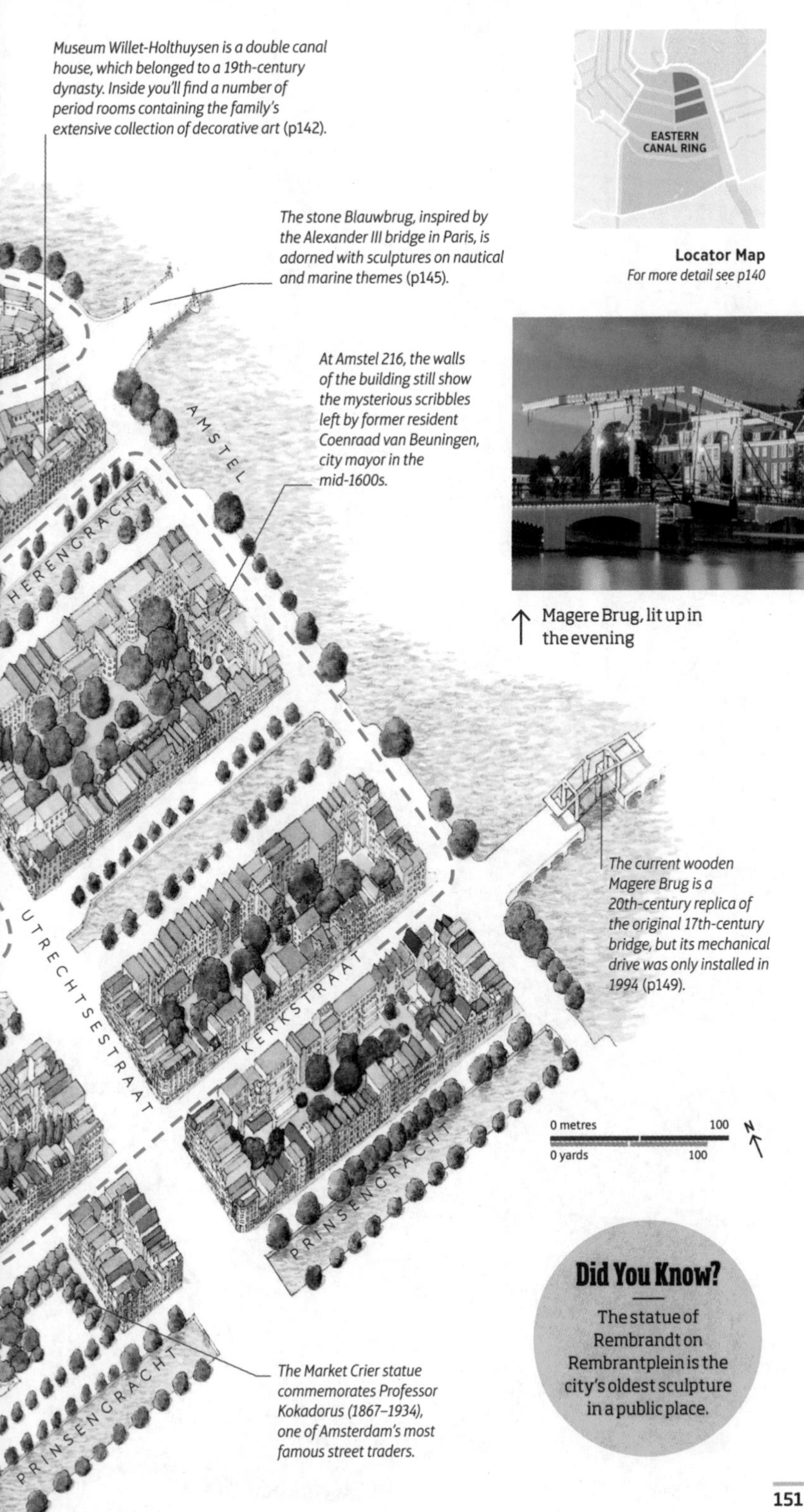

Museum Willet-Holthuysen is a double canal house, which belonged to a 19th-century dynasty. Inside you'll find a number of period rooms containing the family's extensive collection of decorative art (p142).

The stone Blauwbrug, inspired by the Alexander III bridge in Paris, is adorned with sculptures on nautical and marine themes (p145).

At Amstel 216, the walls of the building still show the mysterious scribbles left by former resident Coenraad van Beuningen, city mayor in the mid-1600s.

The current wooden Magere Brug is a 20th-century replica of the original 17th-century bridge, but its mechanical drive was only installed in 1994 (p149).

The Market Crier statue commemorates Professor Kokadorus (1867–1934), one of Amsterdam's most famous street traders.

Locator Map
For more detail see p140

↑ Magere Brug, lit up in the evening

Did You Know?

The statue of Rembrandt on Rembrantplein is the city's oldest sculpture in a public place.

A red-shuttered building on Prinseneiland, the Western Islands

JORDAAN AND THE WESTERN ISLANDS

At the start of the 17th century construction of the Grachtengordel began, just west of the Singel canal. At the same time, city planner Hendrick Staets laid out the marshy area beyond Prinsengracht as an area for workers whose industries were banned from the town centre. Its network of narrow streets and oblique canals followed the course of old paths and drainage ditches. Immigrants fleeing religious persecution also settled here. It is thought that Huguenot refugees called the district *jardin* (garden), later corrupted to "Jordaan". Historically a poor area, it is famous for its *hofjes* (almshouses), of which the Claes Claeszhofje is a fine early example. Further north are the characterful Western Islands, created in the mid-17th century to meet the demand for warehouses.

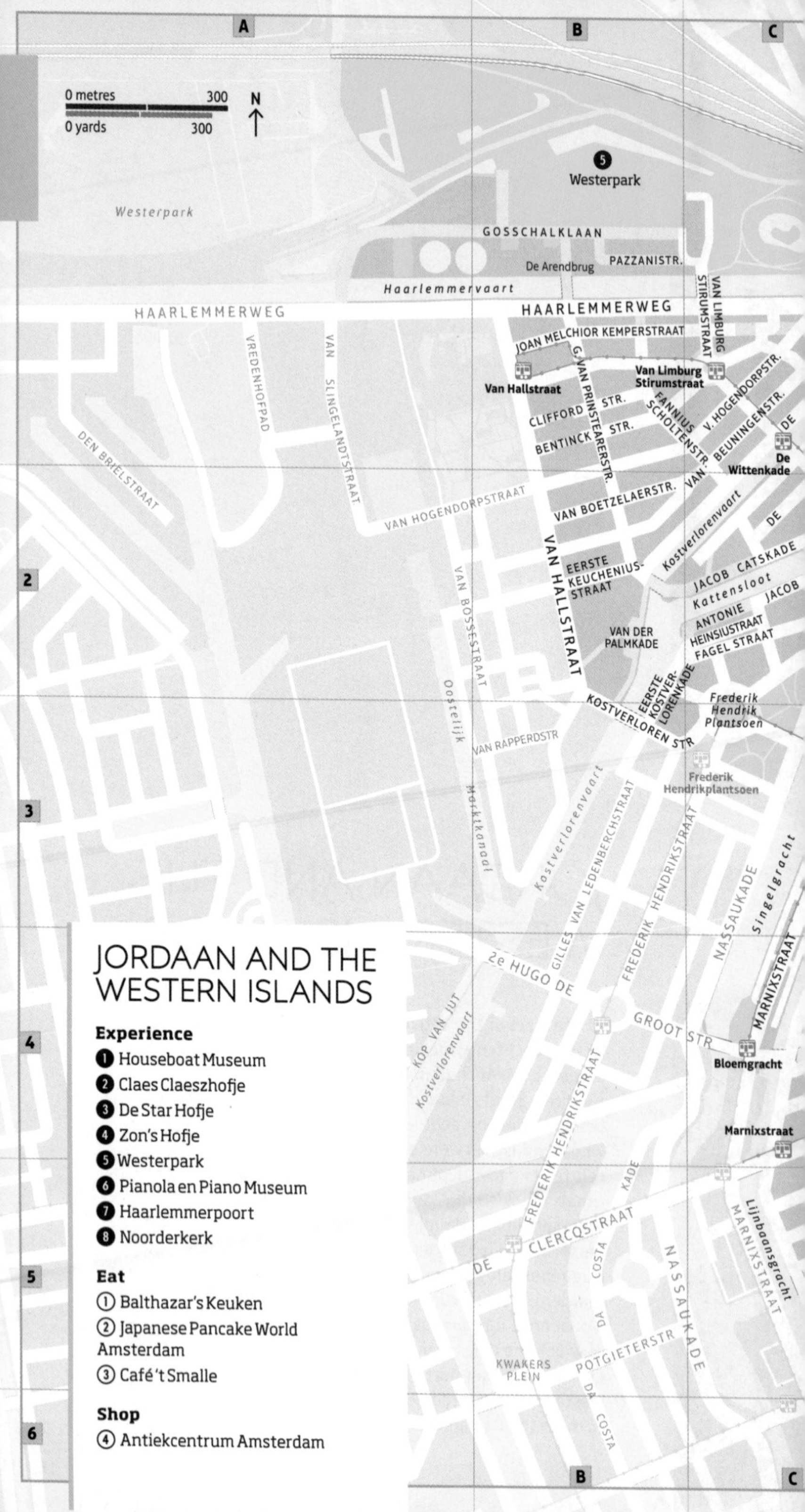
A
B
C
0 metres
300
0 yards
300
N
Westerpark
5 Westerpark
GOSSCHALKLAAN
De Arendbrug
PAZZANISTR.
Haarlemmervaart
HAARLEMMERWEG
HAARLEMMERWEG
STIRUMSTRAAT
VAN LIMBURG
JOAN MELCHIOR KEMPERSTRAAT
VREDENHOFPAD
VAN SLINGELANDTSTRAAT
G. VAN PRINSTEREERSTR.
Van Hallstraat
Van Limburg Stirumstraat
CLIFFORD STR.
BENTINCK STR.
FANNIUS SCHOLTENSTR.
V. HOGENDORPSTR.
VAN BEUNINGENSTR.
DE
De Wittenkade
DEN BRIELSTRAAT
VAN HOGENDORPSTRAAT
VAN BOETZELAERSTR.
Kostverlorenvaart
DE
VAN HALLSTRAAT
EERSTE KEUCHENIUS-STRAAT
JACOB CATSKADE
Kattensloot
ANTONIE HEINSIUSSTRAAT
JACOB
FAGEL STRAAT
VAN BOSSESTRAAT
VAN DER PALMKADE
EERSTE KOSTVER-LORENKADE
KOSTVERLOREN STR
Frederik Hendrik Plantsoen
Oostelijk
VAN RAPPERDSTR
Frederik Hendrikplantsoen
2
3
Marktkanaal
Kostverlorenvaart
GILLES VAN LEDENBERCHSTRAAT
FREDERIK HENDRIKSTRAAT
NASSAUKADE
Singelgracht
MARNIXSTRAAT
JORDAAN AND THE WESTERN ISLANDS
Experience
1 Houseboat Museum
2 Claes Claeszhofje
3 De Star Hofje
4 Zon's Hofje
5 Westerpark
6 Pianola en Piano Museum
7 Haarlemmerpoort
8 Noorderkerk
Eat
① Balthazar's Keuken
② Japanese Pancake World Amsterdam
③ Café 't Smalle
Shop
④ Antiekcentrum Amsterdam
4
5
6
2e HUGO DE GROOT STR
KOP VAN JUT
Kostverlorenvaart
Bloemgracht
FREDERIK HENDRIKSTRAAT
Marnixstraat
KADE
DE CLERCQSTRAAT
COSTA
DA
NASSAUKADE
Lijnbaansgracht
MARNIXSTRAAT
KWAKERS PLEIN
POTGIETERSTR
DA COSTA

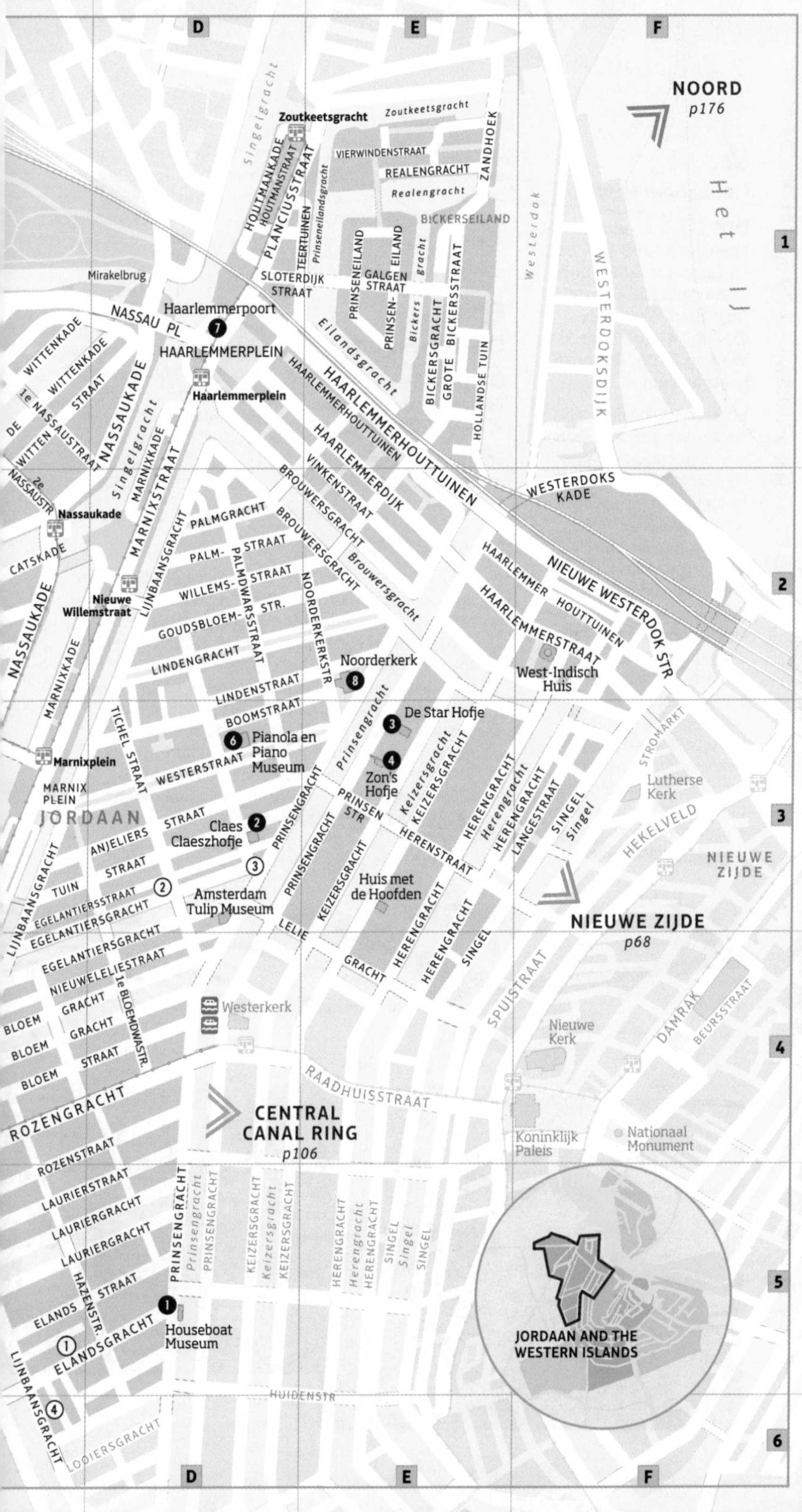

NOORD
p176
Het IJ
Zoutkeetsgracht
Haarlemmerpoort
Haarlemmerplein
Nassaukade
Nieuwe Willemstraat
Marnixplein
JORDAAN
Noorderkerk
De Star Hofje
Zon's Hofje
Pianola en Piano Museum
Claes Claeszhofje
Amsterdam Tulip Museum
Huis met de Hoofden
West-Indisch Huis
Lutherse Kerk
NIEUWE ZIJDE
p68
Westerkerk
Nieuwe Kerk
CENTRAL CANAL RING
p106
Koninklijk Paleis
Nationaal Monument
Houseboat Museum
JORDAAN AND THE WESTERN ISLANDS

Houseboat Museum

D5 Prinsengracht, opposite No 296 5, 7, 17, 19 Jan-Jun & Sep-Dec: 10am-5pm Tue-Sun; Jul & Aug: 10am-5pm daily 1 & 8-24 Jan, 27 Apr, 1st Sat Aug, 25 Dec houseboatmuseum.nl

Houseboats line the canals of Amsterdam, homes to people who prefer the alternative lifestyle of being afloat. Moored on the Prinsengracht canal on the edge of the Jordaan, the *Hendrika Maria* is a showcase of life aboard an Amsterdam houseboat. Built in 1914, it served as a barge and transported coal, sand and gravel until the 1960s, when it was converted into a houseboat.

It is now the world's only houseboat museum. When inside, visitors can make themselves at home. Note the tiny original kitchen with its green-enamel pots and pans, a hand-pump for water and cosy cupboard-beds, and then take a seat in the surprisingly spacious living room, furnished in chintzy 1950s style, where coffee is served.

Claes Claeszhofje

D3 1e Eerste Egelantiersdwarsstraat 5, 13, 17 Occasionally

This is a group of *hofjes*, the earliest of which was founded in 1616 by a textile merchant, Claes Claesz Anslo. Rescued from ruin in the 1960s by the Stichting Diogenes Foundation, the two sets of houses that comprise this *hofje* are now student lodgings. The houses are set around a pretty little courtyard.

One of the oldest surviving and most distinctive is the "Huis met de Schrijvende Hand" (house with the writing hand), at Egelantiersstraat 52. Once the home of a teacher, it dates from the 1630s.

DUTCH HOFJES

Before the Alteration (p53), the Catholic Church usually provided subsidized housing for the poor and elderly, particularly women. During the 17th and 18th centuries, rich merchants and Protestant organizations took on this charitable role and built hundreds of almshouse complexes. Known as *hofjes*, these groups of pretty houses were planned around courtyards or gardens. By providing housing for the elderly and infirm, the *hofjes* marked the beginning of the Dutch welfare system. Visitors are admitted to some but are asked to respect the residents' privacy. Many *hofjes* are found in the Jordaan and some still serve their original purpose.

↑ The cosy lounge, Houseboat Museum

EAT

Balthazar's Keuken

The set menu here changes weekly and embraces seasonal produce, such as halibut in roast carrot sauce.

C5
Elandsgracht 108
balthazarskeuken.nl

Japanese Pancake World Amsterdam

This diner serves *okonomiyaki* (hearty Japanese-style pancakes) with *shogayaki* (beef, wild spinach and onion) toppings, among others.

D3 Tweede Engelantiersgracht 24a
japanesepancake world.com

Café 't Smalle

A local favourite since 1780, this café serves a wide choice of salads, toasted sandwiches and baguettes filled with ham, cheese or steak. Stained-glass windows add a colourful touch.

D3
Engelantiersgracht 12
t-smalle.nl

De Star Hofje's beautiful garden ↓

3 De Star Hofje

E3 Prinsengracht 89-133 3, 5, 13, 17, 18, 21, 22 6am-6pm Mon-Fri, 6am-2pm Sat

De Star Hofje's lovely flower garden makes it one of the prettiest of the district's *hofjes*, and unique lanterns with a royal crown on each add to the charm. The *hofje* consists of a courtyard surrounded on three sides by houses with a water pump in the middle.

It gets its name from the Star Brewery, which stood here until the *hofje* was built in 1804. Officially known as Van Brienen Hofje, legend has it that a merchant, Jan van Brienen, founded this almshouse in gratitude for his release from a vault in which he had been accidentally imprisoned. Since 1995, it has been owned by a housing foundation.

4 Zon's Hofje

E3 Prinsengracht 159-171 3, 5, 7, 17, 18, 21, 22 10am-5pm Mon-Fri

Until it was turned into almshouses for elderly Mennonite widows, this was the site of a clandestine church. The Kleine Zon (little sun) was a splinter group of the Noah's Ark congregation. Look for the carved sun *(zon)* under the 1765 clock in the courtyard.

Houseboats lining the Prinsengracht on a summer's evening

Relaxing under Westerpark's blossom

5

Westerpark

B1 Polonceaukade 5 21, 22, 48, 248 Museum Het Schip: 11am-5pm Tue-Sun westergasfabriek.com hetschip.nl

The wasteland that surrounds Amsterdam's former gasworks (Westergasfabriek) was transformed into a 14-ha (35-acre) green park in the early 2000s. Facilities include playgrounds, bars, restaurants, several performance spaces and the Ketelhuis cinema. The gasworks itself has been redeveloped and is being rented out to various associations that organize music and food festivals, a variety of performances and exhibitions.

Nearby is Het Schip (The Ship), one of the most iconic buildings by the Amsterdam School *(p37)*. Designed by Michel de Klerk in 1919, this apartment block contains 102 homes and the Museum Het Schip, displaying a restored working-class house.

6  

Pianola en Piano Museum

D3 Westerstraat 106 3, 5, 13, 17 11am-5pm Sun & for concerts pianola.nl

Fifteen instruments and some 15,000 piano rolls are on show here, celebrating the automatic pianos that were introduced in 1900. There are regular performances by pianists. Sadly, the museum faces closure as it might lose city council subsidies.

7

Haarlemmerpoort

D1 Haarlemmerplein 50 3, 18, 21, 22 To the public

Originally a defended gateway into Amsterdam, the

JOHNNY JORDAAN

This statue by Kees Verkade depicts Johnny Jordaan (1924-89). Born in the Jordaan, Johannes Hendricus van Musscher became a star in the 1950s as a *levenslied* singer. This Dutch popular music, made up of catchy refrains, reflects on the many realities of life - songs can be sweet and light or bitter and dark. The city's songbird, Jordaan had hits including "Gif mij maar Amsterdam" and "Bij ons in de Jordaan".

By the entrance is a sculpture of three bound figures, inscribed: "Unity is Strength". It commemorates the Jordaanoproer (Jordaan Riot) of 1934 over a reduction in social security.

Haarlemmerpoort marked the beginning of the busy route to Haarlem. The current gateway, dating from 1840, was built for King William II's triumphal entry into the city and officially named Willemspoort. However, as the third gateway to be built on or close to this site, it is still known as the Haarlemmerpoort by Amsterdammers.

Designed by Cornelis Alewijn (1788–1839), the Neo-Classical gatehouse was used as tax offices in the 19th century and was made into flats in 1986. Traffic no longer goes through the gate, since a bridge has been built over the adjoining Westerkanaal. Beyond the Haarlemmerpoort is the peaceful Westerpark, a pleasant retreat.

Noorderkerk

E2 Noordermarkt 44-48 3, 5, 13, 17 18, 21, 22 10:30am-12:30pm Mon, 11am-1pm Sat noorderkerk.org

Built for poor settlers in the Jordaan, the North Church was the first in Amsterdam to be constructed in the shape of a Greek cross. Its layout around a central pulpit allowed all in the encircling pews to see and hear well.

The church was designed by Hendrick de Keyser *(p37)*, who died in 1621, a year after building began. It was completed in 1623. The church is still well attended by a Calvinist congregation, and bears many reminders of the working-class origins of the Jordaan. By the entrance is a sculpture of three bound figures, inscribed: "Unity is Strength". It commemorates the Jordaanoproer (Jordaan Riot) of 1934 over a reduction in social security. On the south façade is a plaque recalling the strike of February 1941, a protest at the Nazis' deportation of Jews.

There are regular concerts held on Saturday afternoons.

SHOP

Antiekcentrum Amsterdam

In a labyrinth of rooms, the biggest antique and curio market in the Netherlands sells everything from glassware and vintage jewellery to dolls.

C6 Elandsgracht 109 11am-6pm Mon & Wed-Fri, 11am-5pm Sat & Sun antiekcentrumamsterdam.nl

↑ A busy market in front of Noorderkerk

The verdant Oosterpark, with its tranquil lake

PLANTAGE

Known as the "plantation", this area was once green parkland beyond the city wall, where 17th-century Amsterdammers spent their leisure time. The area was designated as a space for urban expansion in 1663, but economic crisis in 1672 meant that the government could not find enough buyers for the land. As a result, citizens could buy plots and a multitude of green spaces were the result. From about 1848, it became one of Amsterdam's first suburbs and theatres and dance halls opened their doors. In the 19th century, many middle-class Jews prospered in the area, mainly in the diamond-cutting industry. They formed a large part of the Diamond Workers' Union, whose headquarters were housed in De Burcht.

The area also has a long maritime association. Following defeat in the First Anglo-Dutch War *(p54)*, it was decided that the military ships needed to be better organized to protect the merchant fleet. In 1655, the government built a wharf on Kattenburg island for the military unit and a few years later an arsenal was added to the site. Since 1972, this building has housed the national maritime collection. Across the Nieuwevaart canal, a former thriving shipyard, dating from 1757, houses the Museum 't Kromhout.

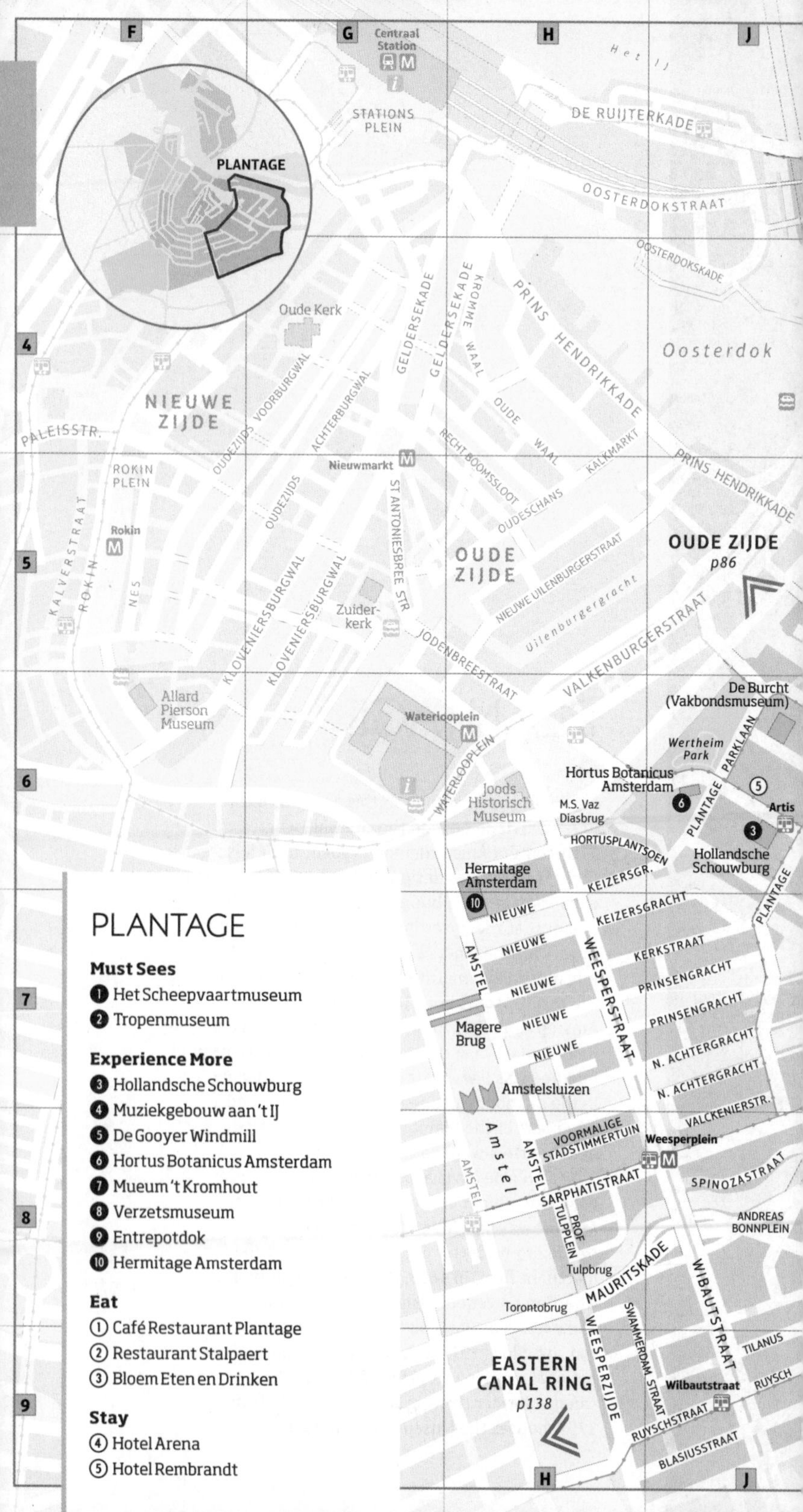
F
G
H
J
4
5
6
7
8
9
Centraal Station
Het IJ
STATIONS PLEIN
DE RUIJTERKADE
OOSTERDOKSTRAAT
OOSTERDOKSKADE
PLANTAGE
Oude Kerk
GELDERSEKADE
KROMME WAAL
PRINS HENDRIKKADE
Oosterdok
NIEUWE ZIJDE
PALEISSTR.
OUDEZIJDS VOORBURGWAL
ACHTERBURGWAL
OUDE WAAL
RECHTBOOMSSLOOT
KALKMARKT
Nieuwmarkt
ROKIN PLEIN
OUDEZIJDS
ST ANTONIESBREE STR
OUDESCHANS
KALVERSTRAAT
Rokin
ROKIN
NES
OUDE ZIJDE
NIEUWE UILENBURGERSTRAAT
Uilenburgergracht
OUDE ZIJDE
p86
KLOVENIERSBURGWAL
Zuiderkerk
JODENBREESTRAAT
VALKENBURGERSTRAAT
De Burcht (Vakbondsmuseum)
Allard Pierson Museum
Waterlooplein
WATERLOOPLEIN
Wertheim Park
PARKLAAN
Hortus Botanicus Amsterdam
Joods Historisch Museum
M.S. Vaz Diasbrug
PLANTAGE
Artis
HORTUSPLANTSOEN
Hollandsche Schouwburg
Hermitage Amsterdam
KEIZERSGR.
KEIZERSGRACHT
NIEUWE
AMSTEL
WEESPERSTRAAT
KERKSTRAAT
PRINSENGRACHT
Magere Brug
N. ACHTERGRACHT
Amstelsluizen
VALCKENIERSTR.
Amstel
VOORMALIGE STADSTIMMERTUIN
Weesperplein
SPINOZASTRAAT
SARPHATISTRAAT
PROF TULPPLEIN
ANDREAS BONNPLEIN
MAURITSKADE
WIBAUTSTRAAT
Tulpbrug
Torontobrug
SWAMMERDAM STRAAT
WEESPERZIJDE
TILANUS
EASTERN CANAL RING
p138
Wilbautstraat
RUYSCH
RUYSCHSTRAAT
BLASIUSSTRAAT
PLANTAGE
Must Sees
1 Het Scheepvaartmuseum
2 Tropenmuseum
Experience More
3 Hollandsche Schouwburg
4 Muziekgebouw aan 't IJ
5 De Gooyer Windmill
6 Hortus Botanicus Amsterdam
7 Mueum 't Kromhout
8 Verzetsmuseum
9 Entrepotdok
10 Hermitage Amsterdam
Eat
① Café Restaurant Plantage
② Restaurant Stalpaert
③ Bloem Eten en Drinken
Stay
④ Hotel Arena
⑤ Hotel Rembrandt

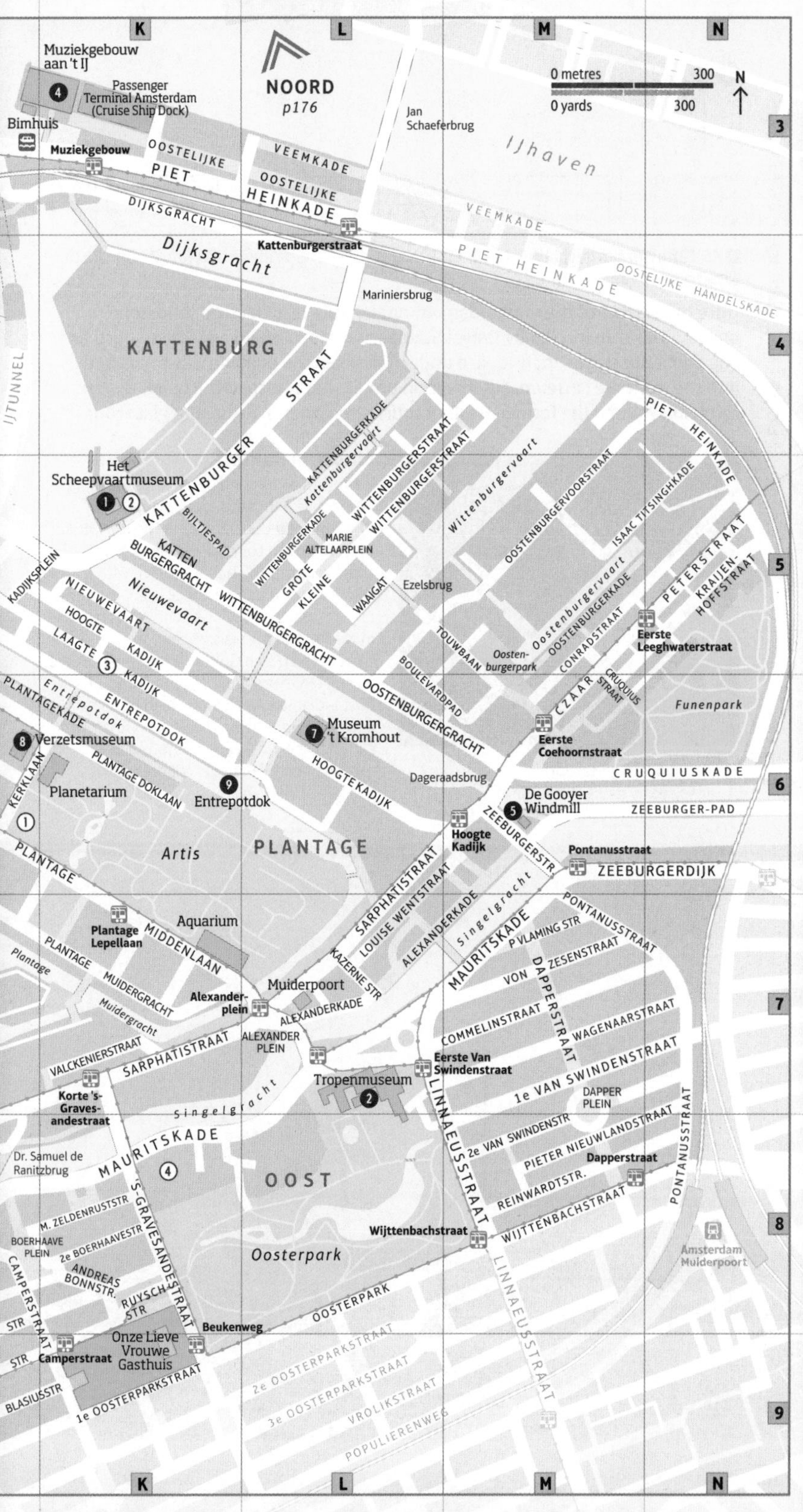
K
L
M
N
3
4
5
6
7
8
9
NOORD
p176
0 metres 300
0 yards 300
N
Muziekgebouw aan 't IJ
Passenger Terminal Amsterdam (Cruise Ship Dock)
Bimhuis
Muziekgebouw
Jan Schaeferbrug
IJhaven
OOSTELIJKE VEEMKADE
PIET HEINKADE
OOSTELIJKE
DIJKSGRACHT
Dijksgracht
Kattenburgerstraat
VEEMKADE
PIET HEINKADE
OOSTELIJKE HANDELSKADE
Mariniersbrug
KATTENBURG
IJTUNNEL
KATTENBURGERSTRAAT
KATTENBURGERKADE
Kattenburgervaart
WITTENBURGERSTRAAT
Wittenburgervaart
OOSTENBURGERVOORSTRAAT
ISAAC TITSINGHKADE
Het Scheepvaartmuseum
BIJLTJESPAD
WITTENBURGERKADE
MARIE ALTELAARPLEIN
GROTE
KLEINE
WAAIGAT
Ezelsbrug
KADIJKSPLEIN
KATTENBURGERGRACHT
WITTENBURGERGRACHT
Nieuwevaart
NIEUWEVAART
HOOGTE KADIJK
LAAGTE KADIJK
Entrepotdok
ENTREPOTDOK
PLANTAGEKADE
TOUWBAAN
Oostenburgerpark
BOULEVARDPAD
OOSTENBURGERGRACHT
Oostenburgervaart
OOSTENBURGERKADE
CONRADSTRAAT
PETERSTRAAT
KRAIJENHOFFSTRAAT
Eerste Leeghwaterstraat
CZAAR PETERSTRAAT
CRUQUIUSSTRAAT
Funenpark
Eerste Coehoornstraat
Verzetsmuseum
Museum 't Kromhout
KERKLAAN
Planetarium
PLANTAGE DOKLAAN
Entrepotdok
HOOGTE KADIJK
Dageraadsbrug
CRUQUIUSKADE
De Gooyer Windmill
ZEEBURGER-PAD
Hoogte Kadijk
ZEEBURGERSTR.
Pontanusstraat
ZEEBURGERDIJK
Artis
PLANTAGE
PLANTAGE MIDDENLAAN
Plantage Lepellaan
Aquarium
SARPHATISTRAAT
LOUISE WENTSTRAAT
ALEXANDERKADE
Singelgracht
MAURITSKADE
PONTANUSSTRAAT
P VLAMING STR
VON ZESENSTRAAT
DAPPERSTRAAT
PLANTAGE MUIDERGRACHT
Plantage Muidergracht
KAZERNE STR
Muiderpoort
Alexanderplein
ALEXANDERKADE
ALEXANDER PLEIN
COMMELINSTRAAT
WAGENAARSTRAAT
VALCKENIERSTRAAT
SARPHATISTRAAT
Eerste Van Swindenstraat
1e VAN SWINDENSTRAAT
Tropenmuseum
DAPPER PLEIN
Korte 's-Gravesandestraat
Singelgracht
LINNAEUSSTRAAT
2e VAN SWINDENSTR
PIETER NIEUWLANDSTRAAT
PONTANUSSTRAAT
Dr. Samuel de Ranitzbrug
MAURITSKADE
OOST
Dapperstraat
REINWARDTSTR.
WIJTTENBACHSTRAAT
M. ZELDENRUSTSTR
'S-GRAVESANDESTRAAT
Wijttenbachstraat
BOERHAAVE PLEIN
2e BOERHAAVESTR
Oosterpark
Amsterdam Muiderpoort
CAMPERSTRAAT
ANDREAS BONNSTR.
RUYSCHSTR
OOSTERPARK
LINNAEUSSTRAAT
STR
Beukenweg
Onze Lieve Vrouwe Gasthuis
Camperstraat
2e OOSTERPARKSTRAAT
BLASIUSSTR
1e OOSTERPARKSTRAAT
3e OOSTERPARKSTRAAT
VROLIKSTRAAT
POPULIERENWEG

1

HET SCHEEPVAARTMUSEUM

K5 Kattenburgerplein 1 22, 48 Nemo 9am-5pm daily 1 Jan, 27 Apr, 25 Dec hetscheepvaartmuseum.nl

Once the arsenal of the Amsterdam Admiralty, this vast Classical sandstone building was constructed by Daniel Stalpaert in 1656 around a massive courtyard. The admiralty stayed in residence until 1973, when the building was converted into the Maritime Museum. A renovation project has returned the building to its former glory, and the former artillery courtyard now has a stunning glass roof.

↑ The modern glass roof, inspired by navigational lines

Museum Guide

Visitors of all ages enjoy the museum's interactive exhibitions and displays of maritime objects. Don't miss the free audio tour. The open courtyard gives access to the three wings of the building, each with its own theme. Oost (East) has displays of maritime objects, paintings, globes and model yachts. In Noord (North), visitors can take a journey back to the Dutch Golden Age using the latest virtual reality technology. Climb aboard the East Indiaman *Amsterdam*: haul up cargo, crawl through the hold and even fire a cannon. The West wing has interactive exhibits geared towards children, such as "Tale of the Whale".

[1] "Tale of the Whale" starts with the first whaling expeditions in the 16th century, when whales were thought to be fearsome sea monsters, and finishes with today's efforts to preserve them from extinction.

[2] Antique nautical maps and modern globes are on display.

[3] The museum has a fine collection of beautifully decorated model boats. It features examples of pleasure craft through the ages, from the 17th century to the present day. Each one is a work of art, with exquisitely painted details.

1

2,300

piles driven into the bed of the Oosterdok support the building.

2

3

↓ The museum sitting majestically in its watery surroundings, with the *Amsterdam* moored outside

The cavernous central hall reflecting the building's grand beginnings

INSIDER TIP
Take a Tour

Free tours often run on Sundays, or you can book a group tour for an insight into either the history of the building, and the meaning behind its decor, or the way different cultures experience love.

TROPENMUSEUM

L7 Linnaeusstraat 2 7, 14, 19 10am-5pm Tue-Sun (daily during school hols) 1 Jan, 27 Apr, 25 Dec tropenmuseum.nl

This fascinating museum reflects the Netherlands' colonial history, as well as the diversity of the country today. The displays of art objects, photographs and film focus on widely different cultures in the tropics and subtropics. Children will love the interactive Tropenmuseum Junior.

The Main Collection

Built to house the Dutch Colonial Institute, this vast complex was finished in 1926 by architects M A and J J Nieukerken. The exterior of what is one of the city's finest historic buildings is decorated with symbols of imperialism, such as stone friezes of peasants planting rice.

In 1978, the Royal Tropical Institute opened this fascinating ethnographic museum. One floor holds treasures from Indonesia, Papua New Guinea and Southeast Asia. The collection aims to show the things that unite all cultures, from love to death. On the upper floors, the exhibitions use static and interactive displays to explore diverse topics, including body art and Afrofuturism. Temporary exhibitions are held in the North Wing on the ground floor and the Park Hall on the second floor.

↑ The museum's exterior, made from red brick

Tropenmuseum Junior

The museum espouses the importance of children learning about different cultures. This immersive Dutch exhibition allows kids to see, hear, smell and taste what it's like to live in a different country. The destination changes every two and a half years. Until early 2020, youngsters board a simulated plane bound for Morocco. Once they've met their guides, they'll experience aspects of Moroccan life *(p31)*.

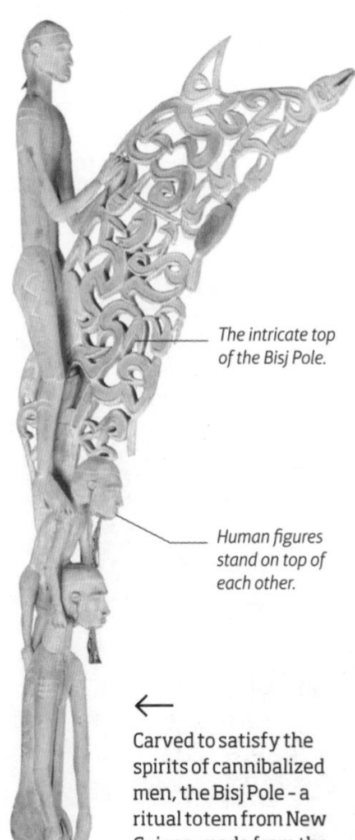

The intricate top of the Bisj Pole.

Human figures stand on top of each other.

← Carved to satisfy the spirits of cannibalized men, the Bisj Pole – a ritual totem from New Guinea, made from the root and trunk of a massive wild nutmeg tree

↑ Made of wood and tree bark, the *Pustaha* (Book of Divinations) containing prescriptions applied by a Toba Batak village healer-priest in North Sumatra

EXPERIENCE MORE

Hollandsche Schouwburg

J6 Plantage Middenlaan 24 14 11am–5pm daily 27 Apr, Rosh Hashanah (Jewish New Year), Yom Kippur jck.nl/en

Part of the Jewish Cultural Quarter *(p92)*, this former theatre is now a memorial to the 104,000 Dutch Jewish victims of World War II. Thousands were detained here before being deported to concentration camps. Postwar, the building was abandoned until 1962. A basalt column with a base in the shape of the Star of David now stands on the site of the stage. Written behind it is: "To the memory of those taken from here".

Following its restoration in 1993, the building became an education centre. On the ground floor, a candle illuminates the names of the war victims. Upstairs, there is a touching permanent exhibition on the persecution of the Jews in the Netherlands from 1940 to 1945.

Muziekgebouw aan 't IJ

K3 Piet Heinkade 1 26 muziekgebouw.nl

A huge glass box that juts into the IJ, this spectacular concert hall opened in 2005. Sharing its complex with the BIMHUIS, Amsterdam's leading jazz venue, Muziekgebouw aan 't IJ is versatile. It is capable of hosting both intimate chamber-music performances and large-scale concerts, with standing room for audiences of up to 1,500 people. As well as classical music, it presents performances of everything from electro to world music. The building also runs an annual programme of contemporary art and photography exhibitions. Order tickets for the coming season online before 1 October for discounts of 20 to 35 per cent.

10,000

windmills once dotted the Dutch landscape.

De Gooyer Windmill

M6 Funenkade 5 7, 14 22 To the public

Of the six remaining windmills within the city's boundaries, De Gooyer, also known as the Funenmolen, is the most central. Dominating the view down the Nieuwevaart, the mill was built around 1725, and was the first cornmill in the Netherlands to use streamlined sails.

↑ Thought-provoking exhibition at the Hollandsche Schouwburg

De Gooyer windmill, a quintessentially Dutch image

It first stood to the west of its present site, but the Oranje Nassau barracks, built in 1814, acted as a windbreak, and the mill was then moved to the Funenkade. The octagonal wooden structure was rebuilt on the stone footings of an earlier water-pumping mill, demolished in 1812.

By 1925, De Gooyer was in a very poor state of repair and was bought by the city council, which fully restored it. Since then, the lower part of the mill, with its neat thatched roof and tiny windows, has been a private home, though its massive sails still creak into action sometimes. Next to the mill is the Brouwerij Het IJ, one of two independent breweries in the city.

Hortus Botanicus Amsterdam

J6 Plantage Middenlaan 2 9, 14 Waterlooplein 10am-5pm daily 1 Jan, 25 Dec dehortus.nl

Beginning life as a small apothecary's herb garden in 1682, this green oasis in the centre of Amsterdam now boasts one of the world's largest botanical collections. Its range of flora expanded when tropical plants were brought back by the Dutch East India Company *(p54)*. In 1706, it became the first place outside Arabia to succeed in cultivating the coffee plant.

The medicinal herb garden has several species of plants that were available in the 17th century and are of great importance to medicine, such as *Acorus calamus*. The glass-domed Palm House, built in 1912, contains a collection of palms, conservatory plants and cycads, including one that is more than 400 years old. The restored orangery has a café and terrace, where art shows with a botanical theme are held.

A modern glass-and-aluminium construction, designed by Moshé Zwarts and Rein Jansma, was opened in 1993 to make room for the tropical, subtropical and desert plants. There is also a butterfly house, with many species flying around, and a shop where you can purchase plants and gardening tools.

EAT

Café Restaurant Plantage

Dine in the leafy courtyard.

J6 Plantage Kerklaan 36 caferestaurant deplantage.nl

Restaurant Stalpaert

Het Scheepvaart-museum's café offers snacks and soups.

K5 Kattenburger-plein 1 hetscheep vaartmuseum.com

Bloem Eten en Drinken

Organic dishes are served on Bloem's sunny waterside terrace.

K5 Entrepotdok 36 Mon bloem36.nl

→ Resistance posters and memorabilia on display in the Verzetsmuseum

INSIDER TIP
Oosterpark

L8

Tai Chi enthusiasts can join other practitioners every morning in the peaceful, uncrowded Oosterpark. Open-air lessons are free of charge and you can just turn up to take part. They take place next to the vintage bandstand. As well as the picturesque setting, Oosterpark has a large population of wild birds that add to the calming atmosphere; grey herons are the most visible, but you may also spot parrots.

Museum 't Kromhout

L6 Hoogte Kadijk 147 7, 14 22 9:30am-3:30pm Tue & 3rd Sun of month kromhout museum.nl

The Museum 't Kromhout is one of the oldest working shipyards in Amsterdam. Ships were built here as early as 1757. As ocean-going ships got bigger in the second half of the 19th century due to industrial developments, the yard, due to its small size, turned to building lighter craft for inland waterways. It is now used only for restoration and repair work. The museum is dedicated to the history of marine engineering, with engines, maritime photographs and a well-equipped, original forge.

Verzetsmuseum

J6 Plantage Kerklaan 61 14 10am-5pm Mon-Fri, 11am-5pm Sat, Sun & public hols 1 Jan, 27 Apr, 25 Dec verzets museum.org

Located in a building that used to be the home of a Jewish choral society, the Resistance Museum holds a fascinating collection of memorabilia recording the activities of Dutch Resistance workers in World War II. It focuses on the courage of the 25,000 people actively involved in the movement. On display are false documents, film clips, slide shows, photographs, weaponry, equipment and personal items belonging to the workers.

By 1945 there were over 300,000 people in hiding in the Netherlands, including Jews and anti-Nazi Dutch. Subsequent events organized by the Resistance, like the dockers' strike against the deportation of the Jews *(p55)*, are brought to life by exhibits showing where the refugees hid and how food was smuggled in. The museum includes a special children's wing, Verzetsmuseum Junior, in which the real-life wartime experiences of children are told. The story begins via a time machine that transports visitors back to the 1940s.

Entrepotdok

K6 14 22

The redevelopment of the old VOC *(p54)* warehouses at

Entrepotdok has revitalized this dockland area. It was the greatest warehouse area in Europe during the mid-19th century, being a customs-free zone for goods in transit. The quayside buildings of Entrepotdok are now a lively complex of offices, homes and eating places. Some of the original façades of the warehouses have been preserved, unlike the interiors, which have been opened up to provide an attractive inner courtyard. Café tables are often set out alongside the canal. On the other side, coloured houseboats are moored side by side, and herons doze at the water's edge.

Hermitage Amsterdam

H7 Amstel 51 4, 14 Waterlooplein City Hall 10am-5pm daily 27 Apr hermitage.nl

The State Hermitage Museum in St Petersburg, Russia, decided upon Amsterdam as the ideal city in which to open an international satellite branch, which would display rotating temporary exhibitions drawn from the Hermitage's rich and extensive collection.

The Hermitage Amsterdam opened in early 2004, in a side wing of the Amstelhof (a former old people's home), with a spectacular exhibition of fine Greek gold jewellery from the 6th to the 2nd centuries BC. Other exhibitions have included the collection of the last Tsars Nicholas and Alexandra, and the Portrait Gallery of the Golden Age. The Amstelhof building, which stands in a stunning position overlooking the Amstel river, has been fully restored.

The Hermitage Amsterdam has taken over the whole complex, with two exhibition wings, an auditorium and a children's wing where youngsters can discover their own creative talents.

There is also a lovely café-restaurant on the first floor where visitors can enjoy an invigorating cup of tea or coffee, a tasty lunch or a refreshing glass of wine.

STAY

Hotel Arena

With 139 rooms and suites, decorated in tones of grey and white, this hotel has views over Oosterpark and a pretty courtyard.

K8 's-Gravesandestraat 55 hotelarena.nl

Hotel Rembrandt

This small hotel in a 19th-century merchant's house has single, double and family-sized en-suite rooms. One has a copy of Rembrandt's *The Night Watch*.

J6 Plantage Middenlaan 17 hotelrembrandt.nl

↑ Portrait Gallery of the Golden Age, Hermitage Amsterdam

A SHORT WALK
PLANTAGE

Distance 2.5 km (1.5 miles) **Nearest tram** 9, 14 (Artis)
Time 25 minutes

With its wide, tree-lined streets and painted, sandstone buildings, the Plantage is a graceful and often overlooked part of the city. Though it seems like a quiet part of town, there is a lot to see and do, with a diverse range of popular attractions which can get very busy on sunny days. The area, which is dominated by the Artis complex, has a strong Jewish tradition, and several monuments commemorate Jewish history in Amsterdam, including a basalt memorial in the Hollandsche Schouwburg. The cafés of the Entrepotdok offer a pleasant setting for a relaxing coffee, within earshot of the zoo.

Entrepotdok was the largest warehouse development in Europe during the 19th century. It has been redeveloped and transformed into an attractive quayside housing, office and leisure complex (p172).

PLANTAGE PARKLAAN

START

Inspired by an Italian palazzo, *De Burcht was the headquarters of the Dutch Diamond Workers' Union.*

PLANTAGE KERKLAAN

FINISH

The old glasshouses at Hortus Botanicus Amsterdam have been restored, and a new one erected to hold tropical and desert plants (p171).

Moederhuis – Aldo van Eyck's refuge for pregnant women – has a colourful, modern façade intended to draw people inside.

Part of the Artis zoo complex, Micropia is the world's first museum dedicated to microbes and micro-organisms, with cutting-edge displays.

Little remains of the Hollandsche Schouwburg, a former theatre which is now a sombre monument to the deported Jews of World War II (p170).

The domed Planetarium explores man's relationship with the stars. Interactive displays show the positions of the planets.

← Greenhouse at Hortus Botanicus Amsterdam

Locator Map
For more detail see p164

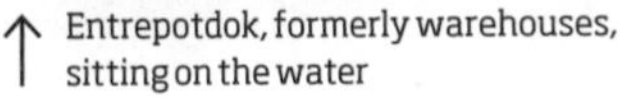
↑ Entrepotdok, formerly warehouses, sitting on the water

More than 900 species, including a pride of lions, live in the Artis zoo complex, which occupies a beautifully laid-out garden site.

Did You Know?

Artis is short for *Natura Artis Magistra*, a Latin phrase meaning "Nature is the teacher of art".

Artis restaurant

PLANTAGE MIDDENLAAN

The historic building that once stood here has been demolished and the new one is under construction.

0 metres 100
0 yards 100
N ↑

→ Lions prowling in their enclosure at Artis

The graphic exterior of EYE

NOORD

Shipbuilders seeking space to build steel-hulled vessels moved to the north shore of the IJ river in the early decades of the 20th century. In 1946, two of the largest naval engineering companies merged to create Nederlandsche Dok en Scheepsbouw Maatschappij (NDSM)– the world's biggest shipbuilding yard. Assembling cargo ships and giant tankers for oil companies, NDSM prospered until the recession of the 1970s, when demand for its ships vanished. The company went out of business in 1984, and, in the 1990s, artists squatted in the abandoned buildings. Made cool by this artistic occupation, the area north of the IJ attracted media and creative industries, including MTV Europe, and the former NDSM site is now the anchor of a district that is rapidly becoming an exciting new cultural hub. Nearby, the former Amsterdam headquarters of the Shell oil company – now known as A'DAM Toren – houses bars, restaurants and hotels with unparalleled views across the IJ.

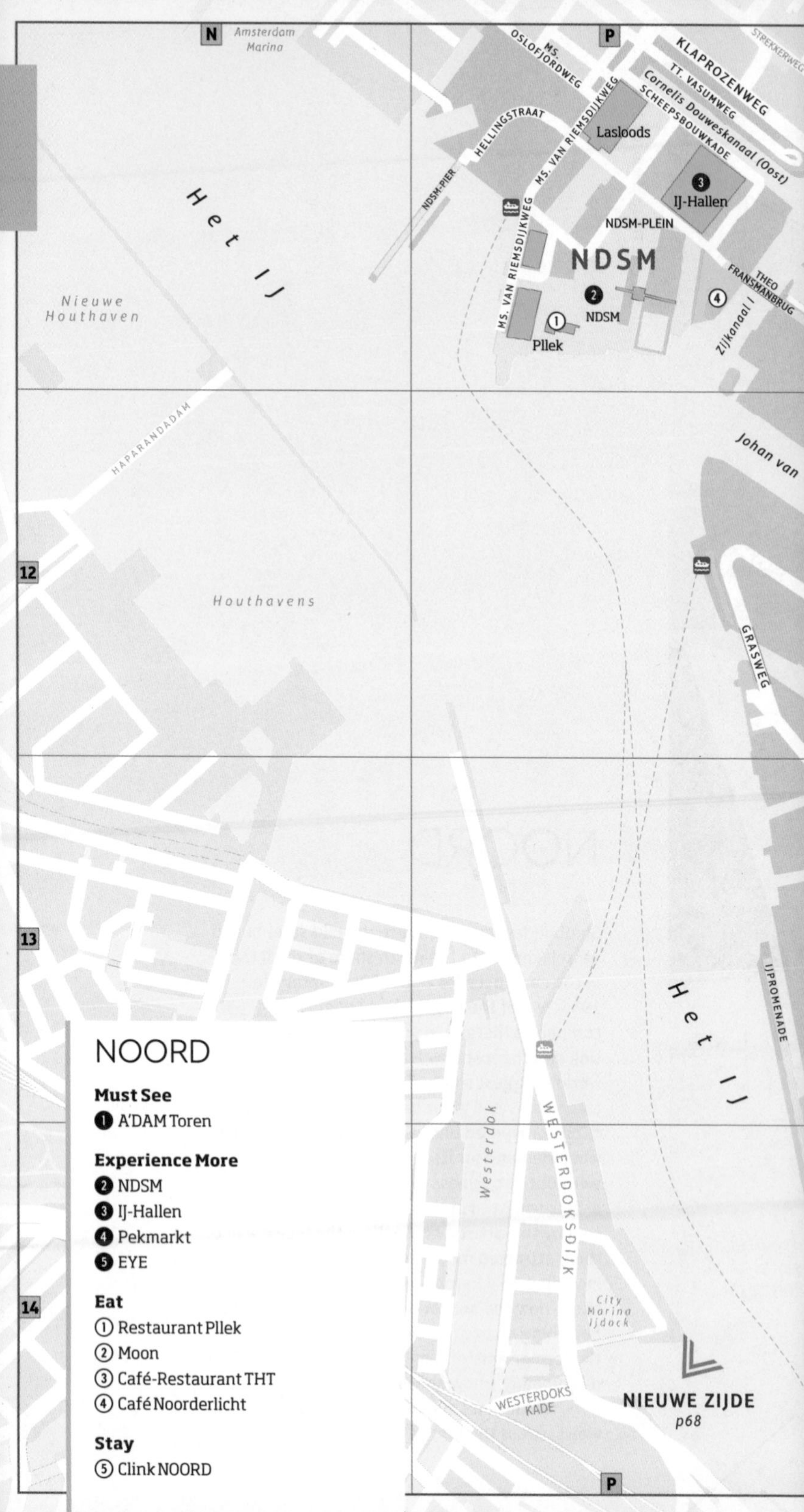

N
Amsterdam Marina
P
KLAPROZENWEG
STREKKERWEG
MS. OSLOFJORDWEG
TT. VASUMWEG
Cornelis Douweskanaal (Oost)
SCHEEPSBOUWKADE
Lasloods
HELLINGSTRAAT
MS. VAN RIEMSDIJKWEG
NDSM-PIER
IJ-Hallen
NDSM-PLEIN
NDSM
Het IJ
Nieuwe Houthaven
THEO FRANSMANBRUG
Zijkanaal I
Pllek
HAPARANDADAM
Johan van
12
Houthavens
GRASWEG
13
IJPROMENADE
Het IJ
WESTERDOKSDIJK
Westerdok
14
City Marina Ijdock
WESTERDOKSKADE
NIEUWE ZIJDE
p68
P
NOORD
Must See
1 A'DAM Toren
Experience More
2 NDSM
3 IJ-Hallen
4 Pekmarkt
5 EYE
Eat
① Restaurant Pllek
② Moon
③ Café-Restaurant THT
④ Café Noorderlicht
Stay
⑤ Clink NOORD

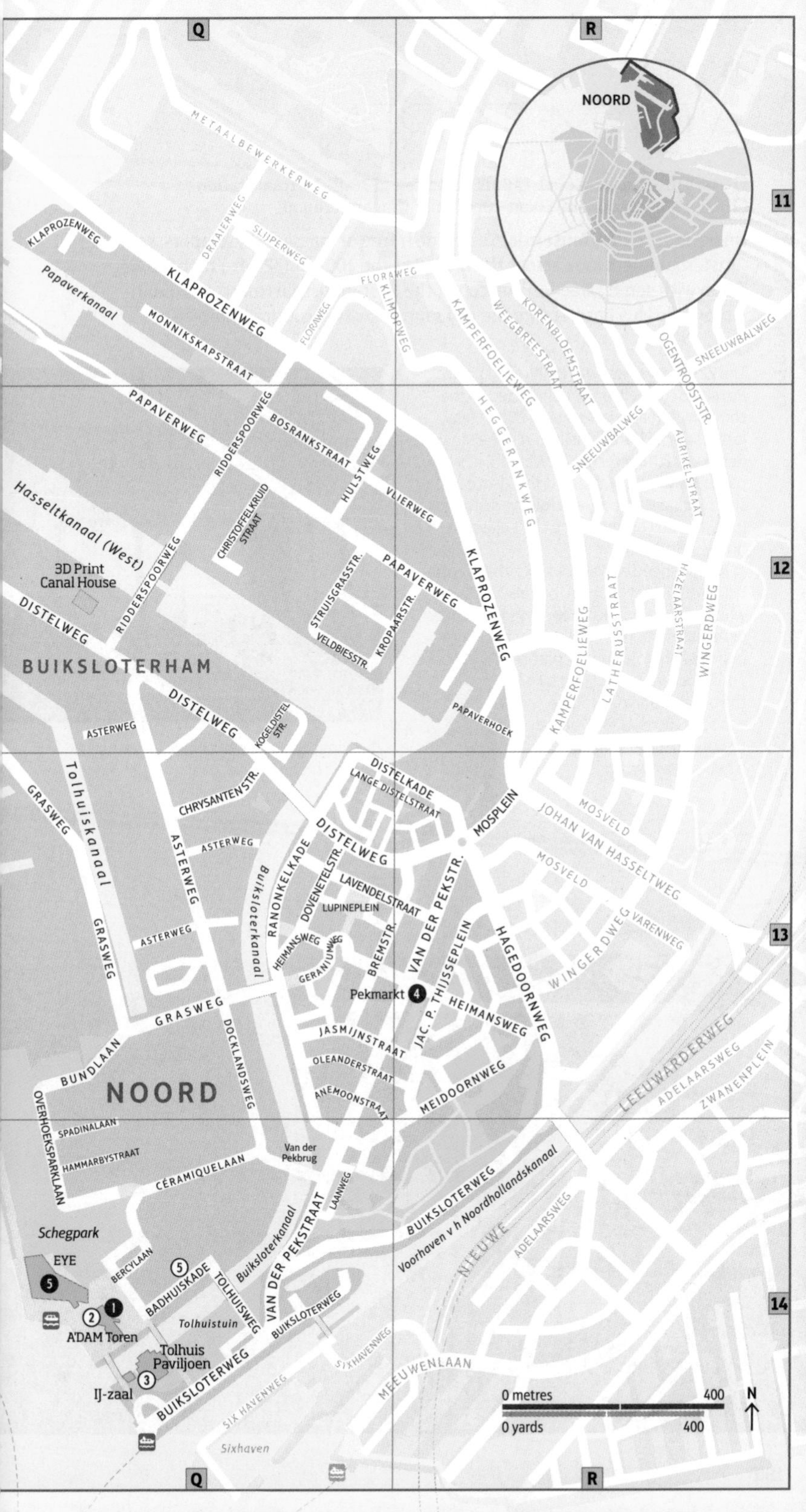

Q
R
NOORD
11
12
13
14
METAALBEWERKERWEG
DRAAIERWEG
SLIJPERWEG
KLAPROZENWEG
Papaverkanaal
MONNIKSKAPSTRAAT
FLORAWEG
KLIMOPWEG
KAMPERFOELIEWEG
WEEGBREESTRAAT
KORENBLOEMSTRAAT
OGENTROOSTSTR.
SNEEUWBALWEG
PAPAVERWEG
RIDDERSPOORWEG
BOSRANKSTRAAT
HULSTWEG
HEGGERANKWEG
AURIKELSTRAAT
VLIERWEG
Hasseltkanaal (West)
CHRISTOFFELKRUID STRAAT
3D Print Canal House
STRUISGRASSTR.
KROPAARSTR.
VELDBIESSTR.
HAZELAARSTRAAT
LATHERUSSTRAAT
WINGERDWEG
DISTELWEG
BUIKSLOTERHAM
PAPAVERHOEK
ASTERWEG
KOGELDISTEL STR.
Tolhuiskanaal
GRASWEG
CHRYSANTENSTR.
DISTELKADE
LANGE DISTELSTRAAT
MOSPLEIN
MOSVELD
JOHAN VAN HASSELTWEG
Buiksloterkanaal
RANONKELKADE
DOVENETELSTR.
LAVENDELSTRAAT
LUPINEPLEIN
VAN DER PEKSTR.
HAGEDOORNWEG
VARENWEG
HEIMANSWEG
GERANIUMWEG
BREMSTR.
JAC. P. THIJSSEPLEIN
Pekmarkt 4
JASMIJNSTRAAT
OLEANDERSTRAAT
ANEMOONSTRAAT
MEIDOORNWEG
LEEUWARDERWEG
ADELAARSWEG
ZWANENPLEIN
BUNDLAAN
DOCKLANDSWEG
OVERHOEKSPARKLAAN
SPADINALAAN
HAMMARBYSTRAAT
CÉRAMIQUELAAN
Van der Pekbrug
LAANWEG
BUIKSLOTERWEG
Voorhaven v h Noordhollandskanaal
NIEUWE
Schegpark
EYE
5
BERCYLAAN
BADHUISKADE
TOLHUISWEG
VAN DER PEKSTRAAT
1
2
A'DAM Toren
Tolhuistuin
Tolhuis Paviljoen
3
IJ-zaal
SIXHAVENWEG
MEEUWENLAAN
SIX HAVENWEG
Sixhaven
0 metres 400
0 yards 400
N

1

A'DAM TOREN

Q14 Overhoeksplein 1 Buiksloterweg 38 Centraal Station
Daily; A'DAM Lookout: 10am-10pm daily adamtoren.nl

Unlike most cities, Amsterdam's skyline is free of massive skyscrapers, so Amsterdammers look across the River IJ at the 100-m- (328-ft-) high A'DAM Toren with some affection. An icon of the post-industrial Noord, this multi-storey colossus has become the city's most exciting cultural complex.

The 22-storey tower was built for oil giant Royal Dutch Shell in 1971 and acted as the company's headquarters until 2009. Many locals still call it the "Shelltoren" (Shell tower). Reborn in 2016 after a massive refit, it is now packed with places to eat, drink, dance and shop, including Moon, a revolving restaurant *(p183)*, as well as one of the city's classiest hotels – Sir Adam.

A high-speed elevator whisks visitors with tickets to A'DAM Lookout, on the 21st floor, which offers an unbeatable 360-degree view of Amsterdam. This is the perfect vantage point for photographers, particularly at sunset. Thrill-seekers, unsatisfied by the observation deck alone, can soar 100 m (328 ft) above the city on "Over the Edge", a two-seater swing.

↑ Diners enjoying the views and food at Moon

TOP 5 A'DAM TOREN SPACES

A'DAM Lookout
Enjoy a cocktail at the rooftop bar or swing over the city.

Moon
This restaurant revolves to give diners unbeatable views of all angles of Amsterdam.

Sir Adam
A cool, boutique hotel, offering guests floor-to-ceiling windows, espresso machines and a pillow menu.

Shelter
Contemporary art and dance music make up the curated programme of events at this club.

Madam
This bar and eatery is on the 20th floor.

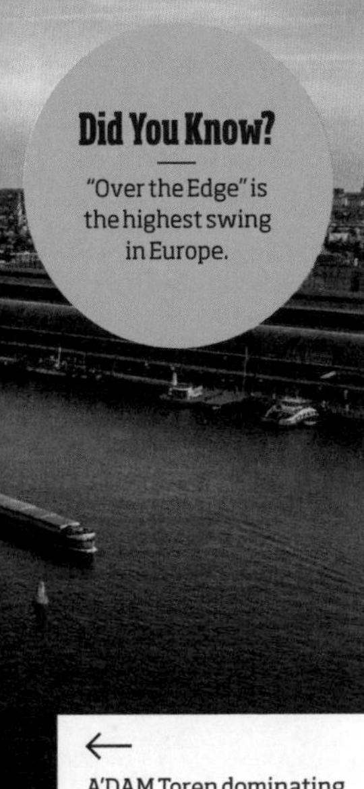

Did You Know?

"Over the Edge" is the highest swing in Europe.

← A'DAM Toren dominating the skyline of Noord and overlooking the River IJ

↑ Bicycles parked in front of repurposed shipping containers at NDSM

EXPERIENCE MORE

2   

NDSM

P11 Neveritaweg 61 ndsm.nl

The giant factory building at the heart of the former NDSM shipyard (on the banks of the River IJ) has become the core of Amsterdam's most vibrant cultural quarter. Some of the city's hottest young creative talents live and work here in spaces created from vintage shipping containers. Those wanting to find out about NDSM's history and future can take a guided tour of the complex and meet some of the "city nomads" who make this area buzz.

Crammed with quirky shops and craft studios, bars, cafés, restaurants and nightspots, the complex also attracts visitors with its festivals, dance events and exhibitions. It even has its own artificial beach – Pllek – where city slickers sunbathe, practise yoga and listen to live music. In the summer months, Sunscreenings takes over the beach for its packed open-air cinema season.

It seems appropriate that this colourful area became the home of the world's largest street-art museum in late 2019. Lasloods, NDSM's cavernous former welding hangar, has been transformed by specially commissioned works created by street-art superstars from around the world. Don't miss Brazilian Eduardo Kobra's huge mural of Anne Frank, *Let Me Be Myself* on the exterior of the building. The artist used 500 cans of spray paint and 40 litres of gloss to complete the 240-sq-m (2,583-sq-ft) work.

STAY

Clink NOORD
For the young, budget-conscious traveller, Clink offers friendly dorms. For those with more discerning tastes, it also has comfortable en-suite rooms.

Q14 Badhuiskade 3
clinkhostels.com

↑ All sorts of interesting items for sale at IJ-Hallen

IJ-Hallen

P11 TT Neveritaweg 15 NDSM Werf 9am-4:30pm 2nd weekend each month ijhallen.nl

For bargain hunters and shopping lovers this flea market is a must. Held in the cavernous IJ-Hallen, it is the largest in Europe. On a busy day, visitors might find as many as 750 stands at this colourful, bustling site. Traders peddle everything from collectable vinyl to vintage clothing from bygone decades. There are also plenty of stalls selling snacks and drinks. Arrive early to find the best stock, but those who arrive later may find the best bargains.

Between April and September the market is held outside, while for the rest of the year it moves indoors into the giant former warehouse building. Look out for the cool graffiti on the walls.

Pekmarkt

R13 Van der Pekstraat Buiksloterweg 11am-5pm Wed, Fri & Sat pekmarkt.nl

Three days a week, Van der Pekstraat comes alive as a farmers' market. Dozens of stalls sell all manner of goods, including craft cheeses, artisan breads and sizzling sausages.

For visitors, the best day to come is Saturday, when art,

REGENERATION OF THE NORTH

After the death of Noord's shipbuilding industry, factories and warehouses stood empty for years. Regeneration gathered pace in the 21st century. Media and creative industries have replaced metal-bashing businesses and the first metro link to the city centre opened in 2018.

A'DAM Toren, a symbol of the regeneration of Noord

vintage clothing and quirky fashion accessories are on sale alongside food and drink.

EYE

Q14 IJpromenade 1 Buiksloterweg Ticket office: 10am–10pm daily; exhibitions: 11am–5pm daily eyefilm.nl/en

Located on the northern bank of the River IJ, the EYE is a merger between the Filmmuseum, housed for almost 40 years in what is now VondelCS *(p132)*, and several other Dutch cinematic organizations. The museum's huge collection tells the story of the Netherlands film industry, from silent films at the end of the 19th century to advances in digital technology and 3D cinema today. There is also a wide display of movie memorabilia, including photographs, soundtracks, technical equipment and posters.

The museum has come a long way from its former 19th-century home in a park's pavilion. The EYE now occupies a sleek white building that, unsurprisingly, is designed to resemble a giant eye. Inside are four cinemas, an exhibition space and a café-restaurant, with a waterside terrace that offers stunning views across the harbour on sunny days.

In the basement, visitors can watch silent films from the museum's vast collection in specially-designed viewing capsules, with three-seater sofas. A room also plays a 360-degree projection of film clips. Entrance to the basement is included in the cost of a cinema or exhibition ticket.

The distinctive EYE building

EAT

Restaurant Pllek

In a space created from upcycled shipping containers and other salvaged materials, Pllek is a food-and-drink hot spot.

P11 TT Neveritaweg 59 pllek.nl

Moon

Perfect for a special occasion; the panorama in this revolving restaurant is spectacular. Menu treats include caviar and oysters.

Q14 Overhoeksplein 3 restaurantmoon.nl

Café-Restaurant THT

Check out this lively café-cum-bar in the summer.

Q14 Tolhuistuin, Tolhuisweg 3 tolhuistuin.nl

Café Noorderlicht

This greenhouse is warm even in winter, when patrons are sheltered from the weather. During the summer months, there's live music outside.

P11 NDSM Plein 102 noorderlichtcafe.nl

A windmill in a tulip field in Noord-Holland

BEYOND AMSTERDAM

Amsterdam is at the northern edge of a region known as the Randstad, the economic powerhouse of the Netherlands. Within easy reach of the capital are the ancient towns of Leiden and Utrecht, as well as Den Haag and Haarlem with their exceptional galleries and museums. The Randstad extends south as far as Rotterdam, a thriving modern city full of avant-garde architecture.

North of Amsterdam, the traditional fishing communities that once depended on the Zuiderzee, before it was closed off from the sea in 1932, have now turned to tourism for their income. Much of the land here was reclaimed from the sea over the last 300 years, and the fertile soil is farmed intensively. Spreading to the southwest, dazzling colours carpet the fields in spring, and the exquisite gardens at Keukenhof are the showcase of the Dutch bulb industry.

BEYOND AMSTERDAM
Must Sees
1 Zuiderzeemuseum
2 Haarlem
3 The Bulbfields
4 Leiden
5 Den Haag
6 Delft
7 Rotterdam
8 Utrecht
9 Paleis Het Loo
North Sea
NOORD-HOLLAND
ZUID-HOLLAND
Den Helder
De Kooy
Van Ewijcksluis
Callantsoog
't Zand
Schagen
Warmenhuizen
Opmeer
Bergen
Alkmaar
Heerhugowaard
Egmond aan Zee
Heiloo
Castricum
Middenbeemster
Heemskerk
Krommenie
Purmerend
Beverwijk
IJmuiden
Zaanstad
Santpoort
Landsmeer
HAARLEM
Zandvoort
Amsterdam
Badhoevedorp
THE BULBFIELDS
Amstelveen
Hoofddorp
Amsterdam Airport Schiphol
Hillegom
Abcoude
Lisse
Aalsmeer
Noordwijk aan Zee
Sassenheim
Uithoorn
Katwijk aan Zee
Kager Plassen
Roelofarendsveen
Mijdrecht
Rijnsburg
LEIDEN
Wassenaar
Alphen aan den Rijn
Scheveningen
Leidschendam
Woerden
Boskoop
Bodegraven
DEN HAAG
Voorburg
Zoetermeer
Rijswijk
Waddinxveen
Monster
Gouda
Pijnacker
Hoek van Holland
Naaldwijk
DELFT
Oudewater
Schoonhoven
Europoort
Maassluis
Rotterdam The Hague
Krimpen aan den IJssel
Lek
Schiedam
ROTTERDAM
Brielle
Ridderkerk
Spijkenisse
N242
N9
A9
A7
A10
N200
N201
A4
N208
A44
N44
N12
A12
A20
A13
A16
N15
A15
S
T
2
3
4

U
V
Woudsend
0 kilometres 10
0 miles 10
N
Den Oever
Koudum
Beam
1
Wieringerwerf
Middenmeer
Medemblik
West - Friesland
Bant
A7
A6
Espel
Blokzijl
N333
Enkhuizen
Emmeloord
N331
Wognum
N302
Hoogkarspel
1
ZUIDERZEEMUSEUM
Hoorn
N50
N302
Oosthuizen
Swifterbant
Kampen
Markermeer
Roggebotsluis
2
N247
Edam
Lelystad
Dronten
Volendam
Kerkbuurt
Biddinghuizen
Wezep
A6
Monnickendam
Marken
N302
Elburg
A50
A28
FLEVOLAND
Almere-Buiten
Almere
A6
Trekkersveld
Zuidelijk-Flevoland
Harderwijk
Epe
A1
Muiden
Weesp
N305
Vaassen
A50
Huizen
N301
A28
Bussum
Putten
3
Uddel
Hilversum
Bunschoten
N201
Nijkerk
N344
Nieuw-Loosdrecht
Baarn
A1
Apeldoorn
Voorthuizen
A27
PALEIS HET LOO
A1
Breukelen
Soest
9
Hoevelaken
UTRECHT
Amersfoort
GELDERLAND
Beekbergen
A2
Maarssen
Bilthoven
N237
A28
Barneveld
N312
Hoenderloo
A50
Soesterberg
N30
Vleuten
8
Lunteren
Otterlo
Zeist
N226
Scherpenzeel
UTRECHT
A12
Ede
Nieuwegein
N224
IJsselstein
Houten
Doorn
Veenendaal
A12
Bennekom
Velp
N225
Arnhem
Wijk bij Duurstede
Wageningen
Oosterbeek
Vianen
Elden
4
A2
Duiven
A27
A325
Tiel
Druten
U
V

GETTING TO KNOW BEYOND AMSTERDAM

Within an hour of Amsterdam lie bustling towns, grand palaces, quaint villages and dazzling bulbfields. Noord-Holland extends north of the city, along the North Sea, while to the south are the diverse sights of Zuid-Holland, and the provinces of Utrecht and Gelderland in the southeast.

PAGE 190

NOORD-HOLLAND

The fertile Noord-Holland peninsula is dotted with pretty fishing villages and historic towns. While away an afternoon exploring the museums of Haarlem – the commercial capital of the region – or promenading along the coast.

Best for
City and beach walks

Home to
Zuiderzee Museum, Haarlem

Experience
The Markermeer aboard a wooden barge

PAGE 196

ZUID-HOLLAND

This province is dominated by two contrasting cities: futuristic Rotterdam and stately Den Haag. Pretty towns like Leiden and Delft – home to the ubiquitous pottery – offer a change of pace. But the real jewels of the south are the spectacular bulbfields north of Leiden, which bloom into a kaleidoscope of colours in spring.

Best for
Sightseeing and floral displays

Home to
Blooming bulbfields, Leiden, Den Haag, Delft and Rotterdam

Experience
Amazing views from Rotterdam's Euromast

PAGE 216

UTRECHT

Founded in AD 47, Utrecht claims to be the oldest town in the Netherlands and dominates the region to which it gives its name. A spectacular Gothic spire towers over its historic centre, which is dotted with museums, medieval churches and historic buildings, like the 16th-century Catharijneconvent. But above all, Utrecht values its unique waterways: locals make the most of the 13th-century wharves, lined with cafés, restaurants and bars, and there are plans, even, to restore a motorway back into a canal.

Best for
Canal-side strolling

Home to
Museums and cathedral

Experience
A trip on the Orient Express with "Dream Journeys" at Nederlands Spoorwegmuseum, where a colourful cast of characters accompanies you on a "train ride" from Paris to Constantinople

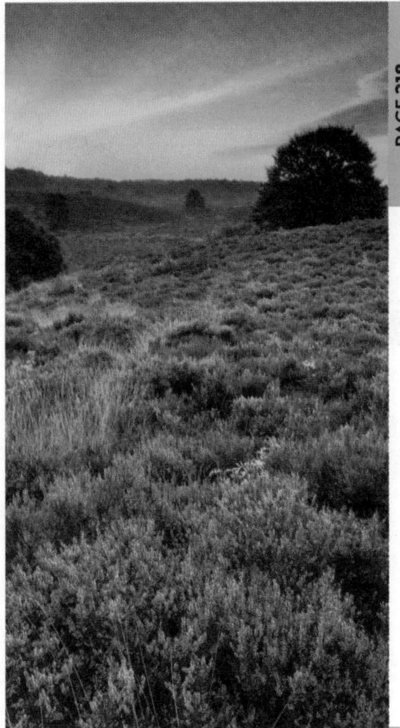

PAGE 218

GELDERLAND

For visitors whose senses have been bombarded by the sights, sounds and smells of Amsterdam, the wide open spaces of rural Gelderland offer a welcome breath of fresh air. This is a region of lush pastures and broad expanses of moor and woodland, where birdsong, the buzz of bees and the scent of wild flowers create a very different sensory experience from Amsterdam's urban hum. Drawn by this pastoral idyll, 17th- and 18th-century Dutch rulers endowed Gelderland with the magnificent palace that is this region's most iconic attraction.

Best for
Unspoiled countryside

Home to
Paleis Het Loo

Experience
A tour of the beautiful formal gardens of the Paleis Het Loo

ZUIDERZEEMUSEUM

U2 Wierdijk, Enkhuizen; 50 km (31 miles) NE of Amsterdam Enkhuizen Leaves from behind train station (Apr-Oct) Indoor museum: 10am-5pm daily; Open-air museum: 10am-5pm Apr-Oct zuiderzeemuseum.nl

Step back in time at this fascinating open-air museum which recreates daily life in a traditional fishing village on the Zuiderzee – a bay of the North Sea – in the early 20th century.

Enkhuizen was one of several villages around the edge of the Zuiderzee whose fishing-based economy was devastated when access to the North Sea was blocked by construction of the Afsluitdijk dam in 1932. The village's fortunes were revived with the opening of this museum complex. The *binnenmuseum* (indoor museum) focuses on the Zuiderzee history, including an impressive display of historic boats. The *buitenmuseum* (open-air museum) consists of rescued buildings, reconstructed to create a typical Zuiderzee village, with demonstrations of local crafts.

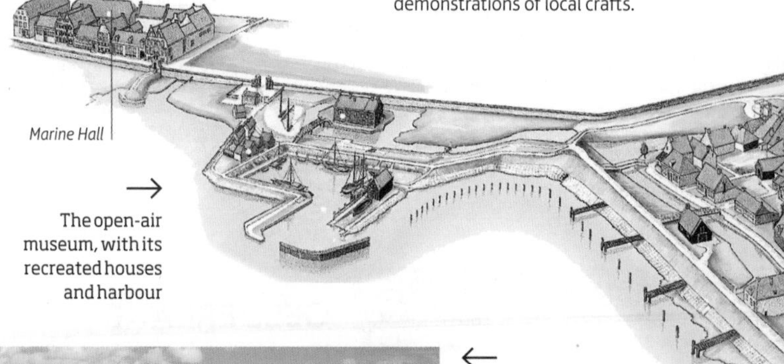

Marine Hall

→ The open-air museum, with its recreated houses and harbour

← Traditional houses, lime kilns and modern boats at the museum

Bottle-shaped lime kilns were used to burn shells to make quicklime.

Barges carry visitors to the open-air museum.

Did You Know?

Herring is preserved by being smoked over smouldering woodchips.

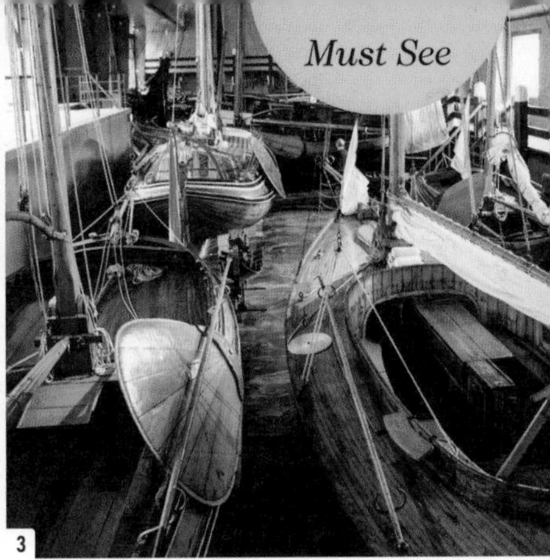

1 Modern Dutch culture is presented on Delft blue tiles at the Contemporary Delft installation by Hugo Kaagman.

2 At the houses from Urk, daily life on the island in 1905, including washing clothes, is recreated by actors.

3 Housed in an old warehouse of the Dutch East India Company, the Marine Hall contains sailing and fishing boats.

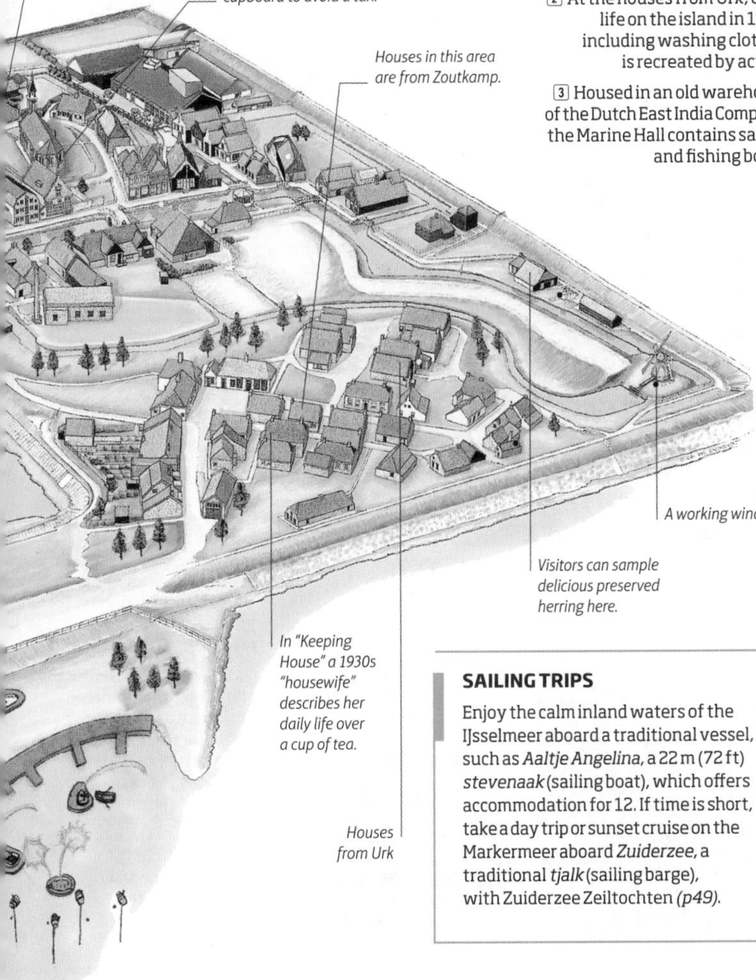

Contemporary Delft installation

The builders of this late 19th-century church disguised the organ in a cupboard to avoid a tax.

Houses in this area are from Zoutkamp.

A working windmill

Visitors can sample delicious preserved herring here.

In "Keeping House" a 1930s "housewife" describes her daily life over a cup of tea.

Houses from Urk

SAILING TRIPS

Enjoy the calm inland waters of the IJsselmeer aboard a traditional vessel, such as *Aaltje Angelina*, a 22 m (72 ft) *stevenaak* (sailing boat), which offers accommodation for 12. If time is short, take a day trip or sunset cruise on the Markermeer aboard *Zuiderzee*, a traditional *tjalk* (sailing barge), with Zuiderzee Zeiltochten *(p49)*.

2

HAARLEM

T3 20 km (12 miles) W of Amsterdam Haarlem
Grote Markt 2; www.haarlemmarketing.nl

A prosperous city in the Golden Age, Haarlem retains much of its 17th-century character, with its brick-paved lanes around the Grote Markt.

Haarlem had grown into a thriving cloth-making centre by the 15th century. Today, the city is the commercial capital of Noord Holland province. It is the centre of the Dutch printing, pharmaceutical and bulb-growing industries, but there is little sign of this in the delightful pedestrianized streets of the historic heart of the city. Most of the sites of interest are within easy walking distance of the Grote Markt, a lively square packed with old buildings, cafés and restaurants. Old bookshops, antique dealers and traditional food shops are all to be discovered in nearby streets.

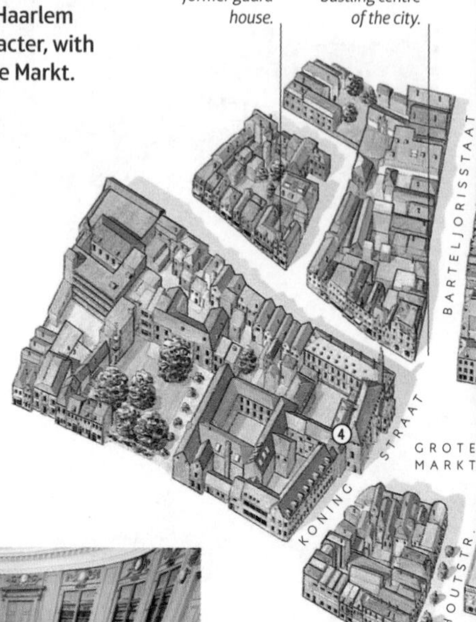

1 The Teylers Museum's two-storey Oval Hall was added in 1779, and contains glass cabinets full of bizarre minerals and cases of intimidating medical instruments.

2 The tree-lined Grote Markt square is bordered with busy pavement restaurants and cafés. It has been the meeting point for the townspeople for centuries.

3 An iconic Haarlem landmark, Molen De Adriaan - a windmill on the river Spaarne - makes for a beautiful photograph at sunset.

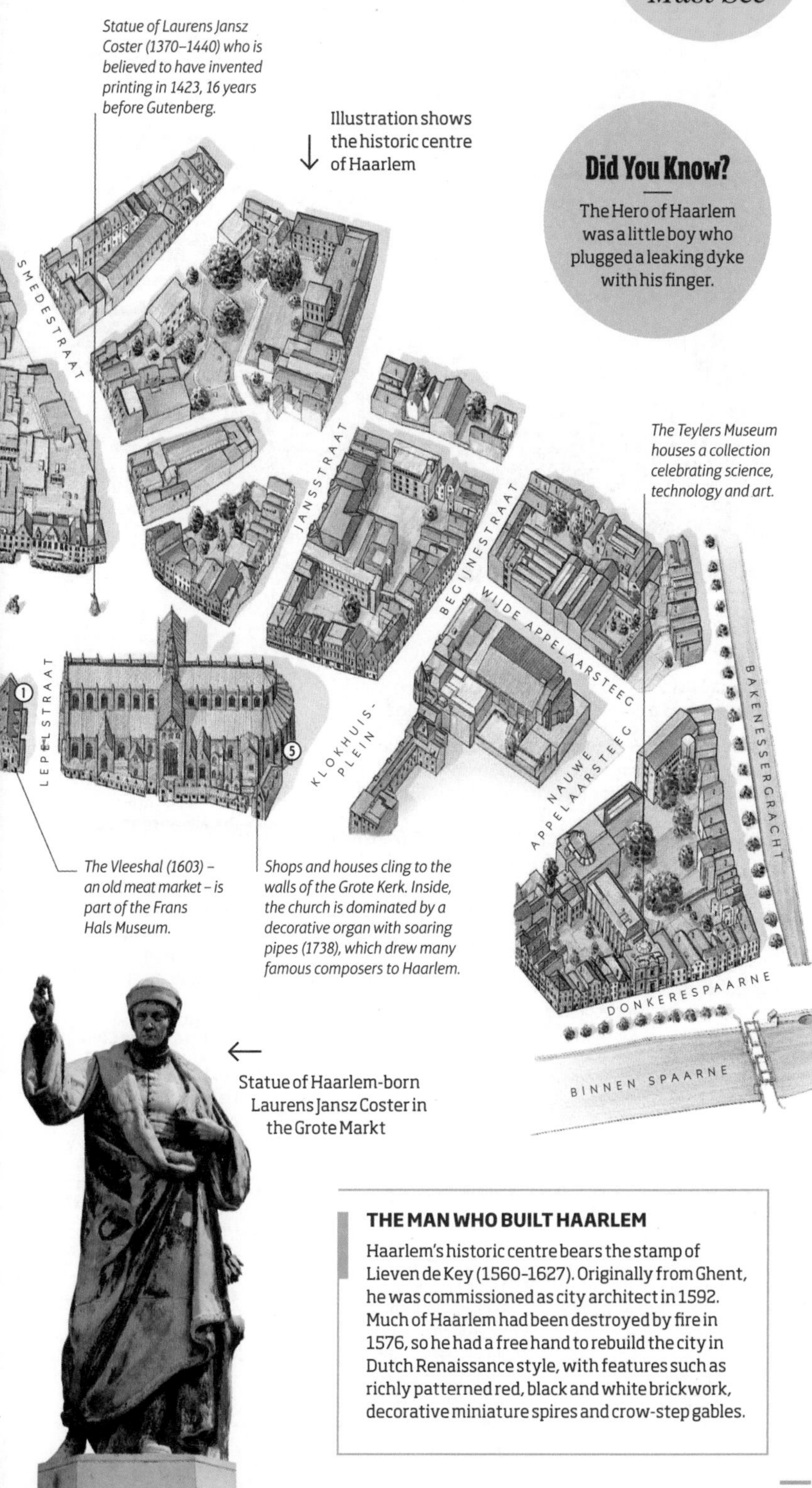

Statue of Laurens Jansz Coster (1370–1440) who is believed to have invented printing in 1423, 16 years before Gutenberg.

Illustration shows the historic centre of Haarlem

Did You Know?

The Hero of Haarlem was a little boy who plugged a leaking dyke with his finger.

The Teylers Museum houses a collection celebrating science, technology and art.

The Vleeshal (1603) – an old meat market – is part of the Frans Hals Museum.

Shops and houses cling to the walls of the Grote Kerk. Inside, the church is dominated by a decorative organ with soaring pipes (1738), which drew many famous composers to Haarlem.

Statue of Haarlem-born Laurens Jansz Coster in the Grote Markt

THE MAN WHO BUILT HAARLEM

Haarlem's historic centre bears the stamp of Lieven de Key (1560-1627). Originally from Ghent, he was commissioned as city architect in 1592. Much of Haarlem had been destroyed by fire in 1576, so he had a free hand to rebuild the city in Dutch Renaissance style, with features such as richly patterned red, black and white brickwork, decorative miniature spires and crow-step gables.

Frans Hals Museum Hal

Grote Markt 16 10am-6pm Tue-Sat; noon-5pm Sun & till 4pm public hols 1 Jan, 24, 25, 31 Dec franshalsmuseum.nl

The heavily ornamented Vleeshal (a meat market) was built in 1603 by the city surveyor, Lieven de Key, and has a steep step gable that disguises the roof line. The extravagantly over-decorated miniature gables above each dormer window bristle with pinnacles. A giant painted ox's head on the building's façade signifies its original function.

This hall, and the Verweyhal, a former gentlemen's club from the 19th century, are venues for exhibitions hosted by the Frans Hals Museum Hof.

The museum challenges contemporary artists to create work inspired by their collection of Golden Age art. The dialogue between the old and new works is surprising, with unexpected associations, as well as the expected differences between them.

②

Frans Hals Museum Hof

Groot Heiligland 62 10am-6pm Tue-Sat; noon-5pm Sun & till 4pm public hols 1 Jan, 24, 25, 31 Dec franshals museum.nl

Frans Hals (c 1582–1666) introduced a new realism into painting. While contemporary painters aimed for an exact likeness, Hals captured the character of his sitters through a more impressionistic technique. In his eighties, he still painted passionate portraits, such as *Governesses of the Old Men's Home* (1664). The Old Men's Home depicted in his painting became the Frans Hals Museum Hof in 1913.

There is also a selection of paintings from the 16th and 17th centuries by other Haarlem artists. Each room displays works by contemporary artists alongside the Old Masters to show interesting points of contrast. The museum will be renovated from the end of 2020; check the website for details.

TOP 5 THINGS TO SEE IN FRANS HALS MUSEUM HOF

Courtyard garden
Enjoy a quiet moment in the beautiful Renaissance garden.

Governors' Portraits
Notable works by Hals: *Governesses of the Old Men's Home* (1664) and *Governors of St Elisabeth Hospital* (1641).

Banquet of the Officers of the Civic Guard of St George (1616)
Hals' group portrait brings to life members of this militia company.

Portrait of Cornelia Claesdr Vooght (1631)
Hals' Baroque-style painting of the wife of Nicolaes van der Meer, sheriff and guard officer.

An Allegory on Tulip Mania (1640)
Satire on the tulip mania by Jan Brueghel II.

The Verweyhal, part of the Frans Hals Museum

③

Museum Haarlem

Groot Heiligland 47 Noon-5pm Mon & Sun, 11am-5pm Tue-Sat Public hols museumhaarlem.nl

St Elisabeth's Gasthuis was built in 1610, around a pretty courtyard. A stone plaque carved above the main doorway in 1612 depicts an invalid being carried off to hospital. After extensive restoration in the 1980s, this almshouse became Haarlem's principal historical museum.

Museum Haarlem focuses on the history of the city and its environs. Changing exhibitions connect the past with the present day.

④

Stadhuis

Grote Markt 2 14 023 11am-4pm Tue-Sat

Haarlem's Stadhuis (town hall) has grown rather haphazardly over the centuries and is an odd mixture of architectural styles dating from 1250. The oldest part of the building is the beamed medieval banqueting hall, originally known as the Gravenzaal. Much of this was destroyed in two great fires in 1347 and 1351, but the 15th-century portraits of the counts of Holland can still be seen.

The wing of the town hall bordering the Grote Markt was designed by Lieven de Key in 1622. It is typical of Dutch Renaissance architecture, with elaborate gables and Classical features.

In a niche above the main entrance is a plump allegorical figure of Justice, bearing a sword in one hand and scales in the other as she smiles benignly upon the pavement cafés in the market below.

A free exhibition on the history of the city is on display in the vaulted cellars.

⑤

Grote Kerk

Grote Markt 22 10am-5pm Mon-Sat (Jul & Aug: also noon-4pm Sun) Public hols bavo.nl

The enormous Gothic edifice of Sint Bavo's great church, often referred to simply as the Grote Kerk, was a favourite subject of the 17th-century Haarlem School artists Pieter Saenredam (1597–1665) and Gerrit Berckheyde (1638–98). Built between 1400 and 1550, the church and its ornate bell tower dominate the market square. The construction of a stone tower commenced in 1502, but the pillars started to subside. A new wooden tower, covered in lead, was erected in 1520.

The church has a high, delicately patterned, vaulted cedarwood ceiling, white upper walls and 28 supporting columns. The intricate choir screen, as well as the magnificent brass lectern in the shape of a preening eagle, was made by master metal worker Jan Fyerens in about 1510. The choirstalls (1512) are painted with coats of arms, and the armrests and misericords are carved with caricatures of animals and human heads. Not far away is the simple stone slab covering the grave of Haarlem's most famous artist, Frans Hals.

The Grote Kerk boasts one of Europe's finest and most flamboyant organs, built in 1738 by Christiaan Müller. In 1740 Handel tried the organ and pronounced it excellent. It also found favour with Mozart, who shouted for joy when he gave a recital on it in 1766. The organ is still in use for concerts.

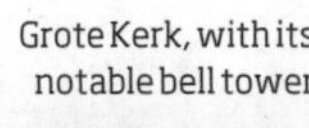

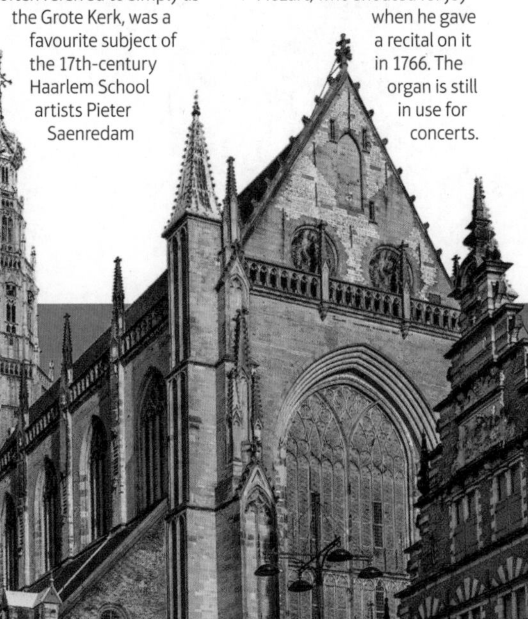

Grote Kerk, with its notable bell tower

Cycling through the endless tulip fields between Haarlem and Leiden ↑

THE BULBFIELDS

T3 Haarlem

Occupying a 30-km (19-mile) strip between Haarlem and Leiden, the Bloembollenstreek is the main bulb-growing area in the Netherlands. The most cultivated bulbs in the Netherlands include gladioli, lilies, daffodils, hyacinths, irises, crocuses and dahlias, but tulips are still far and away the country's most popular flower.

When to Go

From late January, the polders (land reclaimed from the sea) bloom with a series of vividly coloured bulbs, beginning with early crocuses and building to a climax around mid-April, when the tulips flower. Late-blooming flowers, such as lilies, extend the season into late May.

Aalsmeer

This town is home to the world's largest flower auction – the Bloemenveiling Royal FloraHolland. As the 12.5 billion cut flowers and pot plants sold here annually all have a short shelf life, speed is of the essence. A reverse auction is held. The price decreases as the big-screen auction clock counts down and buyers stop the clock at any price point. Visitors can watch the proceedings from a viewing gallery above the trading floor.

Keukenhof

Situated on the outskirts of Lisse, this garden was set up in 1949 as a showcase for Dutch bulb growers and is now planted with some 7 million bulbs. Keukenhof is at its most spectacular from late March to late May, when drifts of daffodils, hyacinths or tulips form. Japanese cherry trees shed snowy blossom early in the season, and there are splashes of azaleas and rhododendrons later in the year.

TOP 5

TOP FIVE DUTCH BULBS

Aladdin Tulips
A lily-shaped flower, which has red petals with yellow tips.

China Pink Tulips
Delicate stems are crowned with vibrant pink flowers.

Tahiti Daffodils
Double-formed, golden-yellow petals nestle in a small orange centre.

Minnow Daffodils
A fragrant, miniature daffodil with cream-coloured blooms.

Blue Jacket Hyacinths
Striped petals form a cone of blue flowers, with a heady scent.

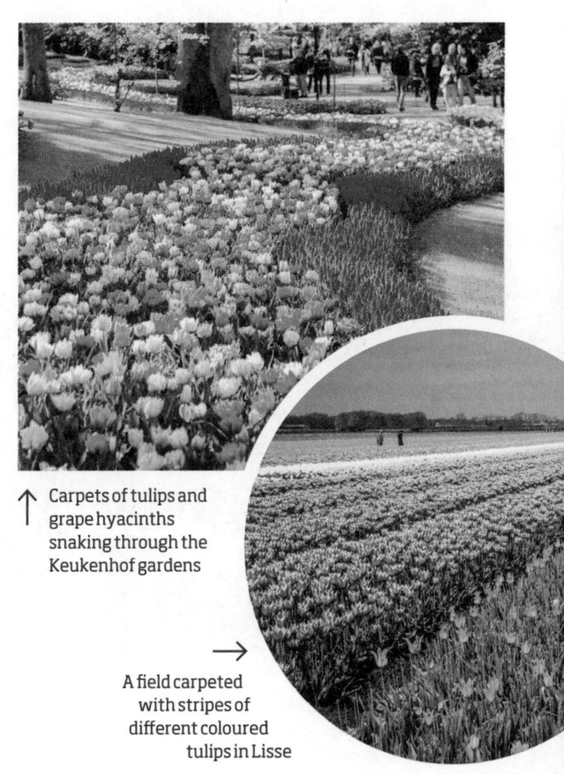

↑ Carpets of tulips and grape hyacinths snaking through the Keukenhof gardens

→ A field carpeted with stripes of different coloured tulips in Lisse

4

LEIDEN

T3 35 km (22 miles) SW of Amsterdam Leiden Centraal Stationsweg 41; www.visitleiden.nl

Leiden is famous for its university, the oldest and most prestigious in the Netherlands. During termtime, the streets are crowded with students cycling between lectures or packing the cafés and bookshops.

The university was founded in 1575 by William of Orange *(p53)*, a year after he relieved the town from a year-long siege by the Spanish. As a reward for their endurance, William offered the citizens of Leiden a choice: the building of a university or the abolition of tax. They chose wisely, and the city's reputation as a centre of intellectual and religious tolerance was firmly established. English Puritan dissidents, victims of persecution in their homeland, were able to settle here in the 17th century before undertaking their epic voyage to the New World.

A number of exceptional museums document Leiden's turbulent history, including the 17th-century Golden Age, when the town was a centre for world-wide trade. This age also saw the birth of the city's most famous son – Rembrandt – in June 1606. Look for the wall plaque on the façade of his birthplace on Weddesteeg.

↑ A café on one of Leiden's picturesque canals, which are lined with modern and 17th-century buildings

1

↑ ⑥ *Museum Volkenkunde (900m)*

Langebrug is lined with student accommodation.

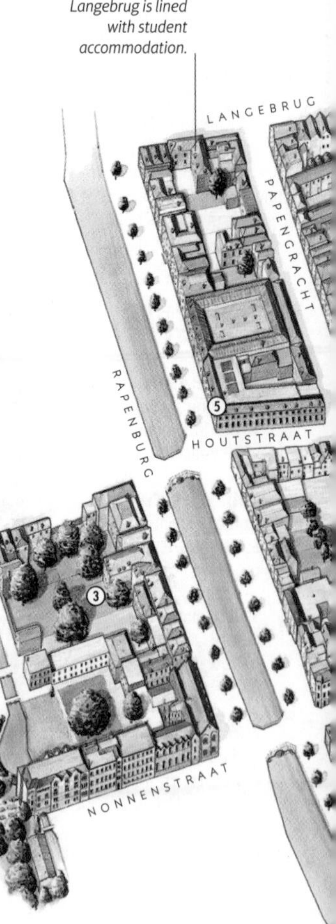

Illustration shows the area around Pieterskerk in Leiden ↑

1 The verdant Hortus Botanicus Leiden contains many beautiful features, such as this waterfall.

2 Artifacts from Ancient Greece are exhibited in the Rijksmuseum van Oudheden.

3 The Rijksmuseum Boerhaave runs a programme of exhibitions, including this one on windmills.

4 Pieterskerk has a dramatic interior, with beautiful vaulting.

↑ *(2) Museum de Lakenhal (750m)*

↑ *(1) Rijksmuseum Boerhaave (500m)*

The university's law faculty lies behind this Classical façade.

Pieterskerk dominates the centre of Leiden.

Hoogstraat is popular for its floating cafés and restaurants.

SCHOOLSTEEG

DIEFSTEEG

BREESTRAAT

MAARSMANSTRAAT

PIETERSKERKCHOORSTEEG

GERECHT

PIETERSKERKHOF

LANGEBRUG

(4)

Neo-Classical Korenbeursbrug

KLOKSTEEG

NIEUWSTEEG

ZONNEVELDSTRAAT

Pieterskerkhof is a cobbled lane with antiquarian bookshops.

John Robinson, pastor of the Pilgrim Fathers, lived in the Jan Pesijnshofje.

EAT

Grand Café van Buuren

Soups, salads and mighty sandwiches, with fillings such as pulled chicken and avocado, feature on the lunch menu here.

Stationsweg 7
grandcafevan buuren.nl

Crabbetje

This upscale seafood restaurant serves platters piled high with sole, lobster and oysters.

St Agatenstraat 5
visrestaurant crabbetje.nl

Rijksmuseum Boerhaave

Lange St Agnietenstraat 10 10am-5pm Tue-Sun & pub hols (daily during school hols) 1 Jan, 27 Apr, 3 Oct & 25 Dec museum boerhaave.nl

This museum is named after the great Dutch professor of medicine, botany and chemistry, Herman Boerhaave (1668–1738). Its collections reflect the development of mathematics, astronomy, physics, chemistry and medicine. Items range in time from a 15th-century astrolabe and surgical equipment of yesteryear to the electron microscope.

Museum De Lakenhal

Oude Singel 28-32 10am-5pm Tue-Fri, noon-5pm Sat & Sun lakenhal.nl

The Lakenhal (cloth hall) was the 17th-century headquarters of Leiden's cloth trade. Built in 1640 in Dutch Classical style by Arent van 's-Gravesande, it now houses the municipal museum.

One of the most famous works of art is Lucas van Leyden's Renaissance triptych of *The Last Judgment* (1526–7), which was rescued from the city's Pieterskerk during the religious struggles of 1566. A wing of the museum, which was built in the 1920s, offers an expansive silver collection, and exhibits covering the local weaving industry. Not to be missed is a big bronze *hutspot*, or cauldron, allegedly left behind by the Spanish when William of Orange broke the siege in 1574. At that time, the cauldron would have contained a wholesome spicy stew that the starving people ate. Traditionally this meal is cooked every year on 3 October, to commemorate Dutch victory over the Spanish *(p53)*.

Hortus Botanicus Leiden

Rapenburg 73 Apr-Oct: 10am-6pm daily; Nov-Mar: 10am-4pm Tue-Sun 3 Oct & 24 Dec-1 Jan hortusleiden.nl

Leiden's botanical garden was founded in 1590 as part of the university. Some of the varied trees and shrubs, including a 350-year-old laburnum, reflect the garden's history.

Today the Hortus Botanicus contains a modern reconstruction of his original walled garden, called the Clusiustuin. Other visual delights include hothouses full of exotic orchids, rose gardens and an exquisite Japanese garden.

Pieterskerk

Pieterskerkhof 1a 11am-6pm daily, unless special events are taking place; check website for details 3 Oct & 31 Dec pieterskerk.com

The magnificent Gothic church dedicated to St Peter was built in the 15th century in rose-pink brick, and stands in a leafy

→ Children looking down microscopes at the Rijksmuseum Boerhaave

→ Museum Volkenkunde, sitting on the river

GREAT VIEW
De Burcht

Sitting between two channels of the Rijn atop a grassy man-made mound, which is thought to be of Saxon origin, this citadel overlooks the town below. Climb this odd 12th-century fortress and peer over the crenelated battlements.

square surrounded by elegant houses. Pieterskerk was deconsecrated in 1971 and is now used as a community centre. The church is worth visiting for its austere interior and its magnificent organ, built by the Hagenbeer brothers in 1642 and enclosed in gilded woodwork. The floor of the nave is covered with worn slabs marking the burial places of 17th-century intellectuals like Puritan leader John Robinson and Golden Age artist Jan Steen. A long-term restoration project started in 2001 and discoveries made during this are displayed in the church.

Rijksmuseum van Oudheden

Rapenburg 28 10am-5pm Tue-Sun (daily during school hols) 1 Jan, 27 Apr, 3 Oct & 25 Dec rmo.nl

The Dutch museum of antiquities, established in 1818, is Leiden's main attraction. The centrepiece of the collection is the Egyptian Temple of Taffeh, reassembled in the main exhibition hall in 1978. It dates from the 1st century AD, and from the 4th century AD was dedicated to Isis, Egyptian goddess of fertility.

The museum's rich collection of Egyptian artifacts, which includes wonderful painted sarcophagi, occupies the first two floors. There are also impressive displays of musical instruments, textiles and shoes, expressive Etruscan bronze work and fragments of Roman mosaics and frescoes.

The presentation has been designed with children in mind, with interactive exhibits and multimedia reconstructions of daily life in ancient Egypt, Greece and Rome.

Museum Volkenkunde

Steenstraat 1 10am-5pm Tue-Sun (daily during school hols) 1 Jan, 27 Apr, 3 Oct & 25 Dec volkenkunde.nl

This outstanding ethnological museum, founded in 1837, houses collections from non-Western cultures. Individual displays are linked together to create a worldwide cultural journey that shows both the differences and connections between cultures. Temporary exhibitions include deep dives into different living conditions across the world, from the Arctic wastes to the hills of China, adding to this eclectic museum's wide appeal.

19

windmills stood on Leiden's walls, where breezes were stronger.

5

DEN HAAG

S4 56 km (35 miles) SW of Amsterdam Centraal Station, Koningin Julianaplein; Station Hollands Spoor (HS), Stationsplein Spui 68; noon-6pm Mon, 10am-6pm Tue-Fri, 10am-5pm Sat, noon-5pm Sun; www.denhaag.com

Den Haag ('s-Gravenhage or The Hague) became the political capital of the Netherlands in 1586 and is home to prestigious institutions such as the Dutch Parliament and International Court of Justice.

Binnenhof

Binnenhof 8a For guided tours only; book via website Sun & public hols prodemos.nl

The former castle of the counts of Holland is now home to the Dutch Parliament and the office of the prime minister of the Netherlands. Known as the Binnenhof, this complex of buildings sits beside the castle's former moat – the Hofvijver. In the centre of the courtyard stands the fairy-tale, double-turreted Gothic Ridderzaal (Hall of the Knights). This was the 13th-century dining hall of Floris V, Count of Holland (1254–96). Since 1904, the hall's function has been mostly ceremonial; it is used for the opening of the Dutch Parliament by the monarch (Prinsjesdag, the third Tuesday in September), and for other state occasions. It is open to visitors when parliament is not in session. Tours take in the Ridderzaal and the debating chambers.

Museum Bredius

Lange Vijverberg 14 11am-5pm Tue-Sun 1 Jan, 27 Apr, Easter & 25 Dec museumbredius.nl

Dr Abraham Bredius was an art historian and collector as well as director of the

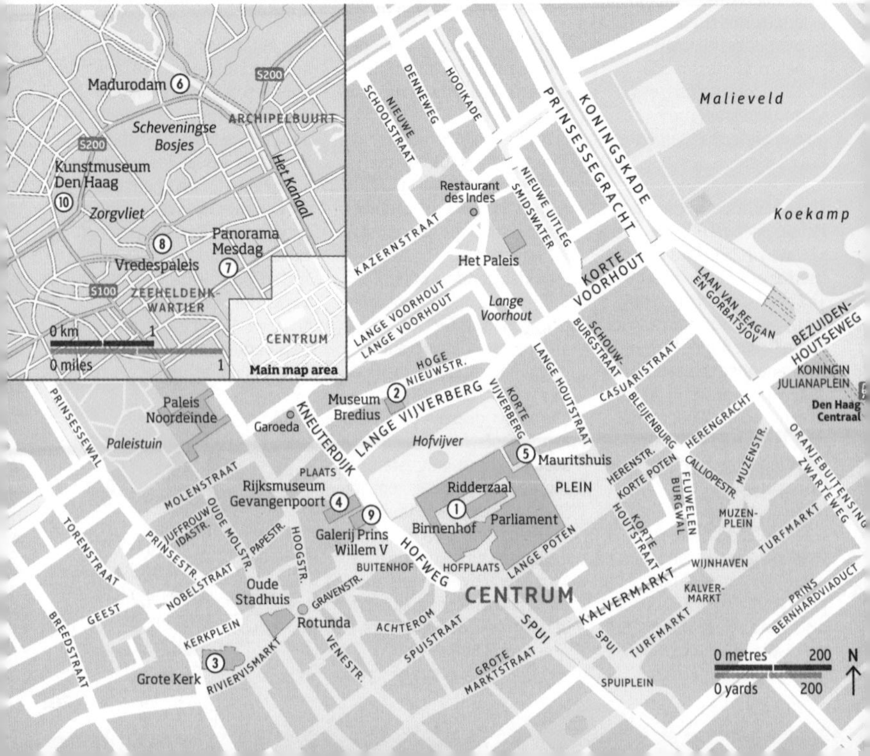

The grand Binnenhof, sitting on the tranquil waters of the Hofvijver lake

Mauritshuis *(p204)* from 1895 to 1922. On his death in 1946, he bequeathed his vast collection of 17th-century art to the city of Den Haag. This bequest is displayed in a distinguished 18th-century merchant's house on the north side of the Hofvijver lake, and features around 200 Golden Age paintings, including famous works by Dutch Masters such as Rembrandt and Jan Steen, as well as others by lesser-known artists.

The building itself has undergone considerable renovation and boasts a fine collection of antique furniture, delicate porcelain and elaborate silverware.

Grote Kerk

Rond de Grote Kerk 12 During summer months; check website for details grotekerkdenhaag.nl

In its present form, the Grote Kerk dates mainly from 1539, but major rebuilding between 1985 and 1987 has restored it to its former glory. Its most impressive feature is a stained-glass window which depicts Charles V, the Holy Roman Emperor *(p53)*, kneeling at the feet of the Virgin Mary.

Rijksmuseum Gevangenpoort

Buitenhof 33 For guided tours only Mon, 1 Jan, 24, 25 & 31 Dec gevangenpoort.nl

The Gevangenpoort (prison gate) was originally the main gateway to the 14th-century castle of the counts of Holland. Later, it was turned into a jail, becoming infamous during a period of violent social unrest in the late 17th century when burgomaster Cornelis de Witt was confined and tortured here. Both he and his brother Jan were subsequently tried for heresy, and torn limb from limb outside the prison gate by a rioting mob.

The gate is now a prison museum. The guided tour explores a unique collection of torture instruments, accompanied by a stereo soundtrack of blood-curdling screams.

The medieval gateway of the Rijksmuseum Gevangenpoort

A delicately carved marble statue in the Grote Kerk

Mauritshuis

Plein 29 1-6pm Mon, 10am-6pm Tue-Sun (to 8pm Thu) 1 Jan, 25 Dec mauritshuis.nl

The Count of Nassau, Johan Maurits, commissioned this graceful house while he was the governor of Brazil. It was completed in 1644 by local architects Pieter Post and Jacob van Campen in Dutch Classical style with influences from Italian Renaissance architecture, and enjoys wonderful views across the Hofvijver (lake). The mansion was bequeathed to the state after Maurits' death in 1679, and has been the home of the Royal Picture Gallery since 1822. The collection is small (laid out over only three floors), but almost every painting is a superb work by one of the Old Masters. This, combined with the exquisite presentation in elegant period rooms, with sparkling chandeliers and immense painted ceilings, makes the Mauritshuis one of the finest galleries in the Netherlands. One of the highlights of the Mauritshuis's collection is Rembrandt's representation of surgeons examining a corpse. This large-scale painting reflects the burgeoning contemporary interest in anatomy and science in the 17th century.

The arrangement of the paintings changes frequently in order to cover all aspects of the collection, so check the current display on the museum's website. Information sheets and an audio tour are available in English.

The Royal Dutch Shell Wing, an exhibition wing, which opened in 2014, is connected to the historic building by an innovative underground foyer, which also houses a brasserie and a museum shop, selling beautiful coffee-table books.

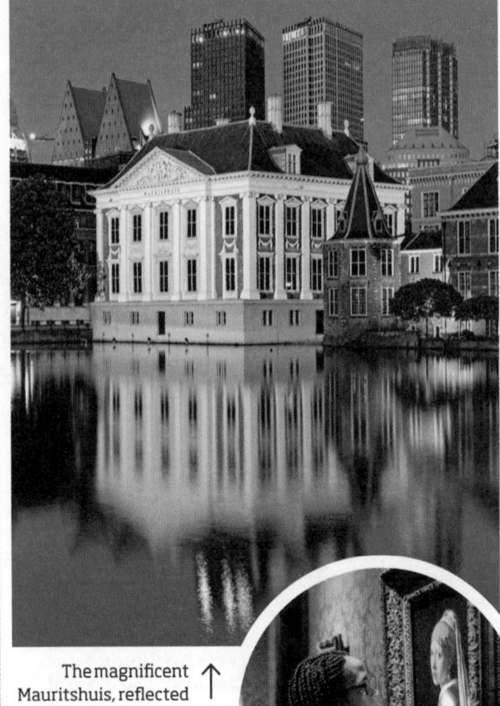

The magnificent Mauritshuis, reflected in the Hofvijver, home to Vermeer's *Girl with a Pearl Earring (right)*

TOP 5 PAINTINGS IN THE MAURITSHUIS

Girl with a Pearl Earring (1665-67)
Johannes Vermeer's most famous portrait.

The Anatomy Lesson of Dr Nicolaes Tulp (1632)
Rembrandt's painting of surgeons examining a corpse.

The Goldfinch (1654)
Tiny, delicate work by Carel Fabritius.

Hunting for Lice (c 1652-53)
Gerard ter Borch's scene of a mother grooming her child's hair.

Roses in a Glass Vase (c 1640-45)
Delicate still life by Jacob van Hulsdonck.

Madurodam

George Maduroplein 1 Daily, check website for details madurodam.nl

Madurodam is a 1:25 scale model of a composite Dutch city. It incorporates replicas of the Binnenhof in Den Haag, the canal houses of Amsterdam, Rotterdam's Europoort and Schiphol airport, along with windmills, polders and bulbfields. At night it is illuminated by tiny lights.

Did You Know?

Johan Maurits built the Mauritshuis with wealth gained from his slave-owning plantations in Dutch Brazil.

The model city was opened by Queen Juliana in 1952. It was conceived by J M L Maduro as a memorial to his son George, who died at Dachau concentration camp in 1945.

Panorama Mesdag

Zeestraat 65 10am-5pm Mon-Sat, 11am-5pm Sun 1 Jan, 25 Dec panorama-mesdag.com

This painted cyclorama is important both as a work of Dutch Impressionism and as a rare surviving example of 19th-century entertainment. The vast painting, the largest circular canvas in Europe, is 120 m (400 ft) in circumference and lines the inside wall of a circular, canopied pavilion. The optical illusion makes visitors feel that they are standing in the old fishing village of Scheveningen.

The astonishingly realistic effect of the painting is achieved through the brilliant use of perspective, enhanced by natural daylight from above. It was painted in 1881 by members of the Dutch Impressionist School, led by H W Mesdag (1831–1915) and his wife, Sientje (1834–1909). George Hendrik Breitner (1857–1923) later added a group of cavalry officers charging along the beach on horseback. Constructed specially for the painting, the building itself has been renovated and extended, creating more space for temporary exhibitions.

STAY

Hotel des Indes

Open since 1884, this grand hotel is redolent of the belle époque, filled with gilt mirrors and chandeliers.

Lange Voorhout 54-56 hoteldesindes thehague.com

Stadsvilla Hotel Mozaic

This small hotel offers stylishly decorated rooms in classic monochrome shades.

Laan Copes van Cattenbuch 38-40 mozaic.nl

→

Miniature buildings in a recreated city, Madurodam

EAT

Restaurant des Indes

The opulent restaurant of Den Haag's grandest hotel *(p205)* serves French-inspired, classically presented steak and seafood such as Dover sole.

Lange Voorhout 54-56
Sun & Mon
desindes.nl

€€€

Garoeda

This long-established restaurant, which opened in 1949, serves Indonesian meat, fish and vegetable dishes, including satay skewers and *rijsttafels* (small dishes served with rice).

Kneuterdijk 18A
garoeda.com

€€€

8

Vredespaleis

Carnegieplein 2
Visitors' centre: Tue-Sun **Public hols & when court is in session**
vredespaleis.nl

In 1899, Den Haag played host to the first international peace conference. This then led to the subsequent formation of the Permanent Court of Arbitration, which had the aim of maintaining world peace. To provide a suitably august home for the court, the Scottish-born philanthropist Andrew Carnegie (1835–1919) donated $1.5 million towards the building of the mock-Gothic Vredespaleis (peace palace), which was designed by French architect Louis Cordonnier.

The enormous palace was completed in 1913, and many of the member nations of the Court of Arbitration contributed to the interior's rich decoration. Today the Vredespaleis is the seat of the United Nations' International Court of Justice, which was formed in 1946 as successor to the Permanent Court of Arbitration. There is a visitors' centre but the building itself is open to the public only on a guided tour (check dates and book tickets via the website).

9

Galerij Prins Willem V

Buitenhof 33 **Noon-5pm Tue-Sun** **1 Jan, 25 Dec** **galerijprinswillemv.nl**

In his youth, Prince William V was a collector of Golden Age paintings. His collection was opened to the public in 1774, inside this former inn, which the prince had converted for use as his *kabinet* – the 18th-century Dutch word for an art gallery. The Galerij is the oldest art gallery in the Netherlands. The 18th-century fashion for

↑ Visitors observing the art at Galerij Prins Willem V

Vredespaleis, home to the International Court of Justice ↓

Admiring artworks in the Kunstmuseum Den Haag

covering every available inch of wall space with paintings has been retained, and so several pictures are hung high and close together. Many of Prince William's original purchases are still to be seen. Old Master paintings by Rembrandt, Jan Steen and Paulus Potter (1625–54) are included in a collection that consists principally of typically Dutch Golden Age landscapes, genre paintings *(p127)*, "conversation pieces" and recreations of important historical events.

10

Kunstmuseum Den Haag

Stadhouderslaan 41 10am-5pm Tue-Sun 25 Dec kunstmuseum.nll

This is one of the city's finest museums. The delightful building was the last work of H P Berlage, the father of the architectural movement known as the Amsterdam School *(p37)*. The museum was completed in 1935, a year after his death, and is built in sandy-coloured brick on two storeys round a central courtyard, with every room open to daylight.

The exhibits are displayed in three sections. Highlights of the superb applied arts section include antique delftware, Islamic and Oriental porcelain and the world's largest collection of paintings by Piet Mondriaan.

Costumes and musical instruments dating from the 15th to the 19th centuries are too fragile to be put on permanent display, but selected items are regularly exhibited.

The labyrinthine basement is the stage for the "Wonderkamers" (the Wonder Rooms), which hold quirky displays of artworks from all the collections, aimed especially at teenage visitors.

With as many as 35 temporary exhibitions each year, the Kunstmuseum has a constantly evolving scene. The extensive exhibition programme offers something for everyone – topics ranging from the role of the colour black in the history of fashion to Picasso's Cubist sculptures have all had their place in the museum's programme. Snaffle up a ticket online before you visit and learn about something interesting in depth.

INTERNATIONAL COURT OF JUSTICE

Den Haag is known the world over for being home to the International Court of Justice - the highest court of the United Nations. The court's 15 judges are elected for nine-year terms by the UN General Assembly and Security Council, and are tasked with settling legal disputes between states submitted by UN members. It's often confused with both the Court of Justice of the European Union, based in Luxembourg, and the European Court of Human Rights, in Strasbourg.

6

DELFT

S4 50 km (31 miles) SW of Amsterdam
Delft Kerkstraat 3; www.delft.nl

The charming town of Delft is known the world over for its blue-and-white pottery, but it is equally famous as the resting place of William of Orange (1533–84) and as the birthplace of artist Jan Vermeer (1632–75).

The origins of Delft date from 1075 and its prosperity was based on weaving and brewing. An explosion at the national arsenal destroyed much of the medieval town in October 1645 and the centre was rebuilt in the late 17th century. The sleepy old town has changed little since then – gabled Gothic and Renaissance houses still line the tree-shaded canals. Activity centres on the market square, bordered by the Stadhuis and Nieuwe Kerk. Visitors can dip into the scores of shops selling antiques and delftware.

INSIDER TIP
Delftware

Instead of buying the famed hand-painted porcelain in the expensive boutiques in the centre of the town, head to a local factory. Their shops are often reasonably priced and you can take a tour.

The centre of Delft, which is illustrated below, boasts two iconic churches

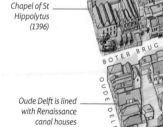

SCHOOLSTRAAT

ST AGATHA PLEIN

HIPPOLYTUSBUURT

OUDE DELFT

NIEUWSTRAAT

THE ASSASSINATION OF WILLIAM OF ORANGE

In 1581, Philip II declared William of Orange *(p53)* an outlaw and offered a reward of 25,000 crowns for his assassination. Balthasar Gérard masqueraded as a French nobleman and gained William's trust. On 10 July 1584, Gérard shot William at his home in Delft, which is now known as Stedelijk Museum Het Prinsenhof. Projected silhouettes here re-enact the assassination.

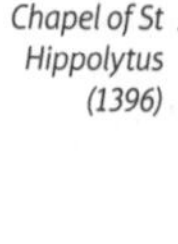

Chapel of St Hippolytus (1396)

BOTER BRUG

OUDE DELFT

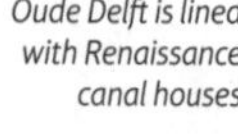

Oude Delft is lined with Renaissance canal houses

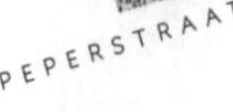

PEPERSTRAAT

↑ The magnificent organ in the white interior of the Oude Kerk, which contains the tombs of eminent Delft citizens

↑ The façade of the Vleeshal - the old meat market - with its animal heads, stands out from the other buildings nearby

Did You Know?

Vermeer's nickname is "The Sphinx of Delft" because so little is known of his life.

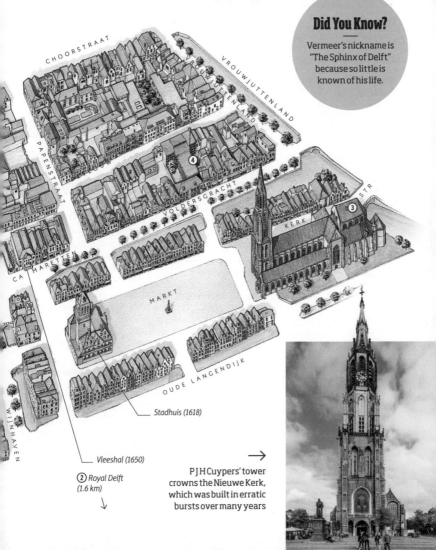

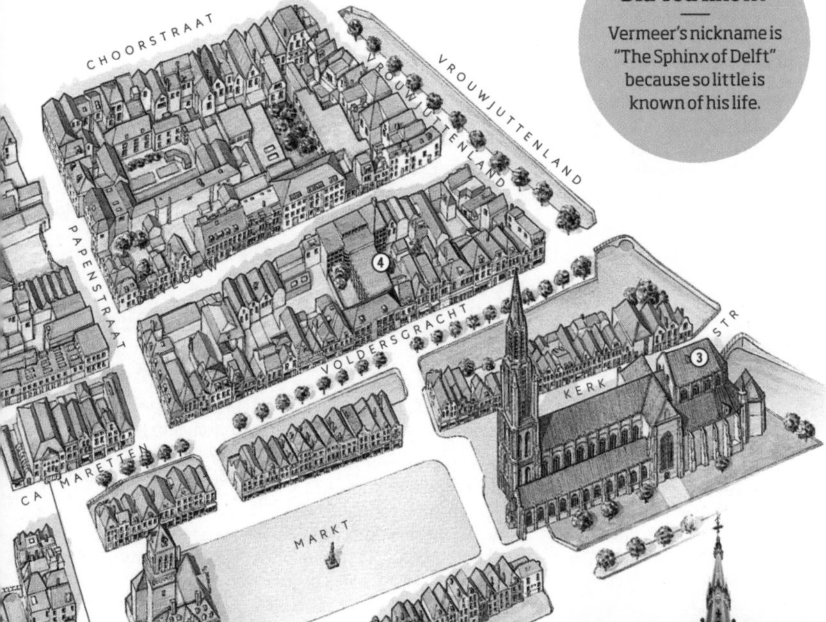

CHOORSTRAAT
VROUWJUTTENLAND
VROUWJUTTENLAND
PAPENSTRAAT
4
VOLDERSGRACHT
STR
3
KERK
CAMARETTEN
MARKT
OUDE LANGENDIJK
WIJNHAVEN

Stadhuis (1618)

Vleeshal (1650)

② Royal Delft (1.6 km) ↓

→ P J H Cuypers' tower crowns the Nieuwe Kerk, which was built in erratic bursts over many years

The Oude Kerk's bell tower, seen from one of Delft's many pretty canals

Oude Kerk

Heilige Geestkerkhof Apr-Oct: 9am-6pm Mon-Sat; Nov-Jan: 11am-4pm Mon-Fri, 10am-5pm Sat; Feb-Mar: 10am-5pm Mon-Sat onkd.nl

Although a church has existed on this site since the 11th century, the original building has been added to many times. The ornate, but leaning, clock tower was built in the 14th century, and the flamboyant Gothic north transept was added in the early 16th century. The interior is dominated by the carved wooden pulpit with overhanging canopy. The simple stone tablet at the east end of the north aisle marks the burial place of Johannes Vermeer. In the north transept lies Admiral Maarten Tromp (1598–1653), who defeated the English fleet in 1652.

Royal Delft

Koninklijke Porceleyne Fles, Rotterdamseweg 196 Apr-Oct: 9am-5pm daily; Nov-Mar: 9am-5pm Mon-Sat, noon-5pm Sun 25 & 26 Dec, 1 Jan royaldelft.com

There were once more than 30 delftware factories in this area. De Porceleyne Fles (established in 1653) is the only factory still producing the typical white pottery with delicate blue hand-painted decorations known as delftware. A visit includes a tour of the factory and the opportunity to watch the artists at work.

There is a small museum displaying pieces produced by the factory. Vermeer's dining room has been recreated, and the Royal Treasury shows the delftware especially designed for the Dutch royal family.

If you fancy trying your hand at creating your own decorative masterpiece, you can sign up for a workshop of earthenware painting with Delft Blue paint. The lunchroom serves afternoon tea (advance booking required), allowing you the chance to sip tea and nibble petits fours from fine Delft Blue crockery.

Nieuwe Kerk

Markt Apr-Oct: 9am-6pm Mon-Sat; Nov-Jan: 11am-4pm Mon-Fri, 10am-5pm Sat; Feb-Mar: 10am-5pm Mon-Sat onkd.nl

Standing in the market square opposite the city hall,

DELFTWARE

The blue-and-white tin-glazed pottery known as delftware was developed from majolica and introduced to the Netherlands by immigrant Italian potters in the 16th century. Settling around Delft and Haarlem, the potters made wall tiles, adopting Dutch motifs such as animals and flowers as decoration. Trade with the east brought samples of delicate Chinese porcelain to the Netherlands, and the market for coarser Dutch majolica crashed. By 1650, local potters had adopted the Chinese model and designed fine plates, vases and bowls decorated with Dutch landscapes, and biblical and genre scenes.

↑ Delftware porcelain clogs

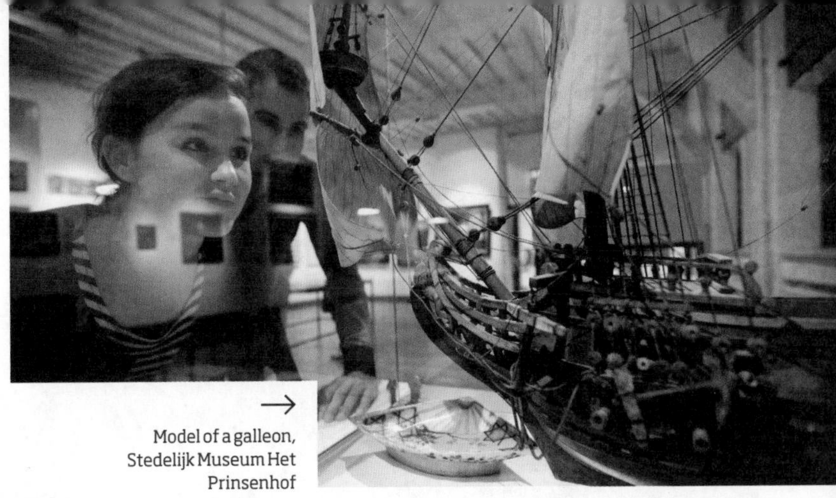

Model of a galleon, Stedelijk Museum Het Prinsenhof

the Nieuwe Kerk was built between 1383 and 1510, but much of the original structure was restored following a fire in 1536 and an explosion at the national arsenal in 1654. Work on the church continued for many years, and it was not until 1872 that P J H Cuypers *(p36)* added the statuesque 100-m (320-ft) tower to the Gothic façade. To climb the tower's 376 steps, buy a token from the church. The climb is quite strenuous but worth it for a great view across Delft and its surroundings. The tower also has a fine series of bells.

The burial vaults of the Dutch royal family are in the crypt of this empty, cavernous church, but the most prominent feature is the mausoleum of William of Orange *(p53)*. The richly decorated tomb was designed by Hendrick de Keyser *(p37)* in 1614 and is carved from black and white marble, with heavy gilded detailing. At its heart is a sculpture of William in his battle dress, and at each corner stand bronze figures representing the Virtues. Close to William is his dog, who died days after him, and at the foot of the tomb is a trumpeting angel – symbol of Fame. Due to ongoing restoration work, parts of the church may be screened off. It is best to check the church's website before visiting.

4  

Vermeer Centrum Delft

Voldersgracht 21
10am-5pm daily
vermeerdelft.nl

Little is known about the life of Delft's most famous and enigmatic artist, Johannes Vermeer (1632–75). In a series of beautiful displays, the Vermeer Centrum uncovers some of the mysteries surrounding this man.

Visitors are introduced to the artist and the city where he lived all his life. Life-size copies of all his paintings are on display, including *Girl with a Pearl Earring* (1665-67). On the upper floors, some of his painting techniques are explained, particularly his use of perspective, colour and light. Changing exhibitions focus on the symbolic messages in his paintings.

---

5   

Stedelijk Museum Het Prinsenhof

St Agathaplein 1 11am-5pm Tue-Sun (daily Mar-Aug) 1 Jan, 27 Apr, 25 Dec
prinsenhof-delft.nl

This tranquil Gothic building, formerly a convent, now houses Delft's historical museum but is better known as the place where William of Orange was assassinated.

He requisitioned the convent in 1572 for his headquarters during the Dutch Revolt. In 1584, by order of Philip II of Spain, William was shot by Balthasar Gérard. The bullet holes in the main staircase wall can still be seen.

The museum houses a rare collection of antique delftware, displayed alongside tapestries, silverware, medieval sculpture and a series of portraits of the Dutch royal family. The museum café has a terrace in the lovely garden.

EAT

Huszár

This lovely waterside brasserie occupies an artfully redesigned industrial space. The menu uses local organic produce. It's easy to imagine Vermeer sitting right here to paint his famous *View of Delft.*

Hooikade 13
huszar.nl

7

ROTTERDAM

T4 65 km (40 miles) SW of Amsterdam Rotterdam Centraal 6 km (4 miles) NW Rotterdam Centraal station and Coolsingel 114; www.rotterdam.info

Rotterdam's ancient heart was ravaged during World War II, due to its prominent port. Much of the city has been rebuilt in experimental styles, resulting in some of Europe's most original and innovative architecture.

EAT

Restaurant de Jong

Chef Jim de Jong's spectacular six-course menu uses local produce.

Nobelstraat 143
restaurantdejong.nl

1   

Maritiem Museum Rotterdam

Leuvehaven 1 10am-5pm Tue-Sat, also 11am-5pm Sun & Mon in Jul & Aug Public hols maritiem museum.nl

Rotterdam occupies a strategic maritime position. The city sits where the Rijn (Rhine), Europe's most important river, meets the North Sea and, as a result, has always been a centre for trade. Today, barges from Rotterdam transport goods deep into the continent, and ocean-going ships carry European exports around the world. Rotterdam is therefore a fitting city for a museum dedicated to the historic seafaring prowess of the Netherlands.

Prince Hendrik, brother of King William III, founded this museum in 1873. Highlights include the oldest model ship in Europe, a miniature version of one of Columbus's cargo ships. Also worth a visit is the museum harbour, where you can explore artfully restored barges and steamships.

Children will love the interactive Professor Splash area where they can play games while learning about ships and what it's like to work in a port.

Historic boats in the Maritiem Museum Rotterdam harbour

The striking tilting yellow cubes of the Kubuswoningen

② 

Kubuswoningen

Overblaak 70
10am-6pm daily
kubuswoning.nl

Much of Oudehaven, the old harbour area of Rotterdam, was bombed in World War II and it has largely been rebuilt in daring and avant-garde styles. The pencil-shaped apartment block, Blaaktoren, and the adjacent "cube houses", Kubuswoningen, were designed by architect Piet Blom (1934–99), and built in 1982–4. The structuralist buildings were designed to integrate with their surroundings, but also to encourage social interaction among its occupants.

The Kubuswoningen are extraordinary apartments, set on concrete stilts and tilted at a crazy angle. Each cube contains three floors. The lowest floor is a triangular living space, with its windows looking down on the street, while the second floor houses the bedrooms and has sky-facing windows. The top floor forms a three-sided pyramid, with 18 windows and 3 hatches, offering amazing views. Residents have specially designed furniture to fit the sloping rooms.

Wereldmuseum Rotterdam

Willemskade 25
10am-5pm Tue-Sun **Public hols**
wereldmuseum.nl

During the 17th century, the city fathers amassed a superb ethnological collection. The Wereldmuseum displays 1,800 artifacts from Indonesia, the Americas and Asia, and presents audiovisual displays of theatre, film, dance and music. The museum reflects 127 of the 170 different nationalities who live in Rotterdam. After exploring the collection, take a break in the café, which offers river views.

EUROPOORT HARBOUR CRUISES

The Europoort, which is the area on the south side of Rotterdam's harbour, stretches along the Rijn between the city and the North Sea. A cruise around this bustling part of the harbour is a rare opportunity to see some of the world's largest ships up close. Visitors who prefer to stay on dry land can see some of these steel behemoths loading and unloading right in the city centre at Spido *(www.spido.nl)*, where wharves and quays service around 32,000 container ships yearly.

④   

Euromast

Parkhaven 20 Apr-Sep: 9:30am-10pm daily; Oct-Mar: 10am-10pm daily euromast.nl

This futuristic structure enjoys sweeping views of Rotterdam. At a height of 100 m (328 ft), the lower section, which was built in 1960, has a viewing platform with a restaurant. In 1970 the Space Tower added another 85 m (279 ft) to the structure to make this the tallest construction in the Netherlands. An exterior "space cabin" ascends 58 m (190 ft) from the viewing platform.

EUROMAST ABSEILING

From May to September, adventurous visitors to Rotterdam can abseil down the 185-m (607-ft) Euromast. A high-speed lift zooms to the top in minutes, but the 100-m (328-ft) descent from the viewing platform takes around 15 minutes. Adrenaline junkies are accompanied by an instructor and must be over 16. The €55 ticket includes admission to the Euromast. See www.abseilen.nl for details.

⑤   

Kunsthal

Westzeedijk 341 10am-5pm Tue-Sat, 11am-5pm Sun & public hols 1 Jan, 27 Apr, 25 Dec kunsthal.nl

From costume and art to inventions and photography, the Kunsthal delivers exciting exhibitions that alternate between traditional "high art" and pop culture. There is no permanent collection.

The eye-catching building was designed in 1998 by Rotterdam's Rem Koolhaas, whose other works include the Beijing headquarters for China Central Television. His innovative use of materials, such as corrugated plastic, and an orange steel girder that sticks out over the edge of the roof draw attention.

Rotterdam's modern architecture, seen from the Euromast tower ↓

Nederlands Fotomuseum

Gebouw Las Palmas, Wilhelminakade 332
11am-5pm Tue-Sun
1 Jan, 27 Apr, 25 Dec
nederlandsfotomuseum.nl

In the heart of Rotterdam's former industrial area, the restored warehouse Las Palmas houses the Dutch Photography Museum, which is an impressive archive of images covering Dutch photographers. Fascinating and ever-changing exhibitions showcase treasures from the archives alongside works by foreign photographers, comparing and contrasting the examples. The large gallery space is very open. Prints are available at the museum shop.

Did You Know?

Covering 105 sq km (41 sq miles), Rotterdam is the biggest port in Europe.

Museum Boijmans Van Beuningen

Museumpark 18-20
11am-5pm Tue-Sun Public hols
boijmans.nl

The museum is named after two art connoisseurs, F J O Boijmans, who bequeathed his paintings to Rotterdam in 1847, and D G van Beuningen, whose heirs donated his collection to the state in 1958. The resulting collection is one of the Netherlands' finest.

First displayed in the nearby Schielandshuis, as the Museum Boijmans, the collection was moved to the present gallery at Museumpark in 1935. Known for its supreme series of Old Master paintings, the collection also covers the whole spectrum of art, including the medieval works of Jan van Eyck, rare glassware, Surrealist paintings and contemporary art.

The museum is vast and the displays change regularly. Signposting to the museum's main sections is clear, however, and attendants are adept at directing visitors. For Bruegel and Rembrandt follow signs to the Old Masters Collection, and for Dalí and Magritte look for the Art: 18th century–1945 section. From 2019 to 2023, the museum will close for renovation; check the website.

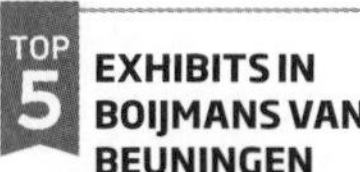

TOP 5 EXHIBITS IN BOIJMANS VAN BEUNINGEN

Tower of Babel (c 1556)
Pieter Bruegel depicts the building of the Old Testament skyscraper.

The Pedlar (c 1502)
Bosch's painting is an allegory of human temptation.

Titus at his Desk (1655)
Rembrandt's portrayal of his frail son.

Three Marys at the Tomb (c 1425-35)
Biblical scene by Jan and Hubertus van Eyck.

Projet pour la toile "Premier Amour" (1952)
Man Ray's jagged geometric abstract painting.

A boat passes a café on one of Utrecht's many canal-side wharfs

8

UTRECHT

U4 57 km (35 miles) SE of Amsterdam Hoog Catharijne Domplein 9; www.visit-utrecht.com

In Utrecht's city centre medieval churches and monasteries stand alongside modern blocks and a vast undercover shopping complex. The Oudegracht (old canal), lined with broad quays, cellar bars and cafés, threads its way through the city.

1 Domkerk

Achter de Dom 1 Daily domkerk.nl

Construction of the cathedral began in 1254. Today, only the north and south transepts, two chapels and the choir remain, along with the 15th-century cloisters and a chapterhouse (1495), which is now part of the university.

Outside the church is a giant boulder, dated 980 and covered with runic symbols. It was presented to Utrecht by the Danish people in 1936, to commemorate Denmark's early conversion to Christianity by missionaries from Utrecht.

The soaring 112-m- (367-ft-) high Domtoren has always stood apart from the cathedral.

2 Museum Catharijneconvent

Lange Nieuwstraat 38 10am-5pm Tue-Fri; from 11am Sat, Sun & public hols 1 Jan, 27 Apr catharijneconvent.nl

The beautiful former convent of St Catherine (1562) is now home to a fascinating museum dealing with the often troubled history of religion in the Netherlands.

On the upper floors, a series of model church interiors highlights the changes in religious philosophies through the ages. They range from the lavish statues and paintings in a Catholic church to the more austere, unadorned interiors typical of Protestant churches.

3 Museum Speelklok

Buurkerk on Steenweg 6 10am-5pm Tue-Sun (daily during school hols) 1 Jan, 27 Apr, 25 Dec museumspeelklok.nl

This magical place displays a collection of mechanical musical instruments, from the 18th century to the present day. Fairground organs compete with music boxes, clocks, carillons, pianolas and automated birds. These instruments are demonstrated on guided tours, during which visitors are encouraged to sing and dance along. The restoration of instruments can be observed in the workshop.

EAT

Meneer Smakers

Bright and friendly canal-side restaurant serving artisan burgers.

Nobelstraat 143
smakers.nl

→ A child hugging a Miffy mascot at the Nijntje Museum

④ 

Nederlands Spoorwegmuseum

Maliebaanstation
10am-5pm Tue-Sun & public hols (daily during school hols) 1 Jan, 27 Apr
spoorwegmuseum.nl

The headquarters of the Dutch railways is based in Utrecht, so it is fitting that the town has a superb railway museum.

Inside, there are modern rail accessories. Outside, visitors can explore steam engines, carriages, trams and signal boxes in five railway "worlds", each with its own theme.

Using costumed actors, the museum's "Dream Journeys" experience recreates a journey on the legendary Orient Express from Paris to Constantinople. It summons up the glamour and romance of the golden age of steam.

⑤  

Nijntje Museum

Agnietenstraat 2
10am-5pm Tue-Sun
1 Jan, 27 Apr, 25 Dec
nijntjemuseum.nl

Reserve your ticket online for the always popular Nijntje Museum. It is dedicated to the most famous *nijntje* (little rabbit) in the Netherlands – Miffy – and her creator, Dick Bruna (1927–2017).

Inside, younger kids can explore ten themed rooms inspired by characters from Bruna's many picture books, listen to story readings, or join a creative workshop. It's a playful learning experience that avoids being either too twee or commercialized.

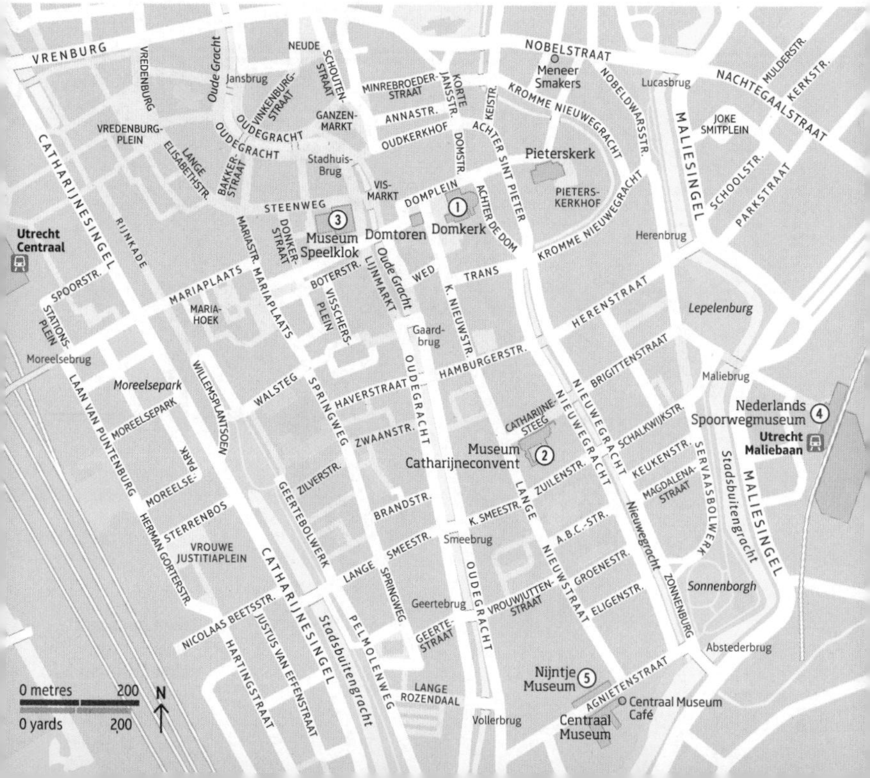

VRENBURG
VREDENBURG
Oude Gracht
Jansbrug
NEUDE
SCHOUTENSTRAAT
NOBELSTRAAT
Meneer Smakers
NOBELDWARSSTR.
Lucasbrug
NACHTEGAALSTRAAT
MULDERSTR.
KERKSTR.
VINKENBURGSTRAAT
MINREBROEDERSTRAAT
KORTE JANSSTR.
KEISTR.
KROMME NIEUWEGRACHT
MALIESINGEL
JOKE SMITPLEIN
VREDENBURGPLEIN
LANGE ELISABETHSTR.
OUDEGRACHT
GANZENMARKT
ANNASTR.
OUDKERKHOF
ACHTER SINT PIETER
Pieterskerk
SCHOOLSTR.
PARKSTRAAT
CATHARIJNESINGEL
BAKKERSTRAAT
Stadhuisbrug
DOMSTR.
VISMARKT
DOMPLEIN
PIETERSKERKHOF
STEENWEG
① Domkerk
ACHTER DE DOM
Herenbrug
Utrecht Centraal
RIJNKADE
③ Museum Speelklok
Domtoren
MARIASTR.
DONKERSTRAAT
SPOORSTR.
STATIONSPLEIN
MARIAPLAATS
MARIAHOEK
BOTERSTR.
VISSCHERSPLEIN
LIJNMARKT
WED
TRANS
K. NIEUWSTR.
HERENSTRAAT
Lepelenburg
Moreelsebrug
Gaardbrug
BRIGITTENSTRAAT
Moreelsepark
WILLEMSPLANTSOEN
WALSTEG
SPRINGWEG
HAVERSTRAAT
HAMBURGERSTR.
Maliebrug
LAAN VAN PUNTENBURG
MOREELSEPARK
ZWAANSTR.
CATHARIJNESTEEG
NIEUWEGRACHT
Nederlands Spoorwegmuseum ④
Utrecht Maliebaan
SCHALKWIJKSTR.
Museum Catharijneconvent ②
SERVAASBOLWERK
Stadsbuitengracht
ZILVERSTR.
GEERTEBOLWERK
ZUILENSTR.
KEUKENSTR.
MAGDALENASTRAAT
STERRENBOS
BRANDSTR.
K. SMEESTR.
LANGE NIEUWSTRAAT
A.B.C.-STR.
Nieuwegracht
VROUWE JUSTITIAPLEIN
HERMAN GORTERSTR.
LANGE SMEESTR.
Smeebrug
GROENESTR.
Sonnenborgh
ZONNENBURG
NICOLAAS BEETSSTR.
Geertebrug
VROUWJUTTENSTRAAT
ELIGENSTR.
HARTINGSTRAAT
JUSTUS VAN EFFENSTRAAT
PELMOLENWEG
GEERTESTRAAT
Abstederbrug
Nijntje Museum ⑤
AGNIETENSTRAAT
Centraal Museum Café
LANGE ROZENDAAL
Vollerbrug
Centraal Museum
0 metres 200
0 yards 200
N

9

PALEIS HET LOO

U3 85 km (53 miles) SE of Amsterdam; Koninklijk Park 1, Apeldoorn Apeldoorn, then bus 10, 102 Gardens & stables: Apr-Sep: 10am-5pm Tue-Sun; Palace: closed for renovation paleishetloo.nl

Regarded as the "Versailles of the Netherlands", the palace's Classical façade belies the opulence of its lavish interior. Don't miss the formal gardens and the collection of vintage cars in the stable.

King William III of England, Stadholder of the Netherlands, built Het Loo in 1686 as a royal hunting lodge. Generations of the House of Orange used the lodge as a summer palace. The main architect was Jacob Roman (1640–1716), but the interior decoration and layout of the gardens were the responsibility of Daniel Marot (1661–1752). After extensive restoration work in 1984, Paleis Het Loo opened as a museum. The palace is closed for renovation until mid-2021, but the gardens and stables remain open.

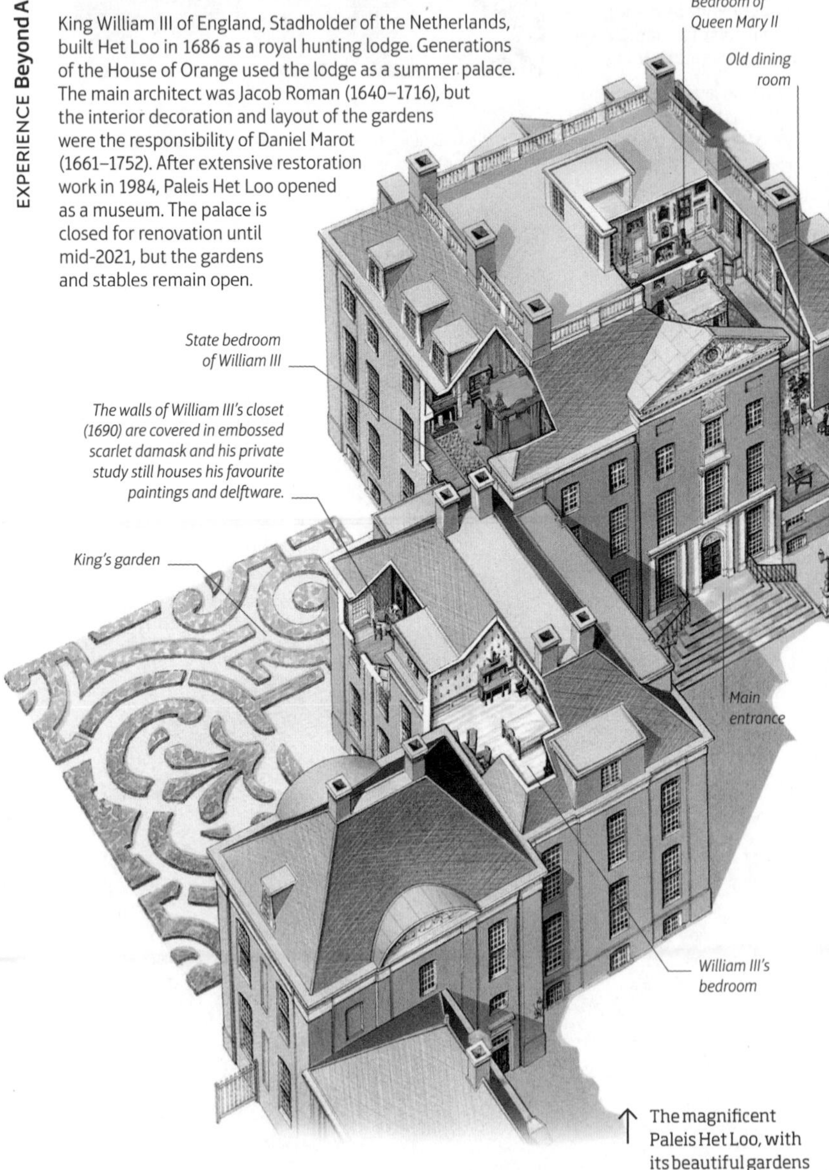

↑ The magnificent Paleis Het Loo, with its beautiful gardens

↑ The flag of the Netherlands flying above the Paleis Het Loo and its formal gardens

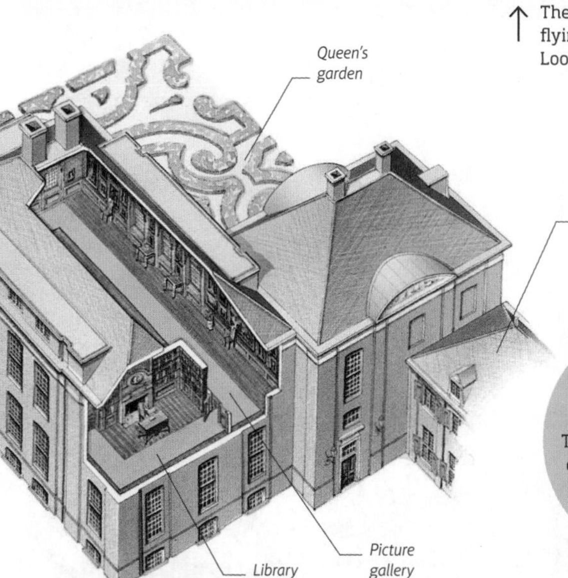
Queen's garden
The east wing houses the royal collections of clocks, dinner services and other household items.
Library
Picture gallery

Did You Know?

The palace hosts a classic car show - the Concours d'Élégance - every July.

1 The luxurious state bedroom of William III (c 1695) has ornate wall coverings and draperies made of rich crimson damask.

2 The gardens combine plants, statuary and fountains in Classical style to reflect the late 17th-century belief that art and nature should exist in harmony.

3 In 1984, six layers of paint were removed from the marbled walls of the old dining room (1686), now hung with tapestries depicting scenes from Ovid's poems.

NEED TO KNOW

Bikes on a bridge at sunrise

BEFORE YOU GO

Forward planning is essential to any successful trip. Be prepared for all eventualities by considering the following points before you travel.

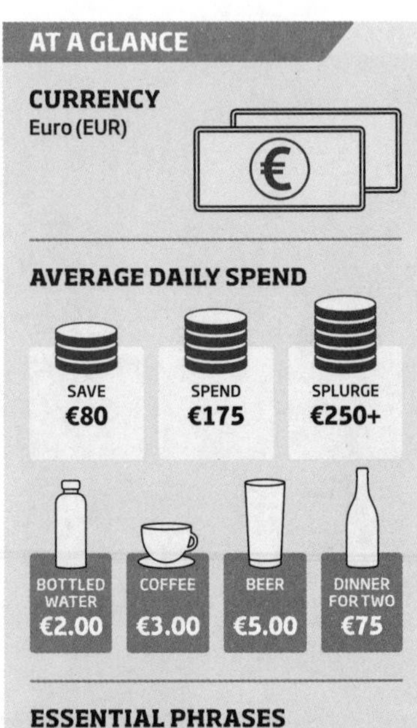

AT A GLANCE
CURRENCY
Euro (EUR)
AVERAGE DAILY SPEND
SAVE
€80
SPEND
€175
SPLURGE
€250+
BOTTLED WATER
€2.00
COFFEE
€3.00
BEER
€5.00
DINNER FOR TWO
€75

ESSENTIAL PHRASES

Hello	Hallo
Goodbye	Dag
Please	Alstublieft
Thank you	Dank u
I'm sorry	Sorry
I don't understand	Ik snap het niet

ELECTRICITY SUPPLY

Power sockets are type C and F, fitting two-pronged plugs. Standard voltage is 230 volts.

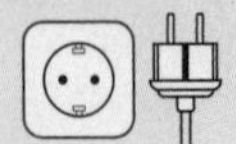

Passports and Visas

For stays of up to three months for the purpose of tourism, EU nationals and citizens of the UK, US, Canada, Australia and New Zealand do not need a visa. For visa information specific to your home country, consult your nearest Netherlands embassy or check online.

Netherlands and You
W netherlandsandyou.nl

Travel Safety Advice

Visitors can get up-to-date travel safety information from the **UK Foreign and Commonwealth Office**, the **US State Department** and the **Australian Department of Foreign Affairs and Trade**.

AUS
W smartraveller.gov.au
UK
W gov.uk/foreign-travel-advice
US
W travel.state.gov

Customs Information

An individual is permitted to carry the following within the EU for personal use:

Tobacco products 800 cigarettes, 400 cigarillos, 200 cigars or 1 kg of smoking tobacco.

Alcohol 10 litres of alcoholic beverages above 22% strength, 20 litres of alcoholic beverages below 22% strength, 90 litres of wine (60 litres of which can be sparkling wine) and 110 litres of beer.

Cash If you plan to enter or leave the EU with €10,000 or more in cash (or the equivalent in other currencies) you must declare it to the customs authorities.

If travelling outside the EU limits vary. It is always best to check the restrictions of your home country or next destination before your departure.

Plant and flower bulbs bought in Amsterdam must have a certificate of inspection from the Plant Protection Service if being taken to the USA or Canada.

Insurance

It is wise to take out an insurance policy covering theft, loss of belongings, medical problems, cancellation and delays.

EU and Australian citizens are eligible for discounted or free emergency medical care in the Netherlands. EU citizens should have an **EHIC** (European Health Insurance Card) and Australians should be registered to **Medicare**.

Visitors from outside these areas must arrange their own private medical insurance.

EHIC
W gov.uk/european-health-insurance-card
Medicare
W humanservices.gov.au/individuals/medicare

Vaccinations

No inoculations are needed for the Netherlands.

Money

Most establishments accept major credit, debit and prepaid currency cards, but it's always a good idea to carry some cash, just in case. Contactless payments are widely accepted.

Booking Accommodation

Amsterdam offers a huge variety of accommodation, comprising luxury five-star hotels, family-run B&Bs, budget hostels and even canal houseboat rentals. During peak season lodgings fill up and prices become inflated, so book in advance. A list of accommodation to suit all needs can be found on the **I amsterdam** website *(p229)*.

Travellers with Specific Needs

Despite its winding canals and cobbled streets, Amsterdam is a surprisingly accessible city.

Assistance at **Schiphol Airport** is available free of charge, but must be booked at the same time as your flight.

Accessible Travel Netherlands reviews the accessibility and user-friendliness of restaurants, shops, transport and public buildings in the city.

Main train stations have tactile guidance lines and mobile ramps, and a carer or companion can travel for free through the **NS Travel Assistance** service. Many trains have wheelchair access doors, and most double-decker trains have wheelchair-accessible toilets.

All main pedestrian crossings have sound alerts for the visually impaired.

Accessible Travel Netherlands
W accessibletravelnl.com
NS Travel Assistance
W ns.nl/en/travel-information/traveling-with-a-functional-disability
Schiphol
W schiphol.nl/en/page/extra-assistance

Language

The Dutch have an excellent level of English, some German, French and usually a few other languages too. In Amsterdam you can easily get by without knowing a word of Dutch, but it's appreciated if you can handle a few niceties in the local language. Asking a local if they speak English can be seen as an insult, the implication being that they are uneducated.

Closures

Mondays Some museums and tourist attractions are closed for the day.
Sundays Some shops close early.
Public holidays Schools, post offices, banks and some shops are closed for the entire day; many museums and attractions close early.

PUBLIC HOLIDAYS

1 Jan	New Year's Day
Mar/Apr	Good Friday
Mar/Apr	Easter Sunday
Mar/Apr	Easter Monday
27 Apr	King's Day
5 May	Liberation Day
May/Jun	Ascension Day
May/Jun	Whit Sunday
May/Jun	Whit Monday
25 Dec	Christmas Day
26 Dec	St Stephen's Day

GETTING AROUND

Amsterdam is known for its excellent public transport system. However, by far the most enjoyable way to explore this vibrant city is on two wheels.

AT A GLANCE

PUBLIC TRANSPORT COSTS

Tickets are valid on all forms of public transport in Amsterdam.

SINGLE

€3.20

Valid for 1 hour, transfers included

DAY PASS

€8.00

Unlimited travel, day or night

3-DAY PASS

€19.00

Unlimited travel, day or night

SPEED LIMIT

MOTORWAY	DUAL CARRIAGEWAYS
130 km/h (80 mph)	**100** km/h (60 mph)

NATIONAL ROADS	URBAN AREAS
80 km/h (50 mph)	**50** km/h (30 mph)

Arriving by Air

Amsterdam's Schiphol airport is a major international transport hub for destinations around the globe. Schiphol is extremely well connected to Amsterdam city centre by train, bus and taxi. Car rental facilities are also available, although driving in Amsterdam is not recommended *(p226)*. For journey times between the airport and city centre, see the table opposite.

Schiphol Travel Taxi is a shared taxi service that can be booked online as either a private or, for a lower fare, shared taxi. A shared fare starts at around €24 for a single trip, and €42 for a return. A shared taxi may take a longer time than expected, as it can make several stops before your destination.

Connexxion Schiphol Hotel Shuttle is a privately run minibus service that will transport you to and from your hotel. Rates vary depending on how far your hotel is from the airport. Discounts are available for group and family bookings.

Connexxion Schiphol Hotel Shuttle
W schipholhotelshuttle.nl
Schiphol Travel Taxi
W schipholtraveltaxi.nl

Train Travel

International Train Travel

Regular high-speed international trains connect Amsterdam's Centraal Station to other major cities across Europe. Reservations for these services are essential.

You can buy tickets and passes for multiple international journeys from **Eurail** or **Interrail**, however you may still need to pay an additional reservation fee depending on what rail service you travel with. Always check that your pass is valid on the service on which you wish to travel before boarding, as you may be fined for travelling without the correct ticket.

Eurostar runs a reliable and regular service from London to Amsterdam via the Channel Tunnel. However, for the return journey you may need to change in Brussels.

GETTING TO AND FROM SCHIPHOL AIRPORT

Transport	Journey time	Average fare
Bus (397)	30 mins	€3
Connexxion Schiphol Hotel Shuttle	from 30 mins	€17
Schiphol Travel Taxi	from 30 mins	€32
Taxi	from 30 mins	€40-60
Train (Sprinter or Intercity)	15-20 mins	€4.30

Thalys runs a high-speed rail service between Paris, Brussels and Amsterdam ten times a day. Look out for the variety of special offers, package deals and half-price last-minute deals that the company offers.

NS International also runs a high-speed service between Brussels, Antwerp, Breda, Rotterdam and Amsterdam.

Students and passengers under the age of 26 can benefit from discounted rail travel. For more information on youth fares visit the **Eurail** or **Interrail** website.

Eurail
W eurail.com
Eurostar
W eurostar.com
Interrail
W interrail.eu
NS International
W nshispeed.nl
Thalys
W thalys.com

Domestic Train Travel

Dutch railways are operated by Nederlandse Spoorwegen **(NS)**.

The NS Service Centre is located in the western hall of Centraal Station, and provides information on all rail journeys, including live updates and information on delays and changes in the schedule.

For venturing further afield, the NS offers a wide range of day trips to a variety of locations across the country. Tickets often include a lunch coupon and reduced entry to many Amsterdam museums and attractions.

Tickets can be bought online, or from the yellow machines at the front and back entrances of Centraal Station.

NS
W ns.nl/en

Public Transport

Centraal Station is the hub for Amsterdam's integrated public transport system **(GVB)**.

9292 provides information on all public transport within the city and the rest of the Netherlands, but it does not make reservations.

9292
W 9292.nl/en
GVB
W en.gvb.nl

Tickets

To travel on the metro, trams and buses you will need an OV-chipkaart. There are two kinds: a disposable card valid for either one hour or one to seven days, and a reloadable pass. Both can be bought and topped up at ticket vending machines at stations, GVB ticket offices, some supermarkets and newsagents operating as OV-chipkaart sales points. Avoid buying your OV-chipkaart at Centraal Station, where queues can be very long.

To validate a journey, hold the OV-chipkaart in front of the grey card readers on entering and leaving a metro or train station, or when getting on and off trams and buses. Don't forget to tap it as you disembark or exit – you will be charged more for your journey if you don't.

On all forms of transport, you will be charged the same distance fee, so no one form of transport is cheaper than another.

Children under 4 travel for free on all forms of public transport. Discounted personalized OV-chipkaarten for seniors and 4–11 year olds can be purchased at a GVB office.

Do bear in mind that Amsterdam's city centre is compact, and most of the major sights and shopping areas are within close walking distance from one another. You will save money and see more of the city on foot.

Buses

The majority of Amsterdam's buses depart from Centraal Station, branching out from the city centre with the same stops as the trams.

Bus 22 connects the centre to the eastern and western parts of the city. Take this bus to visit Jordaan and the Western Islands *(p152)*.

Night buses, numbered 281 to 293, run all night, with services every hour during the week and every half hour at weekends. Fares start at €4.50 per ride.

Long-Distance Bus Travel

Long-distance bus or coach travel can be a cheap option for travellers. **National Express** and **Flixbus** offer a variety of routes to Amsterdam from other European cities. Fares start from £22, with discounts for students and children.

Flixbus
W flixbus.co.uk
National Express
W nationalexpress.com

Trams

The most useful routes go south from Centraal Station along Damrak or Nieuwezijds Voorburgwal (2, 4, 11, 12, 13, 14, 17, 24), diverging after the Singel. Lines 13 and 17 are also useful if you need to travel west into Jordaan.

Trams operate from 6am on weekdays and 7am at weekends, finishing just after midnight, when night buses take over.

Metro

Amsterdam's underground system comprises five lines, three of which start from and terminate at Centraal Station. There are seven stations in the centre. From Amsterdam CS (Centraal Station) you either take the eastern line (51, 53, 54), stopping at Nieuwmarkt, Waterlooplein and Weesperplein, or you can hop on the Noord/Zuidlijn (52) to travel to Rokin, Vijzelgracht and De Pijp.

Taxis

Official taxis have a blue numberplate and display their registration number on the windscreen. They should always run a meter. Taxis are not hailed, but picked up at official taxi stands *(kwaliteitstaxistandplaatsen)* situated at main stations and squares or close to key tourist sights. Taxi apps such as Uber also operate in Amsterdam. The following services can be booked by phone or online:

Amsterdam Taxi Online
W amsterdamtaxi-online.com
Sneltaxi
W sneltaxi.nl
TCA Taxicentrale
W tcataxi.nl/en.html

Driving

Driving in Amsterdam is not recommended. Small inner-city streets, canals, parking shortages and complicated one-way systems all make Amsterdam ill-suited to getting around by car. Public transport is a much more efficient way of travelling around the city.

Driving to Amsterdam

The Netherlands is easily reached by car from most European countries via E-roads, the International European Road Network.

Major roads (N roads) and motorways (A roads) are well maintained. From the A10 ring road, the S-routes (marked by blue signs) will take you to the centre of Amsterdam.

To take your own car into the Netherlands, you will need proof of registration, valid insurance documents, a road safety certificate from the vehicle's country of origin and an international identification disc. Vehicles may also be transported into the country by international ferry or rail.

Car Rental

To rent a car in the Netherlands you must be 19 or over and have held a valid driver's licence for at least a year.

EU driving licences issued by any of the EU member states are valid throughout the European Union. If visiting from outside the EU, you may need to apply for an International Driving Permit (IDP). Check with your local automobile association before you travel.

Driving in Amsterdam

If you do decide to take to the roads in Amsterdam, it is important to be aware of the many one-way systems in place in the city centre. When driving in the canal area, remember that the water should be to your left.

Park-and-ride facilities, available on the outskirts of the city, are much cheaper and less stressful than parking in the city centre.

The **ANWB** (the Royal Dutch Touring Club) provides a breakdown service for members of foreign motoring organizations. A non-member can pay for the ANWB's services, or become a temporary ANWB member for the duration of their stay.

ANWB
W anwb.nl

Rules of the Road

Drive on the right. Unless otherwise signposted, vehicles coming from the right have right of way. Passing or turning is forbidden on roads with a continuous white line.

At all times, drivers must carry a valid driver's licence, registration and insurance documents.

The wearing of seat belts is compulsory, and the use of a mobile phone while driving is prohibited, with the exception of a hands-free system. Headlights should be dipped in built-up areas. It is prohibited to use sidelights only.

The Dutch strictly enforce speed limits *(p224)* on their roads, and use traffic enforcement cameras in urban areas and radar guns on national roads and motorways. The Netherlands strictly enforces its drink-drive limit *(p229)*.

Cycling

By far the best way to get around Amsterdam is by bicycle *(p44)*. The city's traffic system favours cyclists. There is also an excellent network of cycle lanes *(fietspaden)*, dedicated traffic lights and road signs, as well as special routes linking up different parts of the city. There are many bike parking facilities conveniently placed around the city, usually near main stations and busy squares.

Bicycle theft in Amsterdam is rife. Always secure your bike even when parking for just a few minutes to deter potential bike thieves. Hire shops are happy to advise on security matters, and a bike lock will normally be included in the rental price.

Bicycle Hire

Rental costs start at around €10 per day for a basic, single-gear, back-pedal brake bike. Since Amsterdam is so flat, gears are not essential. Bikes with gears and other add-ons will be more expensive.

Deposits are usually paid upfront and refunded on return. You may have to leave your passport or ID for the duration of the rental.

MacBike and **Orange Bike** offer optional extras such as children's seats, paniers, saddlebags and rain gear.

MacBike
W macbike.nl
Orange Bike
W orange-bike.nl

Bicycle Safety

Ride on the right. If you are unsure or unsteady, practise in one of the inner city parks first.

If in doubt, dismount: many novices cross busy junctions on foot; if you do so, switch to the pedestrian section of the crossing. Beware of tram tracks; cross them at an angle to avoid getting stuck.

Do not walk with your bike in a bike lane or cycle on pavements, on the left side of the road, in pedestrian zones, or at night without lights. If caught doing so you will face a hefty fine. The locals usually don't bother, but it is a wise precaution to wear a helmet, particularly if you are planning on cycling on the roads.

Bicycle Tours

Guided bicycle tours are a popular way to discover the city and its environs. The following offer popular city and countryside tours:

Joy Ride Tours
W joyridetours.nl
Mikes Bike Tours
W mikesbiketoursamsterdam.com
Yellowbike Tours and Rental
W yellowbike.nl

Boats and Ferries

The Dutchflyer is a rail and sail service that runs from London to Amsterdam via Harwich and the Hook of Holland.

P&O Ferries operates an overnight service from Hull to Zeebrugge or Rotterdam where you can transfer to Amsterdam's Centraal Station.

The Dutchflyer
W stenaline.co.uk/ferry-to-holland/rail-and-sail
P&O Ferries
W poferries.com/en/portal

AMSTERDAM'S CANALS

For those who wish to explore the city's canals and waterways by boat, the following services are available:

Hop-On, Hop-Off Canal Cruises
These flexible tour boats allow you to explore the city's major sights, shopping areas and attractions at your own pace.

Canal Tours
Many operators offer foreign-language commentaries. Book in advance for lunchtime, evening and dinner cruises.

Small Boat Tours
These tours take you along narrower canals that large canalboats can't navigate. Boats depart every 40 minutes (11am-7pm Apr-Oct) from the Prinsengracht boarding point near the Anne Frank House.

Water Taxis
Exclusive water taxis are much more convenient than canalboats; they are also significantly more expensive.

Private Boat Hire
A licence is not required to rent a boat. Ensure you are clued up on local boating regulations before your maiden voyage.

Canal Bikes
These two- or four-seater pedalboats can be hired for around €10 per hour. They can be left at any of the canal-bike moorings in the city, but must not enter the harbour or western port.

PRACTICAL INFORMATION

A little local know-how goes a long way in Amsterdam. Here you will find all the essential advice and information you will need during your stay.

AT A GLANCE

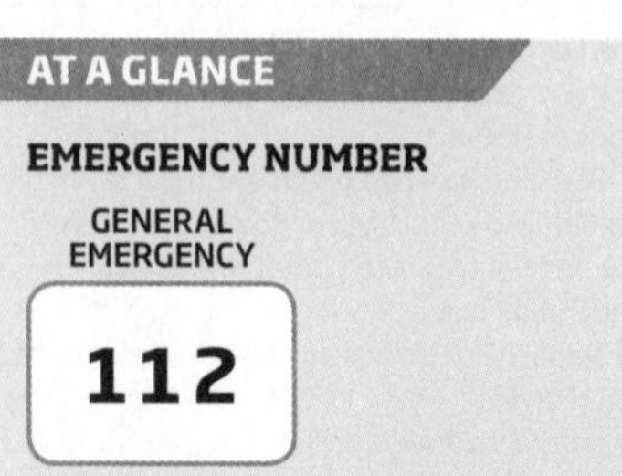

EMERGENCY NUMBER

GENERAL EMERGENCY

112

TIME ZONE

CET/CEST
Central European Summer Time (CEST) runs 31 Mar–27 Oct 2019

TAP WATER

Unless otherwise stated, tap water in the Netherlands is safe to drink.

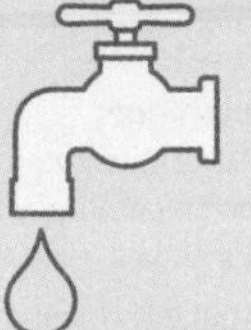

TIPPING

Waiter	5-10%
Hotel Porter	€1 a bag
Housekeeping	€1 a day
Concierge	€1-2
Taxi Driver	Not expected

Personal Security

Pickpockets work crowded tourist areas, trams and trains between the city centre and Schiphol airport. Be alert to your surroundings.

If you have anything stolen, report the crime as soon as possible to the nearest police station. Bring ID with you and get a copy of the crime report in order to claim on your insurance.

Bar and club areas like Leidseplein and Rembrandtplein, the Red Light District and city parks can be dangerous for lone tourists in the early hours.

If you have your passport stolen, or in the event of a serious crime, contact your consulate in Amsterdam, or your embassy in Den Haag.

Health

Minor ailments can be dealt with by a chemist *(drogist)*. For prescriptions go to a pharmacy *(apotheek)*. Details of the nearest 24-hour service are posted in all pharmacy windows.

The **Central Medical Service** *(Centrale Doktersdienst)* will direct you to the nearest pharmacy, and can refer you to a GP or dentist. EU citizens can receive emergency medical and dental treatment in the Netherlands at a reduced charge *(p223)*. You may have to pay upfront for medical treatment and reclaim on your insurance later.

Visitors from outside the EU or Australia are responsible for the payment of hospital and other medical expenses. As such it is important to arrange comprehensive medical insurance.

Central Medical Service
W doktersdienst.info

Smoking, Alcohol and Drugs

The Netherlands has a smoking ban in all public places, including bars, cafés, restaurants and hotels. Confusingly, this also applies to coffee shops, where smoking cannabis is decriminalized, but smoking tobacco is illegal.

Foreign tourists were banned from entering coffee shops in 2013, although Amsterdam police tend to turn a blind eye to this. Soft drugs

such as hashish and cannabis are decriminalized for personal use. Hard drugs are a different matter: anyone caught with them by the police will certainly be prosecuted. Never try to take drugs out of the Netherlands: if caught you will face prosecution.

Alcohol consumption is illegal in parks, and on the streets in nightlife areas such as Leidseplein, Rembrandtplein and the Red Light District. The Netherlands has a strict limit of 0.05% BAC (blood alcohol content) for drivers and cyclists.

ID

In the Netherlands, everyone over the age of 14 is legally required to carry ID, including tourists. You can be fined for not having the correct ID, so carry your passport, or a photocopy of your passport, with you at all times.

Local Customs

Do not photograph prostitutes in the Red Light District – this will anger local sex workers. Avoid using cameras and recording equipment in the area, as someone may mistake your intentions.

Visiting Churches and Cathedrals

Dress respectfully: cover your torso and upper arms; ensure shorts and skirts cover your knees.

Mobile Phones and Wi-Fi

Free Wi-Fi hot spots are widely available in Amsterdam's city centre. Cafés and restaurants usually permit the use of their Wi-Fi on the condition that you make a purchase.

Visitors travelling to Amsterdam with EU mobile phone tariffs won't be affected by data roaming charges. Users will be charged the same rates for data, SMS and voice calls as they would pay at home.

Post

Stamps *(postzegels)* can be bought in shops, supermarkets, newsagents or tobacconists. Send items of value by registered mail from the post office *(postagentschap)*.

Taxes and Refunds

VAT is 21% in the Netherlands. Non-EU residents are entitled to a tax refund subject to certain conditions. Shops that stock the relevant forms will have a sign saying "Tax free for tourists". When leaving the country, present this form at customs, along with the goods receipt and your ID, to receive your refund.

Discount Cards

The following discount cards are available to tourists for a set fee. It is wise to consider carefully how many of the offers you are likely to take advantage of before purchasing, as they can be expensive.

I amsterdam City Card Includes unlimited travel on public transport, a canal tour and free or discounted access to most museums and attractions. Available online and from all tourist offices. Valid for either 24 (€60), 48 (€80), 72 (€95) or 120 (€115) hours.

Museum Card (Museumkaart) Offers discounted admission to over 400 museums in the Netherlands for one year. Available from tourist offices, online and at museums for €64.90 (adults) and €32.45 (under-25s).

CJP Card Under-30s can enjoy discounts on museums, festivals, fashion and more. Available online and from tourist offices.

WEBSITES AND APPS

www.iamsterdam.com
The official tourist information network

Instabridge
Accessable offline, this app directs you to free Wi-Fi hot spots throughout the city centre.

GVB
The official transport app from Amsterdam's public transport provider

NS Reisplanner
The official app of the NS (Dutch national railway)

VaarWater
This app provides information on popular boating routes, timetables and where best to moor.

INDEX

Page numbers in **bold** type refer to main entries

A

B

C

N

O

P

R

S

PHRASE BOOK

IN EMERGENCY

Help!	**Help!**	*Help*
Stop!	**Stop!**	*Stop*
Call a doctor	**Haal een dokter**	*Haal uhn* **dok***-tur*
Call an ambulance	**Bel een ambulance**	*Bell uhn ahm-bew-* **luhns***-uh*
Call the police	**Roep de politie**	*Roop duh poe-***leet***-see*
Call the fire brigade	**Roep de brandweer**	*Roop duh* **brahnt***-vheer*
Where is the nearest telephone?	**Waar is de dichtstbijzijnde telefoon?**	*Vhaar iss duh* **dikhst***-baiy-zaiyn-duh tay-luh-***foan**
Where is the nearest hospital?	**Waar is het dichtstbijzijnde ziekenhuis?**	*Vhaar iss het* **dikhst***-baiy-zaiyn-duh* **zee***-kuh-houws*

COMMUNICATION ESSENTIALS

Yes	**Ja**	*Yaa*
No	**Nee**	*Nay*
Please	**Alstublieft**	*Ahls-tew-***bleeft**
Thank you	**Dank u**	*Dahnk-ew*
Excuse me	**Pardon**	*Pahr-***don**
Hello	**Hallo**	*Hallo*
Goodbye	**Dag**	*Dahgh*
Good night	**Slaap lekker**	*Slaap* **lek***-kah*
morning	**Morgen**	**Mor***-ghuh*
afternoon	**Middag**	**Mid***-dahgh*
evening	**Avond**	**Ah***-vohnd*
yesterday	**Gisteren**	**Ghis***-tern*
today	**Vandaag**	*Vahn-***daagh**
tomorrow	**Morgen**	**Mor***-ghuh*
here	**Hier**	*Heer*
there	**Daar**	*Daar*
What?	**Wat?**	*Vhat*
When?	**Wanneer?**	*Vhan-***eer**
Why?	**Waarom?**	*Vhaar-***om**
Where?	**Waar?**	*Vhaar*
How?	**Hoe?**	*Hoo*

USEFUL PHRASES

How are you?	**Hoe gaat het ermee?**	*Hoo ghaat het er-***may**
Very well, thank you	**Heel goed, dank u**	*Hayl ghoot, dahnk ew*
How do you do?	**Hoe maakt u het?**	*Hoo maakt ew het*
See you soon	**Tot ziens**	*Tot zeens*
That's fine	**Prima**	**Pree***-mah*
Where is/are?	**Waar is/zijn?**	*Vhaar iss/zayn*
How far is it to...?	**Hoe ver is het naar...?**	*Hoo vehr iss het naar...*
How do I get to ...?	**Hoe kom ik naar...?**	*Hoo kom ik naar...*
Do you speak English?	**Spreekt u engels?**	*Spraykt ew* **eng***-uhls*
I don't understand	**Ik snap het niet**	*Ik snahp het neet*
Could you speak slowly?	**Kunt u langzamer praten?**	*Kuhnt ew* **lahng***-zahmer praa-tuh*
I'm sorry	**Sorry**	*Sorry*

USEFUL WORDS

big	**groot**	*ghroaht*
small	**klein**	*klaiyn*
hot	**warm**	*vharm*
cold	**koud**	*khowt*
good	**goed**	*ghoot*
bad	**slecht**	*slekht*
enough	**genoeg**	*ghuh-***noohkh**
well	**goed**	*ghoot*
open	**open**	*open*
closed	**gesloten**	*ghuh-***slow***-tuh*
left	**links**	*links*
right	**rechts**	*rekhts*
straight on	**rechtdoor**	*rehkht dohr*
near	**dichtbij**	*dikht baiy*
far	**ver weg**	*vehr vhekh*
up	**omhoog**	*om-***hoakh**
down	**naar beneden**	*naar buh-***nay***-duh*
early	**vroeg**	*vroohkh*
late	**laat**	*laat*
entrance	**ingang**	**in***-ghahng*
exit	**uitgang**	**ouht***-ghang*
toilet	**wc**	*vhay say*
occupied	**bezet**	*buh-***zett**
free (unoccupied)	**vrij**	*vraiy*
free (no charge)	**gratis**	**ghraah***-tiss*

MAKING A TELEPHONE CALL

I'd like to place a long-distance call	**Ik wil graag interlokaal telefoneren**	*Ik vhil ghraakh* **inter***-loh-kaahl tay-luh-foe-***neh***-ruh*
I'd like to call collect	**Ik wil 'collect call' bellen**	*Ik vhil 'collect call'* **bel***-luh*
I'll try again later	**Ik probeer het later nog wel eens**	*Ik pro-***beer** *het later nokh vhel ayns*
Can I leave a message?	**Kunt u een boodschap doorgeven?**	*Kuhnt ew uhn* **boat***-skhahp* **dohr***-ghay-vuh*
Could you speak a little louder please?	**Wilt u wat harder praten?**	*Vhilt ew vhat* **hahr***up der* **praah***-tuh*
Local call	**Lokaal gesprek**	*Low-***kaahl** *ghuh-***sprek**

SHOPPING

How much does this cost?	**Hoeveel kost dit?**	*Hoo-***vayl** *kost dit*
I would like	**Ik wil graag**	*Ik vhil ghraakh*
Do you have...?	**Heeft u...?**	*Hayft ew...*
I'm just looking	**Ik kijk alleen even**	*Ik kaiyk alleyn* **ay** *-vuh*
Do you take credit cards?	**Neemt u credit cards aan?**	*Naymt ew credit cards aan*
Do you take travellers' cheques?	**Neemt u reischeques aan?**	*Naymt ew* **raiys***-sheks aan*
What time do you open?	**Hoe laat gaat u open?**	*Hoo laat ghaat ew opuh*
What time do you close?	**Hoe laat gaat u dicht?**	*Hoo laat ghaat ew dikht*
This one	**Deze**	**Day***-zuh*
That one	**Die**	*Dee*
expensive	**duur**	*dewr*
cheap	**goedkoop**	*ghoot-***koap**
size	**maat**	*maat*
white	**wit**	*vhit*
black	**zwart**	*zvhahrt*
red	**rood**	*roat*
yellow	**geel**	*ghayl*
green	**groen**	*ghroon*
blue	**blauw**	*blah-ew*

TYPES OF SHOPS

antique shop	**antiekwinkel**	*ahn-***teek***-vhin-kul*
bakery	**bakker**	**bah***-ker*
bank	**bank**	*bahnk*
bookshop	**boekwinkel**	**book***-vhin-kul*
butcher	**slager**	*slaakh-er*
cake shop	**banketbakkerij**	*bahnk-***et***-bahk-er-aiy*
cheese shop	**kaaswinkel**	**kaas***-vhin-kul*
chip shop	**patatzaak**	*pah-***taht***-zaak*
chemist (dispensing)	**apotheek**	*ah-poe-***taiyk**
delicatessen	**delicatessen**	*daylee-kah-***tes***-suh*
department store	**warenhuis**	**vhaar***-uh-houws*
fishmonger	**viswinkel**	**viss***-vhin-kul*
greengrocer	**groenteboer**	**ghroon***-tuh-boor*
hairdresser	**kapper**	**kah***-per*
market	**markt**	*mahrkt*
newsagent	**krantenwinkel**	**krahn***-tuh-vhin-kul*
post office	**postkantoor**	**pohst***-kahn-tor*
shoe shop	**schoenenwinkel**	**sghoo***-nuh-vhin-kul*
supermarket	**supermarkt**	**sew***-per-mahrkt*
tobacconist	**sigarenwinkel**	*see-***ghaa***-ruh-vhin-kul*
travel agent	**reisburo**	**raiys***-bew-roa*

SIGHTSEEING

art gallery	**galerie**	*ghaller-ee*
bus station	**busstation**	**buhs***-stah-shown*
cathedral	**kathedraal**	*kah-tuh-***draal**
church	**kerk**	*kehrk*
closed on public holidays	**op feestdagen gesloten**	*op* **fayst***-daa-ghuh ghuh-***slow***-tuh*
day return	**dagretour**	**dahgh***-ruh-tour*
garden	**tuin**	*touwn*
library	**bibliotheek**	*bee-bee-yo-***tayk**
museum	**museum**	*mew-***zay***-uhm*
railway station	**station**	*stah-***shown**
return ticket	**retourtje**	*ruh-***tour***-tyuh*
single journey	**enkeltje**	**eng***-kuhl-tyuh*
tourist information	**VVV**	*fay fay fay*
town hall	**stadhuis**	*staht-***houws**
train	**trein**	*traiyn*
travel pass	**Ov-chipkaart**	**oh-vay***-chip-kaahrt*

STAYING IN A HOTEL

Do you have a vacant room?	**Zijn er nog kamers vrij?**	*Zaiyn er nokh* **kaa-mer***s vray*
double room with a double bed	**een twee persoonskamer met een twee persoonsbed**	*uhn* **tvhay***-per* **soans***-kaa-mer met uhn* **tvhay***-per* **soans** *beht*
twin room	**een kamer met een lits-jumeaux**	*uhn* **kaa-mer** *met uhn lee-zjoo-***moh**
single room	**eenpersoons-kamer**	**ayn***-per-***soans-kaa-mer**
room with a bath	**kamer met bad**	**kaa-mer** *met baht*
shower	**douche**	*doosh*
porter	**kruier**	**krouw***-yuh*
I have a reservation	**Ik heb gereserveerd**	*Ik hehp ghuh-ray-sehr-***veert**

EATING OUT

Have you got a table?	**Is er een tafel vrij?**	*Iss ehr uhn* **tah***-fuhl vraiy*
I want to reserve a table	**Ik wil een tafel reserveren**	*Ik vhil uhn* **tah***-fuhl ray-sehr-***veer***-uh*
The bill, please	**Mag ik afrekenen**	*Mukh ik* **ahf***-ray-kuh-nuh*
I am a vegetarian	**Ik ben vegetariër**	*Ik ben fay-ghuh-***taahr***-ee-er*
waitress/waiter	**serveerster/ober**	*Sehr-***veer***-ster/***oh***-ber*
menu	**de kaart**	*duh kaahrt*
cover charge	**het couvert**	*het koo-***vehr**
wine list	**de wijnkaart**	*duh* **vhaiyn***-kaart*
glass	**het glas**	*het ghlahss*
bottle	**de fles**	*duh fless*
knife	**het mes**	*het mess*
fork	**de vork**	*duh fork*
spoon	**de lepel**	*duh* **lay***-pul*
breakfast	**het ontbijt**	*het ont-***baiyt**
lunch	**de lunch**	*duh lernsh*
dinner	**het diner**	*het dee-***nay**
main course	**het hoofdgerecht**	*het* **hoaft***-ghuh-rekht*
starter, first course	**het voorgerecht**	*het* **vohr***-ghuh-rekht*
dessert	**het nagerecht**	*het* **naa***-ghuh-rekht*
dish of the day	**het dagmenu**	*het* **dahgh***-munh-ew*
bar	**het cafe**	*het kaa-***fay**
café	**het eetcafe**	*het* **ayt***-kaa-***fay**
rare	**rare**	*rare*
medium	**medium**	*medium*
well done	**doorbakken**	*dohr-***bah***-kuh*

MENU DECODER

aardappels	**aard***-uppuhls*	potatoes
azijn	*aah-***zaiyn**	vinegar
biefstuk	**beef***-stuhk*	steak
bier, pils	*beer, pilss*	beer
boter	*boater*	butter
brood/broodje	*broat/***broat***-yuh*	bread/roll
cake, taart, gebak	*'cake', taahrt, ghuh-***bahk**	cake, pastry
carbonade	*kahr-bow-***naa***-duh*	pork chop
chocola	*show-coa-***laa**	chocolate
citroen	*see-***troon**	lemon
cocktail	*cocktail*	cocktail
droog	*droakh*	dry
eend	*aynt*	duck
ei	*aiy*	egg
garnalen	*ghahr-***naah***-luh*	prawns
gebakken	*ghuh-***bah***-ken*	fried
gegrild	*ghuh-***ghrillt**	grilled
gekookt	*ghuh-***koakt**	boiled
gepocheerd	*ghuh-posh-***eert**	poached
gerookt	*ghuh-***roakt**	smoked
geroosterd brood	*ghuh-***roas***-tert broat*	toast
groenten	**ghroon***-tuh*	vegetables
ham	*hahm*	ham
haring	**haa***-ring*	herring
hutspot	*huht-spot*	hot pot
ijs	*aiyss*	ice, ice cream
jenever	*yuh-***nay***-vhur*	gin
kaas	*kaas*	cheese
kabeljauw	*kah-buhl-***youw**	cod
kip	*kip*	chicken
knoflook	*knoff-loak*	garlic
koffie	*coffee*	coffee
kool, rode of witte	*coal,* **roe***-duh off* vhit-uh	cabbage, red or white
kreeft	*krayft*	lobster
kroket	*crow-***ket**	ragout in bread-crumbs, deep fried
lamsvlees	**lahms***-flayss*	lamb
lekkerbekje	**lek***-kah-bek-yuh*	fried fillet of haddock
mineraalwater	*meener-***aahl***-vhaater*	mineral water
mosterd	**moss***-tehrt*	mustard
niet scherp	*neet skehrp*	mild
olie	**oh***-lee*	oil
paling	**paa***-ling*	eel
pannenkoek	**pah***-nuh-kook*	pancake
patat frites	*pah-***taht** *freet*	chips
peper	**pay***-per*	pepper
poffertjes	**poffer***-tyuhs*	tiny buckwheat pancakes
rijst	*raiyst*	rice
rijsttafel	**raiys***-tah-ful*	Indonesian meal
rode wijn	**roe***-duh vhaiyn*	red wine
rookworst	**roak***-vhorst*	smoked sausage
rundvlees	**ruhnt***-flayss*	beef
saus	*souwss*	sauce
schaaldieren	**skaahl***-deeh-ruh*	shellfish
scherp	*skehrp*	hot (spicy)
schol	*sghol*	plaice
soep	*soup*	soup
stamppot	**stahm***-pot*	sausage stew
suiker	**souw***-ker*	sugar
thee	*tay*	tea
tosti	**toss***-tee*	cheese on toast
uien	**ouw***-yuh*	onions
uitsmijter	**ouht***-smaiy-ter*	fried egg on bread with ham
varkensvlees	**vahr***-kuhns-flayss*	pork
vers fruit	*fehrss frouwt*	fresh fruit
verse jus	**vehr***-suh zjhew*	fresh orange juice
vis	*fiss*	fish/seafood
vlees	*flayss*	meat
water	**vhaa***-ter*	water
witte wijn	**vhih***-tuh vhaiyn*	white wine
worst	*vhorst*	sausage
zout	*zouwt*	salt

NUMBERS

1	**een**	*ayn*
2	**twee**	*tvhay*
3	**drie**	*dree*
4	**vier**	*feer*
5	**vijf**	*faiyf*
6	**zes**	*zess*
7	**zeven**	**zay***-vuh*
8	**acht**	*ahkht*
9	**negen**	**nay***-guh*
10	**tien**	*teen*
11	**elf**	*elf*
12	**twaalf**	*tvhaalf*
13	**dertien**	**dehr***-teen*
14	**veertien**	**feer***-teen*
15	**vijftien**	**faiyf***-teen*
16	**zestien**	**zess***-teen*
17	**zeventien**	**zayvuh***-teen*
18	**achttien**	**ahkh***-teen*
19	**negentien**	**nay-ghuh***-teen*
20	**twintig**	**tvhin***-tukh*
21	**eenentwintig**	**aynuh***-tvhin-tukh*
30	**dertig**	**dehr***-tukh*
40	**veertig**	**feer***-tukh*
50	**vijftig**	**faiyf***-tukh*
60	**zestig**	**zess***-tukh*
70	**zeventig**	**zay***-vuh-tukh*
80	**tachtig**	**tahkh***-tukh*
90	**negentig**	**nayguh***-tukh*
100	**honderd**	**hohn***-durt*
1000	**duizend**	**douw***-zuhnt*
1,000,000	**miljoen**	*mill-***yoon**

TIME

one minute	**een minuut**	*uhn meen-***ewt**
one hour	**een uur**	*uhn ewr*
half an hour	**een half uur**	*uhn hahlf ewr*
half past one	**half twee**	*hahlf tvhay*
a day	**een dag**	*uhn dahgh*
a week	**een week**	*uhn vhayk*
a month	**een maand**	*uhn maant*
a year	**een jaar**	*uhn jaar*
Monday	**maandag**	**maan***-dahgh*
Tuesday	**dinsdag**	**dins***-dahgh*
Wednesday	**woensdag**	**vhoons***-dahgh*
Thursday	**donderdag**	**donder***-dahgh*
Friday	**vrijdag**	**vraiy***-dahgh*
Saturday	**zaterdag**	**zaater***-dahgh*
Sunday	**zondag**	**zon***-dahgh*

ACKNOWLEDGMENTS

The publisher would like to thank the following for their kind permission to reproduce their photographs:

Key: a-above; b-below/bottom; c-centre; f-far; l-left; r-right; t-top

123RF.com:
atosan 105tl; bloodua 202-3t; Nattee Chalermtiragool 50bl, 78br; ekinyalgin 171t; NEMO by Renzo Piano Building Workshop, architects / Markus Gann 99b; giuseppemasci 214tr; Keleny 66-7; macfromlondon 116-7b; marina99 119br; mediagram 126-7b; William Perry 83t, 113; phototraveller 79bl; skyfish555 203bl; tasfoto 194t; topdeq 214-5b; Dennis Van De Water 133br.

4Corners:
Ben Pipe 56-7.

500px: Bart van Dijk 19t, 162-3.

A'DAM Toren:
180-1b; Dennis Bouman 47clb, 180cra.

Alamy Stock Photo:
Mieneke Andeweg-van Rijn 210tl; Anyka 39t; Art Collection 2 53cla; Andrew Balcombe 49crb; Henry Beeker 197br; Sergey Borisov 8-9b; Ger Bosma 41br; Magdalena Bujak 198tr; Nacho Calonge 51bl; Dutch Cities 209tr; eye35 10ca, 61t; eye35.pix 16bl, 86-7; Paul Fearn 73tl; Nick Gammon 30b; Cyrille Gibot 160-1b; Manfred Gottschalk 212bl; Granger Historical Picture Archive 53bl; Chris Harris 43tr; HelloWorld Images 98bc; Hemis.fr / Maurizio Borgese 64tl, / René Mattes 77crb, 142b, 181t; Peter Horree 24cr, 39bl, 53tr, 63t, 134t, 203cr; imageBROKER / Alexander Pöschel 157tr, / Carlos Sanchez 18bl, 152-3, / Hans Zaglitsch 170b; Kim Kaminski 50cl, / © Kobra / DACS, London 2018 *Let Me Be Myself* / 34-5t; Douglas Lander 58tr; Frans Lemmens 192cl, 196; Chon Kit Leong 199ca; Yadid Levy 20bl; Iain Masterton 8bl, 125c; Daryl Mulvihill 42tl, 160t; Paolo Paradiso 48-9t; Mo Peerbacus 147b; Peter Richardson 55cra; S. Vincent 58tl; Marek Slusarczyk 182bl; Pim Smit 60tl, 62tl; Alfred Sonsalla 11t; StockphotoVideo 77br; Peter van Evert 193bl; S R Veejay 28-9b; W.Wiskerke 62tr; World History Archive 54crb, 73ca, 129tr; Bartek Wrzesniowski 45br.

Amsterdam Jewel Cruises:
49cl.

Amsterdam Museum:
75cla, 75cra, Battle of the Slaak on loan foundation Spirit 75crb, Amsterdam Gallery / David, Goliath and His Shield-bearer (1648-50) by Jansz Vinckenbrinck 75cr, Portrait Gallery of the Golden Age, Hermitage Museum 172-3b; Caro Bonink 74-5b; Monique Vermeulen 75br; Barbara Broekman *My town: a celebration of diversity* (2015), Axminster woven woollen carpet in the Schuttersgalerij 3.2 x 38 meters / Monique Vermeulen 43br.

Anne Frank House:
Cris Toala Olivares 111tl, 111tr, 111cla.

AWL Images:
Francesco Riccardo Iacomin 184-5.

BIMHUIS:
41cla; John Post 40-1t.

Bridgeman Images: 73tc.

Collection of the Kunstmuseum Den Haag:
Piet Mondrian *Evolution* (1911) Oil on canvas 183 x 257.5 cm 207t.

Concertgebouw:
Hans Roggen 43c, 51cl.

De Nieuwe Kerk:
Erik en Petra Hesmerg 73cr.

Depositphotos Inc:
microgen 45cl; rognar 8cl; vichie81 188cb.

Dreamstime.com:
A. G. M. 10clb; Mihai Andritoiu 16cl, 68-9; Antonfrolov 24crb, 91br; Asiantraveler 192bl; Atosan 74tr; Izabela Beretka 174bl; Artur Bogacki 96bl, 175tl; Mihai-bogdan Lazar 84cl; Boris Breytman 135, 195b; Devy 51tr, 192bc, Digikhmer 81t, 207bl; Serban Enache 18t, 138-9; Famveldman 44br; Fedecandoniphoto 44-5t; Inna Felker 102-3t; Prochasson Frederic 36tl; Harmen Goedhart 17bl, 120-1; Pablo Hidalgo 36-7b; Peter Hoeks 136tr; Gabriela Insuratelu 80br; JP 32-3t, 166cl; Jjfarq 126tl; Joophoek 60tr; Jorisvo 73br; Pavel Kavalenkau 133t; Kisamarkiza 205b, 206b; Jan Kranendonk 72cl, 85cr, 150clb; Liudmila Laurova 145t; Ethan Le 19bl, 137br, 176-7; Martin Lehmann 26cr; Chon Kit Leong 201t; Kuan Leong Yong 210br; Lornet 22cr; Simone Matteo Giuseppe Manzoni 53tl; Mastroraf 209tl; Fabian Meseberg 39cr; Mike Miltenburg 175br; Martin Molcan 146-7t; Nataliaderiabina 4cb; Olgacov 46b; Alexey Pevnev 37br; Rosshelen 100-1; Sergey Rybin 20crb; Tatiana Savvateeva 59t; Sborisov 117cra; Alfred Georg Sonsalla 91cra; Jacek Sopotnicki 188cla; TasFoto 198bl; Alexander Tolstykh 128-9c; Tomas1111 82-3b, 115t; Tonyv3112 48bl, 114b; Anibal Trejo 98tr; Tupungato 24bl, 148br; Dennis Van De Water 38b, 64tr, 132b, 130cl; VanderWolfImages 182-3b, 212-3t; Victormro 47cr; Björn Wylezich 11br.

Foam Museum:
Foam Talent 2016, Mercatorplein 144b.

Getty Images:
AFP / Bas Czerwinski 50br, / Lex Van Lieshout 217tr, / Koen van Weel 54-5t, / Robin Van Lonkhuijsen 51br; Paulo Amorim 50cla; Archive Photos 53crb; Atlantide Phototravel 17t, 20cr, 106-7; De Agostini / Biblioteca Ambrosiana 52tc; Emmanuel Dunand 13cr; Manfred Gottschalk 209br; EyeEm / Monika Kanokova 32br; Jasper Juinen 51cr; Floris Leeuwenberg 37clb; Yadid Levy 40b; NurPhoto 50cra; PHAS 54bl; Michel Porro 26crb; Premium Archive / Anne Frank Fonds Basel 111br; Smith Collection / Gado 54tl; Ullstein bild Dtl. 55br; Universal History Archive 55bl; Westend61 103br.

Hotel des Indes:
26t.

Hungry Birds:
Pavel Ananich 12clb.

IJ Hallen:
Nichon Glerum 182-3tl.

iStockphoto.com:
ahavelaar 97t; anatols 24tc; AndreyKrav 124-5b; bradleyhebdon 47br; Cloud-Mine-Amsterdam 50cr; danilovi 158-9; Deejpilot 148-9t; dennisvdw 220-1; DutchScenery 149crb; entrechat 49tr; espiegle 65t; freeskyline 22crb; Aleksandar Georgiev 2-3; JacobH 219t; Arie J. Jager 20tc; justhavealook 76bl; KavalenkavaVolha 151cra; klug-photo 204tr; LeoPatrizi 8cla; MadrugadaVerde 189t; MaestroBooks 35br, 55tr; mila103 90bl; Mirrorimage-NL / Kees Verkade © DACS 2018 *Johnny Jordaan bust* 160bl; narvikk 6-7; neirfy 26bl; Olena_Znak 47t; oversnap 37tr; Pidjoe 22bl, 118cl,166-7b; railelectropower 134bl; Rob3rt82 51tl; Prasit Rodphan 128cb; sara_winter 189bl; Siempreverde22 197crb; Bastiaan Slabbers 31br; TasfotoNL 216t; Tolga Tezcan 10-1b; tunart 46tl; VLIET 34bl.

Joods Historisch Museum:
92bc; Liselore Kamping 12t, 92br; Ruud van Zwet 22t; Marijke Volkers 92clb.

Lastplak Collective:
35cb.

Mauritshuis, The Hague:
Galerij Prins Willem V / Frank van der Burg 206cr, Ivo Hoekstra 204cr.

Melkweg:
Emil Varga 12-3b.

Museum Het Rembrandthuis:
11cr, 94, 95cr, 95bl.

Museum Ons' Lieve Heer op Solder:
77bc.

Museum Prinsenhof Delft:
211t; Marco Zwinkels 208bl.

Museum Willet-Holthuysen:
142cr, Caro Bonink 142cra.

National Maritime Museum Amsterdam (Het Scheepvaartmuseum):
Eddo Hartmann 13t; Twycer 167tr, 167cr; Marjo van Rooyen 167c.

NEMO Science Museum:
DigiDaan 30-1t, 31cla; by Renzo Piano Building Workshop, architects / DigiDaan 46cra.

Oude Kerk, Amsterdam:
91tr, NA – Christian Boltanski. © ADAGP, Paris and DACS, London 2018 *Installation at Oude Kerk, Amsterdam. 24 November 2017 - 29 April 2018* / GJ Van Rooij 91tl.

Paleis Het Loos:
Hesmerg 219bc; Stef Verstraaten 219clb, 219br.

Picfair.com:
Johannes Tönne 125tl.

RIJKS Restaurant:
Erik Smits 33br; Jan Kees Steenman 33cl.

Rijksmuseum, Amsterdam:
127bc, 127cra, 127cl; Erik Smits 29br.

Rijksmuseum Boerhaave:
199tc, 200br.

Rijksmuseum van Oudheden:
Mike Bink 199tl.

Robert Harding Picture Library:
dreamtours 29tr; Michael Jenner 110bl; Hans Zaglitsch 79tr.

Stedelijk Museum:
Composition in Red, Black, Blue, Yellow and Grey (1920) by Piet Mondriaan 28tl, Marc Chagall / Chagall ® / © ADAGP, Paris and DACS, London 2018 *Le violoniste (The Fiddler)*, 1912-13 on loan from the Cultural Heritage Agency 131tl; Gert Jan van Rooij 130-1b.

SuperStock:
Art Archive / The aa346722 52crb; age footstock / HelloWorld Images 54cr; Axiom Photographic / Design Pics / Ian Cumming 38cla; imageBROKER 38-9tr; Mauritius / Ernst Wrba 156b; Quint & Lox Limited 52bl, 73cra; World History Archive 55bc.

Tropenmuseum:
Collectie Stichting Nationaal Museum van Wereldculturen. Coll.nr. TM-1389 169br, TM-2357-77 169bl; Jakob van Vliet 169cra; Rob van Esch 168.

Van Gogh Museum, Amsterdam (Vincent van Gogh Foundation):
Vincent van Gogh, *The Bedroom,* Arles, October (1888) 28bl, 128bl; Jan Kees Steenman 13br.

Verzetsmuseum:
172tr.

Vondelpark Openluchttheater:
42-3.

Zuiderzeemuseum:
191tr; Frank Bedijs 191cla; Erik en Petra Hesmerg 191tl; Heliante Moningka 190clb.

Front flap:
123RF.com: ekinyalgin bl, Keleny tc; **Alamy Stock Photo:** imageBROKER / Carlos Sanchez cla; **Dreamstime.com:** Andreykr br; **iStockphoto.com:** LeoPatrizi cra; narvikk cb.

Sheet map cover:
Dreamstime.com: Tomas1111.

Cover images:
Front and Spine: **Dreamstime.com:** Tomas1111. *Back:* **123RF.com:** marina99 cla, William Perry c; **AWL Images:** Francesco Riccardo Iacomino tr; **Dreamstime.com:** Tomas1111 b.

Cartographic Data:
Lovell Johns Ltd.

All other images © Dorling Kindersley
For further information see: www.dkimages.com

MIX
Paper from responsible sources
FSC™ C018179

The information in this DK Eyewitness Travel Guide is checked regularly.

Every effort has been made to ensure that this book is as up-to-date as possible at the time of going to press. Some details, however, such as telephone numbers, opening hours, prices, gallery hanging arrangements and travel information, are liable to change. The publishers cannot accept responsibility for any consequences arising from the use of this book, nor for any material on third party websites, and cannot guarantee that any website address in this book will be a suitable source of travel information. We value the views and suggestions of our readers very highly. Please write to: Publisher, DK Eyewitness Travel Guides, Dorling Kindersley, 80 Strand, London, WC2R 0RL, UK, or email: travelguides@dk.com

Main contributers Robin Gauldie, Robin Pascoe, Christopher Catling
Senior Designer Owen Bennett
Senior Editor Ankita Awasthi Tröger
Project Editor Rebecca Flynn
Project Art Editors Dan Bailey, Toby Truphet, Stuti Tiwari Bhatia, Bharti Karakoti, Priyanka Thakur, Vinita Venugopal
Design Assistant William Robinson
Factchecker Gerard van Vuuren
Editors Jackie Staddon, Danielle Watt
Proofreader Kathryn Glendenning
Indexer Helen Peters
Senior Picture Researcher Ellen Root
Picture Research Harriet Whitaker, Marta Bescos
Illustrators Nick Gibbard, Maltings Partnership, Derrick Stone, Martin Woodward, Arcana (Graham Bell), Richard Bonson, Stephen Conlin, Roy Flooks, Mick Gillah, Kevin Goold, Stephan Gyapay, Chris Orr, Ian Henderson, Philip Winton, John Woodcock
Cartographic Editor James Macdonald
Cartography Simonetta Giori, Reetu Pandey, David Pugh
Cover Designers Maxine Pedliham, Bess Daly
Cover Picture Research Susie Peachey
Senior DTP Designer Jason Little
DTP Coordinator George Nimmo
Senior Producer Stephanie McConnell
Managing Editor Hollie Teague
Art Director Maxine Pedliham
Publishing Director Georgina Dee
This edition updated by Hansa Babra, Sam Cook, Rebecca Flynn, Sumita Khatwani, Lucy Sara-Kelly, Gerard van Vuuren, Tanveer Zaidi

First edition 1995

Published in Great Britain by Dorling Kindersley Limited, 80 Strand, London, WC2R 0RL

Published in the United States by DK Publishing, 1450 Broadway, Suite 801, New York, NY 10018

19 20 21 22 10 9 8 7 6 5 4 3 2 1

A CIP catalogue record for this book is available from the British Library.

A catalog record for this book is available from the Library of Congress.

ISSN: 1542-1554
ISBN: 978-0-2413-6870-1

Printed and bound in China.

www.dk.com